Letters of Anton Chekhov to His Family and Friends

CW00550438

Anton Pavlovich Chekhov

Alpha Editions

This edition published in 2022

ISBN : 9789356718326

Design and Setting By
Alpha Editions
www.alphaedis.com
Email - info@alphaedis.com

TRANSLATOR'S NOTE

Of the eighteen hundred and ninety letters published by Chekhov's family I have chosen for translation these letters and passages from letters which best to illustrate Chekhov's life, character and opinions. The brief memoir is abridged and adapted from the biographical sketch by his brother Mihail. Chekhov's letters to his wife after his marriage have not as yet been published.

BIOGRAPHICAL SKETCH

In 1841 a serf belonging to a Russian nobleman purchased his freedom and the freedom of his family for 3,500 roubles, being at the rate of 700 roubles a soul, with one daughter, Alexandra, thrown in for nothing. The grandson of this serf was Anton Chekhov, the author; the son of the nobleman was Tchertkov, the Tolstoyan and friend of Tolstoy.

There is in this nothing striking to a Russian, but to the English student it is sufficiently significant for several reasons. It illustrates how recent a growth was the educated middle-class in pre-revolutionary Russia, and it shows, what is perhaps more significant, the homogeneity of the Russian people, and their capacity for completely changing their whole way of life.

Chekhov's father started life as a slave, but the son of this slave was even more sensitive to the Arts, more innately civilized and in love with the things of the mind than the son of the slaveowner. Chekhov's father, Pavel Yegorovitch, had a passion for music and singing; while he was still a serf boy he learned to read music at sight and to play the violin. A few years after his freedom had been purchased he settled at Taganrog, a town on the Sea of Azov, where he afterwards opened a "Colonial Stores."

This business did well until the construction of the railway to Vladikavkaz, which greatly diminished the importance of Taganrog as a port and a trading centre. But Pavel Yegorovitch was always inclined to neglect his business. He took an active part in all the affairs of the town, devoted himself to church singing, conducted the choir, played on the violin, and painted ikons.

In 1854 he married Yevgenia Yakovlevna Morozov, the daughter of a cloth merchant of fairly good education who had settled down at Taganrog after a life spent in travelling about Russia in the course of his business.

There were six children, five of whom were boys, Anton being the third son. The family was an ordinary patriarchal household of the kind common at that time. The father was severe, and in exceptional cases even went so far as to chastise his children, but they all lived on warm and affectionate terms. Everyone got up early, the boys went to the high school, and when they returned learned their lessons. All of them had their hobbies. The eldest, Alexandr, would construct an electric battery, Nikolay used to draw, Ivan to bind books, while Anton was always writing stories. In the evening, when their father came home from the shop, there was choral singing or a duet.

Pavel Yegorovitch trained his children into a regular choir, taught them to sing music at sight, and play on the violin, while at one time they had a music teacher for the piano too. There was also a French governess who came to teach the children languages. Every Saturday the whole family went to the evening service, and on their return sang hymns and burned incense. On Sunday morning they went to early mass, after which they all sang hymns in chorus at home. Anton had to learn the whole church service by heart and sing it over with his brothers.

The chief characteristic distinguishing the Chekhov family from their neighbours was their habit of singing and having religious services at home.

Though the boys had often to take their father's place in the shop, they had leisure enough to enjoy themselves. They sometimes went for whole days to the sea fishing, played Russian tennis, and went for excursions to their grandfather's in the country. Anton was a sturdy, lively boy, extremely intelligent, and inexhaustible in jokes and enterprises of all kinds. He used to get up lectures and performances, and was always acting and mimicking. As children, the brothers got up a performance of Gogol's "Inspector General," in which Anton took the part of Gorodnitchy. One of Anton's favourite improvisations was a scene in which the Governor of the town attended church parade at a festival and stood in the centre of the church, on a rug surrounded by foreign consuls. Anton, dressed in his high-school uniform, with his grandfather's old sabre coming to his shoulder, used to act the part of the Governor with extraordinary subtlety and carry out a review of imaginary Cossacks. Often the children would gather round their mother or their old nurse to hear stories.

Chekhov's story "Happiness" was written under the influence of one of his nurse's tales, which were always of the mysterious, of the extraordinary, of the terrible, and poetical.

Their mother, on the other hand, told the children stories of real life, describing how she had travelled all over Russia as a little girl, how the Allies had bombarded Taganrog during the Crimean War, and how hard life had been for the peasants in the days of serfdom. She instilled into her children a hatred of brutality and a feeling of regard for all who were in an inferior position, and for birds and animals.

Chekhov in later years used to say: "Our talents we got from our father, but our soul from our mother."

In 1875 the two elder boys went to Moscow.

After their departure the business went from bad to worse, and the family sank into poverty.

In 1876 Pavel Yegorovitch closed his shop, and went to join his sons in Moscow. While earning their own living, one was a student at the

University, and the other a student at the School of Sculpture and Painting. The house was sold by auction, one of the creditors took all the furniture, and Chekhov's mother was left with nothing. Some months afterwards she went to rejoin her husband in Moscow, taking the younger children with her, while Anton, who was then sixteen, lived on in solitude at Taganrog for three whole years, earning his own living, and paying for his education at the high school.

He lived in the house that had been his father's, in the family of one Selivanov, the creditor who had bought it, and gave lessons to the latter's nephew, a Cossack. He went with his pupil to the latter's house in the country, and learned to ride and shoot. During the last two years he was very fond of the society of the high-school girls, and used to tell his brothers that he had had the most delightful flirtations.

At the same time he went frequently to the theatre and was very fond of French melodramas, so that he was by no means crushed by his early struggle for existence. In 1879 he went to Moscow to enter the University, bringing with him two school-fellows who boarded with his family. He found his father had just succeeded in getting work away from home, so that from the first day of his arrival he found himself head of the family, every member of which had to work for their common livelihood. Even little Mihail used to copy out lectures for students, and so made a little money. It was the absolute necessity of earning money to pay for his fees at the University and to help in supporting the household that forced Anton to write. That winter he wrote his first published story, "A Letter to a Learned Neighbour." All the members of the family were closely bound together round one common centre—Anton. "What will Anton say?" was always their uppermost thought on every occasion.

Ivan soon became the master of the parish school at Voskresensk, a little town in the Moscow province. Living was cheap there, so the other members of the family spent the summer there; they were joined by Anton when he had taken his degree, and the Chekhovs soon had a large circle of friends in the neighbourhood. Every day the company met, went long walks, played croquet, discussed politics, read aloud, and went into raptures over Shtchedrin. Here Chekhov gained an insight into military society which he afterwards turned to account in his play "The Three Sisters."

One day a young doctor called Uspensky came in from Zvenigorod, a small town fourteen miles away. "Look here," he said to Chekhov, "I am going away for a holiday and can't find anyone to take my place.... You take the job on. My Pelageya will cook for you, and there is a guitar there...."

Voskresensk and Zvenigorod played an important part in Chekhov's life as a writer; a whole series of his tales is founded on his experiences there, besides which it was his first introduction to the society of literary and artistic people. Three or four miles from Voskresensk was the estate of a landowner, A. S. Kiselyov, whose wife was the daughter of Begitchev, the director of the Moscow Imperial Theatre. The Chekhovs made the acquaintance of the Kiselyovs, and spent three summers in succession on their estate, Babkino.

The Kiselyovs were musical and cultivated people, and intimate friends of Dargomyzhsky, Tchaykovsky the composer, and the Italian actor Salvini. Madame Kiselyov was passionately fond of fishing, and would spend hours at a time sitting on the river bank with Anton, fishing and talking about literature. She was herself a writer. Chekhov was always playing with the Kiselyov children and running about the old park with them. The people he met, the huntsman, the gardener, the carpenters, the sick women who came to him for treatment, and the place itself, river, forests, nightingales—all provided Chekhov with subjects to write about and put him in the mood for writing. He always got up early and began writing by seven o'clock in the morning. After lunch the whole party set off to look for mushrooms in the woods. Anton was fond of looking for mushrooms, and said it stimulated the imagination. At this time he was always talking nonsense.

Levitan, the painter, lived in the neighbourhood, and Chekhov and he dressed up, blacked their faces and put on turbans. Levitan then rode off on a donkey through the fields, where Anton suddenly sprang out of the bushes with a gun and began firing blank cartridges at him.

In 1886 Chekhov suffered for the second time from an attack of spitting blood. There is no doubt that consumption was developing, but apparently he refused to believe this himself. He went on being as gay as ever, though he slept badly and often had terrible dreams. It was one of these dreams that suggested the subject of his story "The Black Monk."

That year he began to write for the *Novoye Vremya*, which made a special feature of his work. Under the influence of letters from Grigorovitch, who was the first person to appreciate his talent, Chekhov began to take his writing more seriously.

In 1887 he visited the south of Russia and stayed at the Holy Mountains, which gave him the subjects of two of his stories, "Easter Eve" and "Uprooted." In the autumn of that year he was asked by Korsh, a theatrical manager who knew him as a humorous writer, to write something for his theatre. Chekhov sat down and wrote "Ivanov" in a fortnight, sending off every act for rehearsal as it was completed.

By this time he had won a certain amount of recognition, everyone was talking of him, and there was consequently great curiosity about his new play. The performance was, however, only partially a success; the audience, divided into two parties, hissed vigorously and clapped noisily. For a long time afterwards the newspapers were full of discussions of the character and personality of the hero, while the novelty of the dramatic method attracted great attention.

In January, 1889, the play was performed at the Alexandrinsky Theatre in Petersburg and the controversy broke out again.

"Ivanov" was the turning-point in Chekhov's mental development, and literary career. He took up his position definitely as a writer, though his brass plate continued to hang on the door. Shortly after writing "Ivanov," he wrote a one-act play called "The Bear." The following season Solovtsev, who had taken the chief character in "The Bear," opened a theatre of his own in Moscow, which was not at first a success. He appealed to Chekhov to save him with a play for Christmas, which was only ten days off. Chekhov set to work and wrote an act every day. The play was produced in time, but the author was never satisfied with it, and after a short, very successful run took it off the stage. Several years later he completely remodelled it and produced it as "Uncle Vanya" at the Art Theatre in Moscow. At this time he was writing a long novel, of which he often dreamed aloud, and which he liked to talk about. He was for several years writing at this novel, but no doubt finally destroyed it, as no trace of it could be found after his death. He wanted it to embody his views on life, opinions which he expressed in a letter to Plestcheyev in these words:

"I am not a Liberal, not a Conservative.... I should have liked to have been a free artist and nothing more—and I regret that God has not given me the strength to be one. I hate lying and violence in all their forms—the most absolute freedom, freedom from force and fraud in whatever form the two latter may be expressed, that is the programme I would hold to if I were a great artist."

At this time he was always gay and insisted on having people round him while he worked. His little house in Moscow, which "looked like a chest of drawers," was a centre to which people, and especially young people, flocked in swarms. Upstairs they played the piano, a hired one, while downstairs he sat writing through it all. "I positively can't live without visitors," he wrote to Suvorin; "when I am alone, for some reason I am frightened." This gay life which seemed so full of promise was, however, interrupted by violent fits of coughing. He tried to persuade other people, and perhaps himself, that it was not serious, and he would not consent to be properly examined. He was sometimes so weak from haemorrhage that he could see no one, but as soon as the attack was over his mood changed, the doors were thrown open, visitors arrived, there was music again, and Chekhov was once more in the wildest spirits.

The summers of those two years, 1888 and 1889, he spent with his family in a summer villa at Luka, in the province of Harkov. He was in ecstasies beforehand over the deep, broad river, full of fish and crayfish, the pond full of carp, the woods, the old garden, and the abundance of young ladies. His expectations were fulfilled in every particular, and he had all the fishing and musical society he could wish for. Soon after his arrival Plestcheyev came to stay with him on a month's visit.

He was an old man in feeble health, but attractive to everyone. Young ladies in particular were immediately fascinated by him. He used to compose his works aloud, sometimes shouting at the top of his voice, so that Chekhov would run in and ask him if he wanted anything. Then the old man would give a sweet and guilty smile and go on with his work. Chekhov was in constant anxiety about the old man's health, as he was very fond of cakes and pastry, and Chekhov's mother used to regale him on them to such an extent that Anton was constantly having to give him medicine. Afterwards Suvorin, the editor of *Novoye Vremya*, came to stay. Chekhov and he used to paddle in a canoe, hollowed out of a tree, to an old mill, where they would spend hours fishing and talking about literature.

Both the grandsons of serfs, both cultivated and talented men, they were greatly attracted by each other. Their friendship lasted for several years, and on account of Suvorin's reactionary opinions, exposed Chekhov to a great deal of criticism in Russia. Chekhov's feelings for Suvorin began to change at the time of the Dreyfus case, but he never broke entirely with him. Suvorin's feelings for Chekhov remained unchanged.

In the spring of 1889 his brother Nikolay, the artist, fell ill with consumption, and his illness occupied Anton entirely, and completely prevented his working. That summer Nikolay died, and it was under the influence of this, his first great sorrow, that Chekhov wrote "A Dreary Story." For several months after the death of his brother he was extremely restless and depressed.

In 1890 his younger brother Mihail was taking his degree in law at Moscow, and studying treatises on the management of prisons. Chekhov got hold of them, became intensely interested in prisons, and resolved to visit the penal settlement of Sahalin. He made up his mind to go to the Far East so unexpectedly that it was difficult for his family to believe that he was in earnest.

He was afraid that after Kennan's revelations about the penal system in Siberia, he would, as a writer, be refused permission to visit the prisons in

Sahalin, and therefore tried to get a free pass from the head of the prison administration, Galkin-Vrasskoy. When this proved fruitless he set off in April, 1890, with no credentials but his card as a newspaper correspondent.

The Siberian railway did not then exist, and only after great hardships, being held up by floods and by the impassable state of the roads, Chekhov succeeded in reaching Sahalin on the 11th of July, having driven nearly 3,000 miles. He stayed three months on the island, traversed it from north to south, made a census of the population, talked to every one of the ten thousand convicts, and made a careful study of the convict system. Apparently the chief reason for all this was the consciousness that "We have destroyed millions of men in prisons.... It is not the superintendents of the prisons who are to blame, but all of us." In Russia it was not possible to be a "free artist and nothing more."

Chekhov left Sahalin in October and returned to Europe by way of India and the Suez Canal. He wanted to visit Japan, but the steamer was not allowed to put in at the port on account of cholera.

In the Indian Ocean he used to bathe by diving off the forecastle deck when the steamer was going at full speed, and catching a rope which was let down from the stern. Once while he was doing this he saw a shark and a shoal of pilot fish close to him in the water, as he describes in his story "Gusev."

The fruits of this journey were a series of articles in *Russkaya Myssl* on the island of Sahalin, and two short stories, "Gusev" and "In Exile." His articles on Sahalin were looked on with a favourable eye in Petersburg, and, who knows, it is possible that the reforms which followed in regard to penal servitude and exile would not have taken place but for their influence.

After about a month in Moscow, Chekhov went to Petersburg to see Suvorin. The majority of his Petersburg friends and admirers met him with feelings of envy and ill-will. People gave dinners in his honour and praised him to the skies, but at the same time they were ready to "tear him to pieces." Even in Moscow such people did not give him a moment for work or rest. He was so prostrated by the feeling of hostility surrounding him that he accepted an invitation from Suvorin to go abroad with him. When Chekhov had completed arrangements for equipping the Sahalin schools with the necessary books, they set off for the South of Europe. Vienna delighted him, and Venice surpassed all his expectations and threw him into a state of childlike ecstasy.

Everything fascinated him—and then there was a change in the weather and a steady downpour of rain. Chekhov's spirits drooped. Venice was damp and seemed horrible, and he longed to escape from it.

He had had just such a change of mood in Singapore, which interested him immensely and suddenly filled him with such misery that he wanted to cry.

After Venice Chekhov did not get the pleasure he expected from any Italian town. Florence did not attract him; the sun was not shining. Rome gave him the impression of a provincial town. He was feeling exhausted, and to add to his depression he had got into debt, and had the prospect of spending the summer without any money at all.

Travelling with Suvorin, who did not stint himself, drew him into spending more than he intended, and he owed Suvorin a sum which was further increased at Monte Carlo by Chekhov's losing nine hundred roubles at roulette. But this loss was a blessing to him in so far as, for some reason, it made him feel satisfied with himself. At the end of April, 1891, after a stay in Paris, Chekhov returned to Moscow. Except at Vienna and for the first days in Venice and at Nice, it had rained the whole time. On his return he had to work extremely hard to pay for his two tours. His brother Mihail was at this time inspector of taxes at Alexino, and Chekhov and his household spent the summer not far from that town in the province of Kaluga, so as to be near him. They took a house dating from the days of Catherine. Chekhov's mother had to sit down and rest halfway when she crossed the hall, the rooms were so large. He liked the place with its endless avenues of lime-trees and poetical river, while fishing and gathering mushrooms soothed him and put him in the mood for work. Here he went on with his story "The Duel," which he had begun before going abroad. From the windows there was the view of an old house which Chekhov described in "An Artist's Story," and which he was very eager to buy. Indeed from this time he began thinking of buying a country place of his own, not in Little Russia, but in Central Russia. Petersburg seemed to him more and more idle, cold and egoistic, and he had lost all faith in his Petersburg acquaintances. On the other hand, Moscow no longer seemed to him as before "like a cook," and he grew to love it. He grew fond of its climate, its people and its bells. He always delighted in bells. Sometimes in earlier days he had gathered together a party of friends and gone with them to Kamenny Bridge to listen to the Easter bells. After eagerly listening to them he would set off to wander from church to church, and with his legs giving way under him from fatigue would, only when Easter night was over, make his way homewards. Meanwhile his father, who was fond of staying till the end of the service, would return from the parish church, and all the brothers would sing "Christ is risen" in chorus, and then they all sat down to break their fast. Chekhov never spent an Easter night in bed.

Meanwhile in the spring of 1892 there began to be fears about the crops. These apprehensions were soon confirmed. An unfortunate summer was followed by a hard autumn and winter, in which many districts were famine-stricken. Side by side with the Government relief of the starving population there was a widespread movement for organizing relief, in which various societies and private persons took part. Chekhov naturally was drawn into this movement. The provinces of Nizhni-Novogorod and Voronezh were in the greatest distress, and in the former of these two provinces, Yegorov, an old friend of Chekhov's Voskresensk days, was a district captain (Zemsky Natchalnik). Chekhov wrote to Yegorov, got up a subscription fund among his acquaintance, and finally set off himself for Nizhni-Novogorod. As the starving peasants were selling their horses and cattle for next to nothing, or even slaughtering them for food, it was feared that as spring came on there would be no beasts to plough with, so that the coming year threatened to be one of famine also.

Chekhov organized a scheme for buying up the horses and feeding them till the spring at the expense of a relief fund, and then, as soon as field labour was possible, distributing them among the peasants who were without horses.

After visiting the province of Nizhni-Novogorod, Chekhov went with Suvorin to Voronezh. But this expedition was not a successful one. He was revolted by the ceremonious dinners with which he was welcomed as an author, while the whole province was suffering from famine. Moreover travelling with Suvorin tied him down and hindered his independent action. Chekhov longed for intense personal activity such as he displayed later in his campaign against the cholera.

In the winter of the same year his long-cherished dream was realized: he bought himself an estate. It was in the province of Moscow, near the hamlet of Melihovo. As an estate it had nothing to recommend it but an old, badly laid out homestead, wastes of land, and a forest that had been felled. It had been bought on the spur of the moment, simply because it had happened to turn up. Chekhov had never been to the place before he bought it, and only visited it when all the formalities had been completed. One could hardly turn round near the house for the mass of hurdles and fences. Moreover the Chekhovs moved into it in the winter when it was under snow, and all boundaries being obliterated, it was impossible to tell what was theirs and what was not. But in spite of all that, Chekhov's first impression was favourable, and he never showed a sign of being disappointed. He was delighted by the approach of spring and the fresh surprises that were continually being revealed by the melting snow. Suddenly it would appear that a whole haystack belonged to him which he had supposed to be a neighbour's, then an avenue of lime-trees came to light which they had not distinguished before under the snow. Everything that was amiss in the place, everything he did not like, was at once abolished or altered. But in spite of all the defects of the house and its surroundings, and the appalling road from the station (nearly nine miles) and the lack of rooms, so many visitors came that there was nowhere to put them, and beds had sometimes to be made up in the passages. Chekhov's household at this time consisted of his father and mother, his sister, and his younger brother Mihail. These were all permanent inmates of Melihovo.

As soon as the snow had disappeared the various duties in the house and on the land were assigned: Chekhov's sister undertook the flower-beds and the kitchen garden, his younger brother undertook the field work. Chekhov himself planted the trees and looked after them. His father worked from morning till night weeding the paths in the garden and making new ones.

Everything attracted the new landowner: planting the bulbs and watching the flight of rooks and starlings, sowing the clover, and the goose hatching out her goslings. By four o'clock in the morning Chekhov was up and about. After drinking his coffee he would go out into the garden and would spend a long time scrutinizing every fruit-tree and every rose-bush, now cutting off a branch, now training a shoot, or he would squat on his heels by a stump and gaze at something on the ground. It turned out that there was more land than they needed (639 acres), and they farmed it themselves, with no bailiff or steward, assisted only by two labourers, Frol and Ivan.

At eleven o'clock Chekhov, who got through a good deal of writing in the morning, would go into the dining-room and look significantly at the clock. His mother would jump up from her seat and her sewing-machine and begin to bustle about, crying: "Oh dear! Antosha wants his dinner!"

When the table was laid there were so many homemade and other dainties prepared by his mother that there would hardly be space on the table for them. There was not room to sit at the table either. Besides the five permanent members of the family there were invariably outsiders as well. After dinner Chekhov used to go off to his bedroom and lock himself in to "read." Between his after-dinner nap and tea-time he wrote again. The time between tea and supper (at seven o'clock in the evening) was devoted to walks and outdoor work. At ten o'clock they went to bed. Lights were put out and all was stillness in the house; the only sound was a subdued singing and monotonous recitation. This was Pavel Yegorovitch repeating the evening service in his room: he was religious and liked to say his prayers aloud.

From the first day that Chekhov moved to Melihovo the sick began flocking to him from twenty miles around. They came on foot or were brought in carts, and often he was fetched to patients at a distance. Sometimes from early in the morning peasant women and children were standing before his door waiting. He would go out, listen to them and sound them, and would never let one go away without advice and medicine. His expenditure on drugs was considerable, as he had to keep a regular store of them. Once some wayfarers brought Chekhov a man they had picked up by the roadside in the middle of the night, stabbed in the stomach with a pitchfork. The peasant was carried into his study and put down in the middle of the floor, and Chekhov spent a long time looking after him, examining his wounds and bandaging them up. But what was hardest for Chekhov was visiting the sick at their own homes: sometimes there was a journey of several hours, and in this way the time essential for writing was wasted.

The first winter at Melihovo was cold; it lasted late and food was short. Easter came in the snow. There was a church at Melihovo in which a service was held only once a year, at Easter. Visitors from Moscow were staying with Chekhov. The family got up a choir among themselves and sang all the Easter matins and mass. Pavel Yegorovitch conducted as usual. It was out of the ordinary and touching, and the peasants were delighted: it warmed their hearts to their new neighbours.

Then the thaw came. The roads became appalling. There were only three broken-down horses on the estate and not a wisp of hay. The horses had to be fed on rye straw chopped up with an axe and sprinkled with flour. One of the horses was vicious and there was no getting it out of the yard. Another was stolen in the fields and a dead horse left in its place. And so for a long time there was only one poor spiritless beast to drive which was nicknamed Anna Petrovna. This Anna Petrovna contrived to trot to the station, to take Chekhov to his patients, to haul logs and to eat nothing but straw sprinkled with flour. But Chekhov and his family did not lose heart. Always affectionate, gay and plucky, he cheered the others, work went ahead, and in less than three months everything in the place was changed: the house was furnished with crockery; there was the ring of carpenters' axes; six horses were bought, and all the field work for the spring had been completed in good time and in accordance with the rules of agricultural science. They had no experience at all, but bought masses of books on the management of the land, and every question, however small, was debated in common.

Their first successes delighted Chekhov. He had thirty acres under rye, thirty under oats, and fully thirty under hay. Marvels were being done in the kitchen garden: tomatoes and artichokes did well in the open air. A dry spring and summer ruined the oats and the rye; the peasants cut the hay in return for half the crop, and Chekhov's half seemed a small stack; only in the kitchen garden things went well.

The position of Melihovo on the highroad and the news that Chekhov the author had settled there inevitably led to new acquaintances. Doctors and members of the local Zemstvos began visiting Chekhov; acquaintance was made with the officials of the district, and Chekhov was elected a member of the Serpuhov Sanitary Council.

At that time cholera was raging in the South of Russia. Every day it came nearer and nearer to the province of Moscow, and everywhere it found favourable conditions among the population weakened by the famine of autumn and winter. It was essential to take immediate measures for meeting the cholera, and the Zemstvo of Serpuhov worked its hardest. Chekhov as a doctor and a member of the Sanitary Council was asked to take charge of a section. He immediately gave his services for nothing. He had to drive about among the manufacturers of the district persuading them to take adequate measures to combat the cholera. Owing to his efforts the whole section containing twenty-five villages and hamlets was covered with a network of the necessary institutions. For several months Chekhov scarcely got out of his chaise. During that time he had to drive all over his section, receive patients at home, and do his literary work. He returned home shattered and exhausted, but always behaved as though he were doing something trivial; he cracked little jokes and made everyone laugh as before, and carried on conversations with his dachshund, Quinine, about her supposed sufferings.

By early autumn the place had become unrecognizable. The outhouses had been rebuilt, unnecessary fences had been removed, rose-trees had been planted, a flower-bed had been laid out; in the fields before the gates Chekhov was planning to dig a big new pond. With what interest he watched each day the progress of the work upon it! He planted trees round it and dropped into it tiny carp and perch which he brought with him in a jar from Moscow. The pond became later on more like an ichthyological station than a pond, as there was no kind of fish in Russia, except the pike, of which Chekhov had not representatives in this pond. He liked sitting on the dam on its bank and watching with ecstasy shoals of little fish coming suddenly to the surface and then hiding in its depths. An excellent well had been dug in Melihovo before this. Chekhov had been very anxious that it should be in Little Russian style with a crane. But the position did not allow of this, and it was made with a big wheel painted yellow like the wells at Russian railway stations. The question where to dig this well and whether the water in it would be good greatly interested Chekhov. He wanted exact information and a theory based on good grounds, seeing that nine-tenths of Russia uses water out of wells, and has done so since time immemorial; but whenever he questioned the well-sinkers who came to him, he received the same vague answer: "Who can tell? It's in God's hands. Can you find out beforehand what the water will be like?"

But the well, like the pond, was a great success, and the water turned out to be excellent.

He began seriously planning to build a new house and farm buildings. Creative activity was his passion. He was never satisfied with what he had ready-made; he longed to make something new. He planted little trees, raised pines and fir-trees from seed, looked after them as though they were his children, and, like Colonel Vershinin in his "Three Sisters," dreamed as he looked at them of what they would be like in three or four hundred years.

The winter of 1893 was a severe one with a great deal of snow. The snow was so high under the windows that the hares who ran into the garden stood on their hind-legs and looked into the window of Chekhov's study. The swept paths in the garden were like deep trenches. By then Chekhov had finished his work in connection with the cholera and he began to live the life of a hermit. His sister found employment in Moscow; only his father and mother were left with him in the house, and the hours seemed very long. They went to bed even earlier than in the summer, but Chekhov would wake up at one in the morning, sit down to his work and then go back to bed and sleep again. At six o'clock in the morning all the household was up. Chekhov wrote a great deal that winter. But as soon as visitors arrived, life was completely transformed. There was singing, playing on the piano, laughter. Chekhov's mother did her utmost to load the tables with dainties; his father with a mysterious air would produce various specially prepared cordials and liqueurs from some hidden recess; and then it seemed that Melihovo had something of its own, peculiar to it, which could be found in no other country estate. Chekhov was always particularly pleased at the visits of Miss Mizinov and of Potapenko. He was particularly fond of them, and his whole family rejoiced at their arrival. They stayed up long after midnight on such days, and Chekhov wrote only by snatches. And every time he wrote five or six lines, he would get up again and go back to his visitors.

"I have written sixty kopecks' worth," he would say with a smile.

Braga's "Serenade" was the fashion at that time, and Chekhov was fond of hearing Potapenko play it on the violin while Miss Mizinov sang it.

Having been a student at the Moscow University, Chekhov liked to celebrate St. Tatyana's Day. He never missed making a holiday of it when he lived in Moscow. That winter, for the first time, he chanced to be in Petersburg on the 12th of January. He did not forget "St. Tatyana," and assembled all his literary friends on that day in a Petersburg restaurant. They made speeches and kept the holiday, and this festivity initiated by him was so successful that the authors went on meeting regularly afterwards.

Though Melihovo was his permanent home, Chekhov often paid visits to Moscow and Petersburg. He frequently stayed at hotels, and there he sometimes had difficulties over his passport. As a landowner he had no need of credentials from the police in the Serpuhov district, and found his University diploma sufficient. In Petersburg and Moscow, under the old passport regulations they would not give him a passport because he resided permanently in the provinces. Misunderstandings arose, sometimes developing into disagreeable incidents and compelling Chekhov to return home earlier than he had intended. Someone suggested to Chekhov that he should enter the Government service and immediately retire from it, as retired officials used at that time to receive a permanent passport from the department in which they had served. Chekhov sent a petition to the Department of Medicine for a post to be assigned to him, and received an appointment as an extra junior medical clerk in that Department, and soon afterwards sent in his resignation, after which he had no more trouble.

Chekhov spent the whole spring of 1893 at Melihovo, planted roses, looked after his fruit-trees, and was enthusiastic over country life. That summer Melihovo was especially crowded with visitors. Chekhov was visited not only by his friends, but also by people whose acquaintance he neither sought nor desired. People were sleeping on sofas and several in a room; some even spent the night in the passage. Young ladies, authors, local doctors, members of the Zemstvo, distant relations with their sons— all these people flitted through Melihovo. Life was a continual whirl, everyone was gay; this rush of visitors and the everlasting readiness of Chekhov's mother to regale them with food and drink seemed like a return to the good old times of country life in the past. Chekhov was the centre on which all attention was concentrated. Everyone sought him, lived in him, and caught up every word he uttered. When he was with friends he liked taking walks or making expeditions to the neighbouring monastery. The chaise, the cart, and the racing droshky were brought out. Chekhov put on his white tunic, buckled a strap round his waist, and got on the racing droshky. A young lady would sit sideways behind him, holding on to the strap. The white tunic and strap used to make Chekhov call himself an Hussar. The party would set off; the "Hussar" in the racing droshky would lead the way, and then came the cart and the chaise full of visitors.

The numbers of guests necessitated more building, as the house would not contain them all. Instead of a farm, new buildings close to the house itself were begun. Some of the farm buildings were pulled down, others were put up after Chekhov's own plans. A new cattle yard made its appearance, and by it a hut with a well and a hurdle fence in the Little Russian style, a bathhouse, a barn, and finally Chekhov's dream—a lodge. It was a little house with three tiny rooms, in one of which a bedstead was put with difficulty, and in another a writing-table. At first this lodge was intended only for visitors, but afterwards Chekhov moved into it and there he wrote his "Seagull." This little lodge was built among the fruit-bushes, and to reach it one had to pass through the orchard. In spring, when the apples and cherries were in blossom, it was pleasant to live in this lodge, but in winter it was so buried in the snow that pathways had to be cut to it through drifts as high as a man.

Chekhov suffered terribly about this time from his cough. It troubled him particularly in the morning. But he made light of it. He was afraid of worrying his family. His younger brother once saw his handkerchief spattered with blood, and asked what it meant. Chekhov seemed disconcerted and said:

"Oh, nothing; it is no matter.... Don't tell Masha and Mother."

The cough was the reason for Chekhov's going in 1894 to the Crimea. He stayed in Yalta, though he evidently did not like it and longed to be home.

Chekhov's activity in the campaign against the cholera resulted in his being elected a member of the Zemstvo. He was keenly interested in everything to do with the new roads to be constructed, and the new hospitals and schools it was intended to open. Besides this public work the neighbourhood was indebted to him for the making of a highroad from the station of Lopasnya to Melihovo, and for the building of schools at Talezh, Novoselka, and Melihovo. He made the plans for these schools himself, bought the material, and superintended the building of them. When he talked about them his eyes kindled, and it was evident that if he had had the means he would have built, not three, but a multitude.

At the opening of the school at Novoselka, the peasants brought him the ikon and offered him bread and salt. Chekhov was much embarrassed in responding to their gratitude, but his face and his shining eyes showed that he was pleased. Besides the schools he built a fire-station for the village and a belfry for the church, and ordered a cross made of looking-glass for the cupola, the flash of which in the sun or moonlight was visible more than eight miles away.

Chekhov spent the year 1894 at Melihovo, began writing "The Seagull," and did a great deal of work. He paid a visit to Tolstoy at Yasnaya Polyana, and returned enchanted with the old man and his family. Chekhov was already changing; he looked haggard, older, sallower. He coughed, he was tortured by intestinal trouble. Evidently he was now aware of the gravity of his illness, but, as before, made no complaint and tried to hide it from others.

In 1896 "The Seagull" was performed at the Alexandrinsky Theatre in Petersburg. It was a fiasco. The actors did not know their parts; in the theatre there was "a strained condition of boredom and bewilderment." The notices in the press were prejudiced and stupid. Not wishing to see or meet anyone, Chekhov kept out of sight after the performance, and by next morning was in the train on his way back to Melihovo. The subsequent performances of "The Seagull," when the actors understood it, were successful.

Chekhov had collected a large number of books, and in 1896 he resolved to present them to the public library in his native town of Taganrog. Whole bales of books were sent by Chekhov from Petersburg and Moscow, and Iordanov, the mayor of Taganrog, sent him lists of the books needed. At the same time, at Chekhov's suggestion, something like an Information Bureau was instituted in connection with the Taganrog Library. There were to be catalogues of all the important commercial firms, all the existing regulations and government enactments on all current questions, everything, in fact, which might be of immediate service to a reader in any practical difficulty. The library at Taganrog has now developed into a fine educational institution, and is lodged in a special building designed and equipped for it and dedicated to the memory of Chekhov.

Chekhov took an active interest in the census of the people in 1896. It will be remembered that he had made a census of the whole convict population of the island of Sahalin on his own initiative and at his own expense in 1890. Now he was taking part in a census again. He studied peasant life in all its aspects; he was on intimate terms with his peasant neighbours, to whom he was now indispensable as a doctor and a friend always ready to give them good counsel.

Just before the census was completed Chekhov was taken ill with influenza, but that did not prevent his carrying out his duties. In spite of headache, he went from hut to hut and village to village, and then had to work at putting together his materials. He was absolutely alone in his work. The Zemsky Natchalniks, upon whom the government relied principally to carry out the census, were inert, and for the most part the work was left to private initiative.

In February, 1897, Chekhov was completely engrossed by a project of building a "People's Palace" in Moscow. "People's Palaces" had not been thought of; the common people spent their leisure in drink-shops. The "People's Palace" in Moscow was designed on broad principles; there was to be a library, a reading-room, lecture-rooms, a museum, a theatre. It was proposed to run it by a company of shareholders with a capital of half a million roubles. Owing to various causes in no way connected with Chekhov, this scheme came to nothing.

In March he paid a visit to Moscow, where Suvorin was expecting him. He had hardly sat down to dinner at The Hermitage when he had a sudden haemorrhage from the lungs. He was taken to a private hospital, where he remained till the 10th of April. When his sister, who knew nothing of his illness, arrived in Moscow, she was met by her brother Ivany who gave her a card of admission to visit the invalid at the hospital. On the card were the words: "Please don't tell father or mother." His sister went to the hospital. There casting a casual glance at a little table, she saw on it a diagram of the lungs, in which the upper part of the left lung was marked with a red pencil. She guessed at once that this was what was affected in Chekhov's case. This and the sight of her brother alarmed her. Chekhov, who had always been so gay, so full of spirits and vitality, looked terribly ill; he was forbidden to move or to talk, and had hardly the strength to do so.

He was declared to be suffering from tuberculosis of the lungs, and it was essential to try and ward it off at all costs, and to escape the unwholesome northern spring. He recognized himself that this was essential.

When he left the hospital he returned to Melihovo and prepared to go abroad. He went first to Biarritz, but there he was met by bad weather. A fashionable, extravagant way of living did not suit his tastes, and although he was delighted with the sea and the life led (especially by the children) on the beach, he soon moved on to Nice. Here he stayed for a considerable time at the Pension Russe in the Rue Gounod. He seemed to be fully satisfied with the life there. He liked the warmth and the people he met, M. Kovalevsky, V. M. Sobolesky, V. T. Nemirovitch-Dantchenko, the artist V. T. Yakobi and I. N. Potapenko. Prince A. I. Sumbatov arrived at Nice too, and Chekhov used sometimes to go with him to Monte Carlo to roulette.

Chekhov followed all that he had left behind in Russia with keen attention: he was anxious about the *Chronicle of Surgery*, which he had more than once saved from ruin, made arrangements about Melihovo, and so on.

He spent the autumn and winter in Nice, and in February, 1898, meant to go to Africa. He wanted to visit Algiers and Tunis, but Kovalevsky, with whom he meant to travel, fell ill, and he had to give up the project. He contemplated a visit to Corsica, but did not carry out that plan either, as he was taken seriously ill himself. A wretched dentist used contaminated forceps in extracting a tooth, and Chekhov was attacked by periostitis in a malignant form. In his own words, "he was in such pain that he climbed up the wall."

As soon as the spring had come he felt an irresistible yearning for Russia. He was weary of enforced idleness; he missed the snow and the Russian country, and at the same time he was depressed at having gained no weight in spite of the climate, good nourishment, and idleness.

While he was at Nice France was in the throes of the Dreyfus affair. Chekhov began studying the Dreyfus and Zola cases from shorthand notes, and becoming convinced of the innocence of both, wrote a heated letter to Suvorin, which led to a coolness between them.

He spent March, 1898, in Paris. He sent three hundred and nineteen volumes of French literature from Paris to the public library at Taganrog.

The lateness of the spring in Russia forced Chekhov to remain in Paris till May, when he returned to Melihovo. Melihovo became gay and lively on his arrival. Visitors began coming again; he was as hospitable as ever, but he was quieter, no longer jested as in the past, and perhaps owing to his illness talked little. But he still took as much pleasure in his roses.

After a comparatively good summer there came days of continual rain, and on the 14th of September Chekhov went away to Yalta. He had to choose between Nice and Yalta. He did not want to go abroad, and preferred the Crimea, reckoning that he might possibly seize an opportunity to pay a brief visit to Moscow, where his plays were to appear at the Art Theatre. His choice did not disappoint him. That autumn in Yalta was splendid; he felt well there, and the progress of his disease led him to settle in Yalta permanently.

Chekhov obtained a piece of land at Autka, and the same autumn began building. He spent whole days superintending the building. Stone and plaster was brought, Turks and Tatars dug the ground and laid the foundation, while he planted little trees and watched with fatherly anxiety every new shoot on them. Every stone, every tree there is eloquent of Chekhov's creative energy. That same autumn he bought the little property of Kutchuka. It was twenty-four miles from Yalta, and attracted him by its wildness and primitive beauty. To reach it one had to drive along the road at a giddy height. He began once more dreaming and drawing plans. The possible future began to take a different shape to him now, and he was already dreaming of moving from Melihovo, farming and gardening and living there as in the country. He wanted to have hens, cows, a horse and donkeys, and, of course, all of this would have been quite possible and might have been realized if he had not been slowly dying. His dreams remained dreams, and Kutchuka stands uninhabited to this day.

The winter of 1898 was extremely severe in the Crimea. The cold, the snow, the stormy sea, and the complete lack of people akin to him in spirit and of "interesting women" wearied Chekhov; he began to be depressed. He was irresistibly drawn to the north, and began to fancy that if he moved for the winter to Moscow, where his plays were being acted with such success and where everything was so full of interest for him, it would be no worse for his health than staying in Yalta, and he began dreaming of buying a house in Moscow. He wanted at one moment to get something small and snug in the neighbourhood of Kursk Station, where it might be possible to stay the three winter months in every comfort; but when such a house was found his mood changed and he resigned himself to life at Yalta.

The January and February of 1899 were particularly irksome to Chekhov: he suffered from an intestinal trouble which poisoned his existence. Moreover consumptive patients from all over Russia began appealing to him to assist them to come to Yalta. These invalids were almost always poor, and on reaching Yalta mostly ended their lives in miserable conditions, pining for their native place. Chekhov exerted himself on behalf of everyone, printed appeals in the papers, collected money, and did his utmost to alleviate their condition.

After the unfavourable winter came an exquisite warm spring, and on the 12th of April Chekhov was in Moscow and by May in Melihovo. His father had died the previous October, and with his death a great link with the place was broken. The consciousness of having to go away early in the autumn gradually brought Chekhov to decide to sell the place.

On the 25th of August he went back to his own villa at Yalta, and soon afterwards Melihovo was sold, and his mother and sister joined him. During the last four and a half years of his life Chekhov's health grew rapidly worse. His chief interest was centred in Moscow, in the Art Theatre, which had just been started, and the greater part of his dramatic work was done during this period.

Chekhov was ill all the winter of 1900, and only felt better towards the spring. During those long winter months he wrote "In the Ravine." The detestable spring of that year affected his mood and his health even more. Snow fell on the 5th of March, and this had a shattering effect on him. In April he was again very ill. An attack of intestinal trouble prevented him from eating, drinking, or working. As soon as it was over Chekhov, homesick for the north, set off for Moscow, but there he was met by severe weather. Returning in August to Yalta, he wrote "The Three Sisters."

He spent the autumn in Moscow, and at the beginning of December went to the French Riviera, settled in Nice, and dreamed again of a visit to Africa, but went instead to Rome. Here, as usual, he met with severe weather. Early in February he returned to Yalta. That year there was a soft, sunny spring. Chekhov spent whole days in the open air, engaged in his favourite occupations; he planted and pruned trees, looked after his garden, ordered all sorts of seeds, and watched them coming up. At the same time he was working on behalf of the invalids coming to Yalta, who appealed to him for help, and also completing the library he had founded at Taganrog, and planning to open a picture gallery there.

In May, 1901, Chekhov went to Moscow and was thoroughly examined by a physician, who urged him to go at once to Switzerland or to take a koumiss cure. Chekhov preferred the latter.

On the 25th of May he married Olga Knipper, one of the leading actresses at the Art Theatre, and with her went off to the province of Ufa for the koumiss cure. On the way they had to wait twenty-four hours for a steamer, in very unpleasant surroundings, at a place called Pyany Bor ("Drunken Market"), in the province of Vyatka.

In the autumn of 1901 Tolstoy was staying, for the sake of his health, at Gaspra. Chekhov was very fond of him and frequently visited him. Altogether that autumn was an eventful one for him: Kuprin, Bunin and Gorky visited the Crimea; the writer Elpatyevsky settled there also, and Chekhov felt fairly well. Tolstoy's illness was the centre of general attention, and Chekhov was very uneasy about him.

In 1902 there was suddenly a change for the worse: violent haemorrhage exhausted him till the beginning of February; he was for over a month confined to his study. It was at this time that the incident of Gorky's election to the Academy and subsequent expulsion from it led Chekhov to write a letter to the Royal President of the Academy asking that his own name should be struck off the list of Academicians.

Chekhov had hardly recovered when his wife was taken seriously ill. When she was a little better he made a tour by the Volga and the Kama as far as Perm. On his return he settled with his wife in a summer villa not far from Moscow; he spent July there and returned home to Yalta in August. But the longing for a life of movement and culture, the desire to be nearer to the theatre, drew him to the north again, and in September he was back in Moscow. Here he was not left in peace for one minute; swarms of visitors jostled each other from morning till night. Such a life exhausted him; he ran away from it to Yalta in December, but did not escape it there. His cough was worse; every day he had a high temperature, and these symptoms were followed by an attack of pleurisy. He did not get up all through the Christmas holidays; he still had an agonizing cough, and it was in this enforced idleness that he thought out his play "The Cherry Orchard."

It is quite possible that if Chekhov had taken care of himself his disease would not have developed so rapidly or proved fatal. The feverish energy of his temperament, his readiness to respond to every impression, and his thirst for activity, drove him from south to north and back again, regardless of his health and of the climate. Like all invalids, he ought to have gone on living in the same place, at Nice or at Yalta, until he was better, but he lived exactly as though he had been in good health. When he arrived in the north he was always excited and absorbed by what was going on, and this exhilaration he mistook for an improvement in his health; but he had only to return to Yalta for the reaction to set in, and it would seem to him at once that his case was hopeless, that the Crimea had no beneficial effect on consumptives, and that the climate was wretched.

The spring of 1903 passed fairly favourably. He recovered sufficiently to go to Moscow and even to Petersburg. On returning from Petersburg he began preparing to go to Switzerland. But his state of health was such that his doctor in Moscow advised him to give up the idea of Switzerland and even of Yalta, and to stay somewhere not very far from Moscow. He followed this advice and settled at Nar. Now that it was proposed that he should stay the winter in the north, all that he had created in Yalta—his house and his garden—seemed unnecessary and objectless. In the end he returned to Yalta and set to work on "The Cherry Orchard."

In October, 1903, the play was finished and he set off to produce it himself in Moscow. He spent days at a time in the Art Theatre, producing his "Cherry Orchard," and incidentally supervising the setting and performance of the plays of other authors. He gave advice and criticized, was excited and enthusiastic.

On the 17th of January, 1904, "The Cherry Orchard" was produced for the first time. The first performance was the occasion of the celebration of the twenty-fifth anniversary of Chekhov's literary activity. A great number of addresses were read and speeches were made. Chekhov was many times called before the curtain, and this expression of universal sympathy exhausted him to such a degree that the very day after the performance he began to think with relief of going back to Yalta, where he spent the following spring.

His health was completely shattered, and everyone who saw him secretly thought the end was not far off; but the nearer Chekhov was to the end, the less he seemed to realize it. Ill as he was, at the beginning of May he set off for Moscow. He was terribly ill all the way on the journey, and on arrival took to his bed at once. He was laid up till June.

On the 3rd of June he set off with his wife for a cure abroad to the Black Forest, and settled in a little spa called Badenweiler. He was dying, although he wrote to everyone that he had almost recovered, and that health was coming back to him not by ounces but by hundredweights. He was dying, but he spent the time dreaming of going to the Italian lakes and returning to Yalta by sea from Trieste, and was already making inquiries about the steamers and the times they stopped at Odessa.

He died on the 2nd of July.

His body was taken to Moscow and buried in the Novodyevitchy Monastery, beside his father's tomb.

TO HIS BROTHER MIHAIL.

TAGANROG, July 1, 1876.

DEAR BROTHER MISHA,

I got your letter when I was fearfully bored and was sitting at the gate yawning, and so you can judge how welcome that immense letter was. Your writing is good, and in the whole letter I have not found one mistake in spelling. But one thing I don't like: why do you style yourself "your worthless and insignificant brother"? You recognize your insignificance? ... Recognize it before God; perhaps, too, in the presence of beauty, intelligence, nature, but not before men. Among men you must be conscious of your dignity. Why, you are not a rascal, you are an honest man, aren't you? Well, respect yourself as an honest man and know that an honest man is not something worthless. Don't confound "being humble" with "recognizing one's worthlessness." ...

It is a good thing that you read. Acquire the habit of doing so. In time you will come to value that habit. Madame Beecher-Stowe has wrung tears from your eyes? I read her once, and six months ago read her again with the object of studying her—and after reading I had an unpleasant sensation which mortals feel after eating too many raisins or currants.... Read "Don Quixote." It is a fine thing. It is by Cervantes, who is said to be almost on a level with Shakespeare. I advise my brothers to read—if they haven't already done so—Turgenev's "Hamlet and Don Quixote." You won't understand it, my dear. If you want to read a book of travel that won't bore you, read Gontcharov's "The Frigate Pallada."

... I am going to bring with me a boarder who will pay twenty roubles a month and live under our general supervision. Though even twenty roubles is not enough if one considers the price of food in Moscow and mother's weakness for feeding boarders with righteous zeal. [Footnote: This letter

- 23 -

was written by Chekhov when he was in the fifth class of the Taganrog high school.]

TO HIS COUSIN, MIHAIL CHEKHOV.

TAGANROG, May 10, 1877.

... If I send letters to my mother, care of you, please give them to her when you are alone with her; there are things in life which one can confide in one person only, whom one trusts. It is because of this that I write to my mother without the knowledge of the others, for whom my secrets are quite uninteresting, or, rather, unnecessary.... My second request is of more importance. Please go on comforting my mother, who is both physically and morally broken. She has found in you not merely a nephew but a great deal more and better than a nephew. My mother's character is such that the moral support of others is a great help to her. It is a silly request, isn't it? But you will understand, especially as I have said "moral," i.e., spiritual support. There is no one in this wicked world dearer to us than our mother, and so you will greatly oblige your humble servant by comforting his worn-out and weary mother....

TO HIS UNCLE, M. G. CHEKHOV.

MOSCOW, 1885.

... I could not come to see you last summer because I took the place of a district doctor friend of mine who went away for his holiday, but this year I hope to travel and therefore to see you. Last December I had an attack of spitting blood, and decided to take some money from the Literary Fund and go abroad for my health. I am a little better now, but I still think that I shall have to go away. And whenever I go abroad, or to the Crimea, or to the Caucasus, I will go through Taganrog.

... I am sorry I cannot join you in being of service to my native Taganrog.... I am sure that if my work had been there I should have been calmer, more cheerful, in better health, but evidently it is my fate to remain in Moscow. My home and my career are here. I have work of two sorts. As a doctor I should have grown slack in Taganrog and forgotten my medicine, but in Moscow a doctor has no time to go to the club and play cards. As a writer I am no use except in Moscow or Petersburg.

My medical work is progressing little by little. I go on steadily treating patients. Every day I have to spend more than a rouble on cabs. I have a lot of friends and therefore many patients. Half of them I have to treat for nothing, but the other half pay me three or five roubles a visit.... I need hardly say I have not made a fortune yet, and it will be a long time before I do, but I live tolerably and need nothing. So long as I am alive and well the position of the family is secure. I have bought new furniture, hired a good piano, keep two servants, give little evening parties with music and singing. I have no debts and do not want to borrow. Till quite recently we used to run an account at the butcher's and grocer's, but now I have stopped even that, and we pay cash for everything. What will come later, there is no knowing; as it is we have nothing to complain of....

TO N. A. LEIKIN.

MOSCOW, October, 1885.

... You advise me to go to Petersburg, and say that Petersburg is not China. I know it is not, and as you are aware, I have long realized the necessity of going there; but what am I to do? Owing to the fact that we are a large family, I never have a ten-rouble note to spare, and to go there, even if I did it in the most uncomfortable and beggarly way, would cost at least fifty roubles. How am I to get the money? I can't squeeze it out of my family and don't think I ought to. If I were to cut down our two courses at dinner to one, I should begin to pine away from pangs of conscience.... Allah only knows how difficult it is for me to keep my balance, and how easy it would be for me to slip and lose my equilibrium. I fancy that if next month I should earn twenty or thirty roubles less, my balance would be gone, and I should be in difficulties. I am awfully apprehensive about money matters and, owing to this quite uncommercial cowardice in pecuniary affairs, I avoid loans and payments on account. I am not difficult to move. If I had money I should fly from one city to another endlessly.

TO A. S. SUVORIN.

MOSCOW, February 21, 1886.

... Thank you for the flattering things you say about my work and for having published my story so soon. You can judge yourself how refreshing, even inspiring, the kind attention of an experienced and gifted writer like yourself has been to me.

I agree with what you say about the end of my story which you have cut out; thank you for the helpful advice. I have been writing for the last six years, but you are the first person who has taken the trouble to advise and explain.

... I do not write very much—not more than two or three short stories weekly.

TO D. V. GRIGOROVITCH.

MOSCOW, March 28, 1886.

Your letter, my kind, fervently beloved bringer of good tidings, struck me like a flash of lightning. I almost burst into tears, I was overwhelmed, and now I feel it has left a deep trace in my soul! May God show the same tender kindness to you in your age as you have shown me in my youth! I can find neither words nor deeds to thank you. You know with what eyes ordinary people look at the elect such as you, and so you can judge what your letter means for my self-esteem. It is better than any diploma, and for a writer who is just beginning it is payment both for the present and the future. I am almost dazed. I have no power to judge whether I deserve this high reward. I only repeat that it has overwhelmed me.

If I have a gift which one ought to respect, I confess before the pure candour of your heart that hitherto I have not respected it. I felt that I had a gift, but I had got into the habit of thinking that it was insignificant. Purely external causes are sufficient to make one unjust to oneself, suspicious, and morbidly sensitive. And as I realize now I have always had plenty of such causes. All my friends and relatives have always taken a condescending tone to my writing, and never ceased urging me in a friendly way not to give up real work for the sake of scribbling. I have hundreds of friends in Moscow, and among them a dozen or two writers, but I cannot recall a single one who reads me or considers me an artist. In Moscow there is a so-called Literary Circle: talented people and mediocrities of all ages and colours gather once a week in a private room of a restaurant and exercise their tongues. If I went there and read them a single passage of your letter, they would laugh in my face. In the course of the five years that I have been knocking about from one newspaper office to another I have had time to assimilate the general view of my literary insignificance. I soon got used to looking down upon my work, and so it has gone from bad to worse. That is the first reason. The second is that I am a doctor, and am up to my ears in medical work, so that the proverb about trying to catch two hares has given to no one more sleepless nights than me.

I am writing all this to you in order to excuse this grievous sin a little before you. Hitherto my attitude to my literary work has been frivolous, heedless, casual. I don't remember a *single* story over which I have spent more than twenty-four hours, and "The Huntsman," which you liked, I wrote in the bathing-shed! I wrote my stories as reporters write their notes about fires, mechanically, half-unconsciously, taking no thought of the reader or myself.... I wrote and did all I could not to waste upon the story the scenes and images dear to me which—God knows why—I have treasured and kept carefully hidden.

The first impulse to self-criticism was given me by a very kind and, to the best of my belief, sincere letter from Suvorin. I began to think of writing something decent, but I still had no faith in my being any good as a writer. And then, unexpected and undreamed of, came your letter. Forgive the comparison: it had on me the effect of a Governor's order to clear out of the town within twenty-four hours—i.e., I suddenly felt an imperative need to hurry, to make haste and get out of where I have stuck....

I agree with you in everything. When I saw "The Witch" in print I felt myself the cynicism of the points to which you call my attention. They would not have been there had I written this story in three or four days instead of in one.

I shall put an end to working against time, but cannot do so just yet.... It is impossible to get out of the rut I have got into. I have nothing against going hungry, as I have done in the past, but it is not a question of myself.... I give to literature my spare time, two or three hours a day and a bit of the night, that is, time which is of no use except for short things. In the summer, when I have more time and have fewer expenses, I will start on some serious work.

I cannot put my real name on the book because it is too late: the design for the cover is ready and the book printed. [Footnote: "Motley Tales" is meant.] Many of my Petersburg friends advised me, even before you did, not to spoil the book by a pseudonym, but I did not listen to them, probably out of vanity. I dislike my book very much. It's a hotch-potch, a disorderly medley of the poor stuff I wrote as a student, plucked by the censor and by the editors of comic papers. I am sure that many people will be disappointed when they read it. Had I known that I had readers and that you were watching me, I would not have published this book.

I rest all my hopes on the future. I am only twenty-six. Perhaps I shall succeed in doing something, though time flies fast.

Forgive my long letter and do not blame a man because, for the first time in his life, he has made bold to treat himself to the pleasure of writing to Grigorovitch.

Send me your photograph, if possible. I am so overwhelmed with your kindness that I feel as though I should like to write a whole ream to you. God grant you health and happiness, and believe in the sincerity of your deeply respectful and grateful

A. CHEKHOV.

TO N. A. LEIKIN.

MOSCOW, April 6, 1886.

... I am ill. Spitting of blood and weakness. I am not writing anything.... If I don't sit down to write to-morrow, you must forgive me—I shall not send you a story for the Easter number. I ought to go to the South but I have no money.... I am afraid to submit myself to be sounded by my colleagues. I am inclined to think it is not so much my lungs as my throat that is at fault.... I have no fever.

TO MADAME M. V. KISELYOV.

BABKINO, June, 1886.

LOVE UNRIPPLED [Footnote: Parody of a feminine novel.]

(A NOVEL) Part I.

It was noon.... The setting sun with its crimson, fiery rays gilded the tops of pines, oaks, and fir-trees.... It was still; only in the air the birds were singing, and in the distance a hungry wolf howled mournfully.... The driver turned round and said:

"More snow has fallen, sir."

"What?"

"I say, more snow has fallen."

"Ah!"

Vladimir Sergeitch Tabatchin, who is the hero of our story, looked for the last time at the sun and expired.

A week passed.... Birds and corncrakes hovered, whistling, over a newly-made grave. The sun was shining. A young widow, bathed in tears, was standing by, and in her grief sopping her whole handkerchief....

MOSCOW,

September 21, 1886.

... It is not much fun to be a great writer. To begin with, it's a dreary life. Work from morning till night and not much to show for it. Money is as scarce as cats' tears. I don't know how it is with Zola and Shtchedrin, but in my flat it is cold and smoky.... They give me cigarettes, as before, on holidays only. Impossible cigarettes! Hard, damp, sausage-like. Before I begin to smoke I light the lamp, dry the cigarette over it, and only then I begin on it; the lamp smokes, the cigarette splutters and turns brown, I burn my fingers ... it is enough to make one shoot oneself!

... I am more or less ill, and am gradually turning into a dried dragon-fly.

... I go about as festive as though it were my birthday, but to judge from the critical glances of the lady cashier at the *Budilnik*, I am not dressed in the height of fashion, and my clothes are not brand-new. I go in buses, not in cabs.

But being a writer has its good points. In the first place, my book, I hear, is going rather well; secondly, in October I shall have money; thirdly, I am beginning to reap laurels: at the refreshment bars people point at me with their fingers, they pay me little attentions and treat me to sandwiches. Korsh caught me in his theatre and straight away presented me with a free pass.... My medical colleagues sigh when they meet me, begin to talk of literature and assure me that they are sick of medicine. And so on....

September 29.

... Life is grey, there are no happy people to be seen.... Life is a nasty business for everyone. When I am serious I begin to think that people who have an aversion for death are illogical. So far as I understand the order of things, life consists of nothing but horrors, squabbles, and trivialities mixed together or alternating!

December 3.

This morning an individual sent by Prince Urusov turned up and asked me for a short story for a sporting magazine edited by the said Prince. I refused, of course, as I now refuse all who come with supplications to the foot of my pedestal. In Russia there are now two unattainable heights: Mount Elborus and myself.

The Prince's envoy was deeply disappointed by my refusal, nearly died of grief, and finally begged me to recommend him some writers who are versed in sport. I thought a little, and very opportunely remembered a lady writer who dreams of glory and has for the last year been ill with envy of my literary fame. In short, I gave him your address.... You might write a story "The Wounded Doe"—you remember, how the huntsmen wound a doe; she looks at them with human eyes, and no one can bring himself to kill her. It's not a bad subject, but dangerous because it is difficult to avoid sentimentality—you must write it like a report, without pathetic phrases, and begin like this: "On such and such a date the huntsmen in the Daraganov forest wounded a young doe...." And if you drop a tear you will strip the subject of its severity and of everything worth attention in it.

December 13.

... With your permission I steal out of your last two letters to my sister two descriptions of nature for my stories. It is curious that you have quite a masculine way of writing. In every line (except when dealing with children) you are a man! This, of course, ought to flatter your vanity, for speaking generally, men are a thousand times better than women, and superior to them.

In Petersburg I was resting—i.e., for days together I was rushing about town paying calls and listening to compliments which my soul abhors. Alas and alack! In Petersburg I am becoming fashionable like Nana. While Korolenko, who is serious, is hardly known to the editors, my twaddle is being read by all Petersburg. Even the senator G. reads me.... It is gratifying, but my literary feeling is wounded. I feel ashamed of the public which runs after lap-dogs simply because it fails to notice elephants, and I am deeply convinced that not a soul will know me when I begin to work in earnest.

TO HIS BROTHER NIKOLAY.

MOSCOW, 1886.

... You have often complained to me that people "don't understand you"! Goethe and Newton did not complain of that.... Only Christ complained of it, but He was speaking of His doctrine and not of Himself.... People understand you perfectly well. And if you do not understand yourself, it is not their fault.

I assure you as a brother and as a friend I understand you and feel for you with all my heart. I know your good qualities as I know my five fingers; I value and deeply respect them. If you like, to prove that I understand you, I can enumerate those qualities. I think you are kind to the point of softness, magnanimous, unselfish, ready to share your last farthing; you have no envy nor hatred; you are simple-hearted, you pity men and beasts; you are trustful, without spite or guile, and do not remember evil.... You have a gift from above such as other people have not: you have talent. This talent places you above millions of men, for on earth only one out of two millions is an artist. Your talent sets you apart: if you were a toad or a tarantula, even then, people would respect you, for to talent all things are forgiven.

You have only one failing, and the falseness of your position, and your unhappiness and your catarrh of the bowels are all due to it. That is your utter lack of culture. Forgive me, please, but *veritas magis amicitiae*.... You see, life has its conditions. In order to feel comfortable among educated people, to be at home and happy with them, one must be cultured to a certain extent. Talent has brought you into such a circle, you belong to it, but ... you are drawn away from it, and you vacillate between cultured people and the lodgers *vis-a-vis*.

Cultured people must, in my opinion, satisfy the following conditions:

1. They respect human personality, and therefore they are always kind, gentle, polite, and ready to give in to others. They do not make a row because of a hammer or a lost piece of india-rubber; if they live with anyone they do not regard it as a favour and, going away, they do not say "nobody can live with you." They forgive noise and cold and dried-up meat and witticisms and the presence of strangers in their homes.

2. They have sympathy not for beggars and cats alone. Their heart aches for what the eye does not see.... They sit up at night in order to help P...., to pay for brothers at the University, and to buy clothes for their mother.

3. They respect the property of others, and therefor pay their debts.

4. They are sincere, and dread lying like fire. They don't lie even in small things. A lie is insulting to the listener and puts him in a lower position in the eyes of the speaker. They do not pose, they behave in the street as they do at home, they do not show off before their humbler comrades. They are not given to babbling and forcing their uninvited confidences on others. Out of respect for other people's ears they more often keep silent than talk.

5. They do not disparage themselves to rouse compassion. They do not play on the strings of other people's hearts so that they may sigh and make much of them. They do not say "I am misunderstood," or "I have become second-rate," because all this is striving after cheap effect, is vulgar, stale, false....

6. They have no shallow vanity. They do not care for such false diamonds as knowing celebrities, shaking hands with the drunken P., [Translator's Note: Probably Palmin, a minor poet.] listening to the raptures of a stray spectator in a picture show, being renowned in the taverns.... If they do a pennyworth they do not strut about as though they had done a hundred roubles' worth, and do not brag of having the entry where others are not admitted.... The truly talented always keep in obscurity among the crowd, as far as possible from advertisement.... Even Krylov has said that an empty barrel echoes more loudly than a full one.

7. If they have a talent they respect it. They sacrifice to it rest, women, wine, vanity.... They are proud of their talent.... Besides, they are fastidious.

8. They develop the aesthetic feeling in themselves. They cannot go to sleep in their clothes, see cracks full of bugs on the walls, breathe bad air, walk on a floor that has been spat upon, cook their meals over an oil stove. They seek as far as possible to restrain and ennoble the sexual instinct.... What they want in a woman is not a bed-fellow ... They do not ask for the cleverness which shows itself in continual lying. They want especially, if

they are artists, freshness, elegance, humanity, the capacity for motherhood.... They do not swill vodka at all hours of the day and night, do not sniff at cupboards, for they are not pigs and know they are not. They drink only when they are free, on occasion.... For they want *mens sana in corpore sano.*

And so on. This is what cultured people are like. In order to be cultured and not to stand below the level of your surroundings it is not enough to have read "The Pickwick Papers" and learnt a monologue from "Faust." ...

What is needed is constant work, day and night, constant reading, study, will.... Every hour is precious for it.... Come to us, smash the vodka bottle, lie down and read.... Turgenev, if you like, whom you have not read.

You must drop your vanity, you are not a child ... you will soon be thirty. It is time!

I expect you.... We all expect you.

TO MADAME M. V. KISELYOV.

MOSCOW, January 14, 1887.

... Even your praise of "On the Road" has not softened my anger as an author, and I hasten to avenge myself for "Mire." Be on your guard, and catch hold of the back of a chair that you may not faint. Well, I begin.

One meets every critical article with a silent bow even if it is abusive and unjust—such is the literary etiquette. It is not the thing to answer, and all who do answer are justly blamed for excessive vanity. But since your criticism has the nature of "an evening conversation on the steps of the Babkino lodge" ... and as, without touching on the literary aspects of the story, it raises general questions of principle, I shall not be sinning against the etiquette if I allow myself to continue our conversation.

In the first place, I, like you, do not like literature of the kind we are discussing. As a reader and "a private resident" I am glad to avoid it, but if you ask my honest and sincere opinion about it, I shall say that it is still an open question whether it has a right to exist, and no one has yet settled it.... Neither you nor I, nor all the critics in the world, have any trustworthy data that would give them the right to reject such literature. I do not know which are right: Homer, Shakespeare, Lopez da Vega, and, speaking generally, the ancients who were not afraid to rummage in the "muck heap," but were morally far more stable than we are, or the modern writers, priggish on paper but coldly cynical in their souls and in life. I do not know which has bad taste—the Greeks who were not ashamed to describe love as it really is in beautiful nature, or the readers of Gaboriau, Marlitz, Pierre Bobo. [Footnote: P. D. Boborykin.] Like the problems of non-resistance to evil, of free will, etc., this question can only be settled in the future. We can only refer to it, but are not competent to decide it. Reference to Turgenev and Tolstoy—who avoided the "muck heap"—does not throw light on the question. Their fastidiousness does not prove anything; why, before them there was a generation of writers who regarded as dirty not only accounts of "the dregs and scum," but even descriptions of peasants and of officials below the rank of titular councillor. Besides, one period, however brilliant, does not entitle us to draw conclusions in favour of this or that literary tendency. Reference to the demoralizing effects of the literary tendency we are discussing does not decide the question either. Everything in this world is relative and approximate. There are people who can be demoralized even by children's books, and who read with particular pleasure the piquant passages in the Psalms and in Solomon's Proverbs, while there are others who become only the purer from closer knowledge of the filthy side of life. Political and social writers, lawyers, and doctors who are initiated into all the mysteries of human sinfulness are not reputed to be immoral; realistic writers are often more moral than archimandrites. And, finally, no literature can outdo real life in its cynicism, a wineglassful won't make a man drunk when he has already emptied a barrel.

2. That the world swarms with "dregs and scum" is perfectly true. Human nature is imperfect, and it would therefore be strange to see none but righteous ones on earth. But to think that the duty of literature is to unearth the pearl from the refuse heap means to reject literature itself. "Artistic" literature is only "art" in so far as it paints life as it really is. Its vocation is to be absolutely true and honest. To narrow down its function to the particular task of finding "pearls" is as deadly for it as it would be to make Levitan draw a tree without including the dirty bark and the yellow leaves. I agree that "pearls" are a good thing, but then a writer is not a confectioner, not a provider of cosmetics, not an entertainer; he is a man bound, under contract, by his sense of duty and his conscience; having put his hand to the plough he mustn't turn back, and, however distasteful, he must conquer his squeamishness and soil his imagination with the dirt of life. He is just like any ordinary reporter. What would you say if a newspaper correspondent out of a feeling of fastidiousness or from a wish to please his readers would describe only honest mayors, high-minded ladies, and virtuous railway contractors?

To a chemist nothing on earth is unclean. A writer must be as objective as a chemist, he must lay aside his personal subjective standpoint and must understand that muck heaps play a very respectable part in a landscape, and that the evil passions are as inherent in life as the good ones.

3. Writers are the children of their age, and therefore, like everybody else, must submit to the external conditions of the life of the community. Thus, they must be perfectly decent. This is the only thing we have a right to ask of realistic writers. But you say nothing against the form and executions of "Mire." ... And so I suppose I have been decent.

4. I confess I seldom commune with my conscience when I write. This is due to habit and the brevity of my work. And so when I express this or that opinion about literature, I do not take myself into account.

5. You write: "If I were the editor I would have returned this feuilleton to you for your own good." Why not go further? Why not muzzle the editors themselves who publish such stories? Why not send a reprimand to the Headquarters of the Press Department for not suppressing immoral newspapers?

The fate of literature would be sad indeed if it were at the mercy of individual views. That is the first thing. Secondly, there is no police which could consider itself competent in literary matters. I agree that one can't dispense with the reins and the whip altogether, for knaves find their way even into literature, but no thinking will discover a better police for literature than the critics and the author's own conscience. People have been trying to discover such a police since the creation of the world, but they have found nothing better.

Here you would like me to lose one hundred and fifteen roubles and be put to shame by the editor; others, your father among them, are delighted with the story. Some send insulting letters to Suvorin, pouring abuse on the paper and on me, etc. Who, then, is right? Who is the true judge?

6. Further you write, "Leave such writing to spiritless and unlucky scribblers such as Okrects, Pince-Nez, [Footnote: The pseudonym of Madame Kisselyov.] or Aloe." [Footnote: The pseudonym of Chekhov's brother Alexandr.]

Allah forgive you if you were sincere when you wrote those words! A condescending and contemptuous tone towards humble people simply because they are humble does no credit to the heart. In literature the lower ranks are as necessary as in the army—this is what the head says, and the heart ought to say still more.

Ough! I have wearied you with my drawn-out reflections. Had I known my criticism would turn out so long I would not have written it. Please forgive me! ...

You have read my "On the Road." Well, how do you like my courage? I write of "intellectual" subjects and am not afraid. In Petersburg I excite a regular furore. A short time ago I discoursed upon non-resistance to evil, and also surprised the public. On New Year's Day all the papers presented me with a compliment, and in the December number of the *Russkoye Bogatstvo*, in which Tolstoy writes, there is an article thirty-two pages long by Obolensky entitled "Chekhov and Korolenko." The fellow goes into raptures over me and proves that I am more of an artist than Korolenko.

He is probably talking rot, but, anyway, I am beginning to be conscious of one merit of mine: I am the only writer who, without ever publishing anything in the thick monthlies, has merely on the strength of writing newspaper rubbish won the attention of the lop-eared critics—there has been no instance of this before.... At the end of 1886 I felt as though I were a bone thrown to the dogs.

... I have written a play [Footnote: "Calchas," later called "Swansong."] on four sheets of paper. It will take fifteen to twenty minutes to act.... It is much better to write small things than big ones: they are unpretentious and successful.... What more would you have? I wrote my play in an hour and five minutes. I began another, but have not finished it, for I have no time.

TO HIS UNCLE, M. G. CHEKHOV.

MOSCOW, January 18, 1887.

... During the holidays I was so overwhelmed with work that on Mother's name-day I was almost dropping with exhaustion.

I must tell you that in Petersburg I am now the most fashionable writer. One can see that from papers and magazines, which at the end of 1886 were taken up with me, bandied my name about, and praised me beyond my deserts. The result of this growth of my literary reputation is that I get a number of orders and invitations—and this is followed by work at high pressure and exhaustion. My work is nervous, disturbing, and involving strain. It is public and responsible, which makes it doubly hard. Every newspaper report about me agitates both me and my family.... My stories are read at public recitations, wherever I go people point at me, I am overwhelmed with acquaintances, and so on, and so on. I have not a day of peace, and feel as though I were on thorns every moment.

... Volodya [Translator's Note: He had apparently criticized the name Vladimir, which means "lord of the world."] is right.... It is true that a man cannot possess the world, but a man can be called "the lord of the world." Tell Volodya that out of gratitude, reverence, or admiration of the virtues of the best men—those qualities which make a man exceptional and akin to the Deity—peoples and historians have a right to call their elect as they like, without being afraid of insulting God's greatness or of raising a man to God. The fact is we exalt, not a man as such, but his good qualities, just that divine principle which he has succeeded in developing in himself to a high degree. Thus remarkable kings are called "great," though bodily they may not be taller than I. I. Loboda; the Pope is called "Holiness," the patriarch used to be called "Ecumenical," although he was not in relations with any planet but the earth; Prince Vladimir was called "the lord of the world," though he ruled only a small strip of ground, princes are called "serene" and "illustrious," though a Swedish match is a thousand times brighter than they are—and so on. In using these expressions we do not lie or exaggerate, but simply express our delight, just as a mother does not lie when she calls her child "my golden one." It is the feeling of beauty that speaks in us, and beauty cannot endure what is commonplace and trivial; it induces us to make comparisons which Volodya may, with his intellect, pull to pieces, but which he will understand with his heart. For instance, it is usual to compare black eyes with the night, blue with the azure of the sky, curls with waves, etc., and even the Bible likes these comparisons; for instance, "Thy womb is more spacious than heaven," or "The Sun of righteousness arises," "The rock of faith," etc. The feeling of beauty in man knows no limits or bounds. This is why a Russian prince may be called "the lord of the world"; and my friend Volodya may have the same name, for names are given to people, not for their merits, but in honour and commemoration of remarkable men of the past.... If your young scholar does not agree with me, I have one more argument which will be sure to appeal to him: in exalting people even to God we do not sin against love, but, on the contrary, we express it. One must not humiliate people—that is the chief thing. Better say to man "My angel" than hurl "Fool" at his head—though men are more like fools than they are like angels.

TO HIS SISTER.

TAGANROG, April 2, 1887.

The journey from Moscow to Serpuhov was dull. My fellow-travellers were practical persons of strong character who did nothing but talk of the prices of flour....

... At twelve o'clock we were at Kursk. An hour of waiting, a glass of vodka, a tidy-up and a wash, and cabbage soup. Change to another train. The carriage was crammed full. Immediately after Kursk I made friends with my neighbours: a landowner from Harkov, as jocose as Sasha K.; a lady who had just had an operation in Petersburg; a police captain; an officer from Little Russia; and a general in military uniform. We settled social questions. The general's arguments were sound, short, and liberal; the police captain was the type of an old battered sinner of an hussar yearning for amorous adventures. He had the affectations of a governor: he opened his mouth long before he began to speak, and having said a word he gave a long growl like a dog, "er-r-r." The lady was injecting morphia, and sent the men to fetch her ice at the stations.

At Belgrade I had cabbage soup. We got to Harkov at nine o'clock. A touching parting from the police captain, the general and the others.... I woke up at Slavyansk and sent you a postcard. A new lot of passengers got in: a landowner and a railway inspector. We talked of railways. The inspector told us how the Sevastopol railway stole three hundred carriages from the Azov line and painted them its own colour. [Footnote: See the story "Cold Blood."]

... Twelve o'clock. Lovely weather. There is a scent of the steppe and one hears the birds sing. I see my old friends the ravens flying over the steppe.

The barrows, the water-towers, the buildings—everything is familiar and well-remembered. At the station I have a helping of remarkably good and rich sorrel soup. Then I walk along the platform. Young ladies. At an upper window at the far end of the station sits a young girl (or a married lady, goodness knows which) in a white blouse, beautiful and languid. [Footnote: See the story "Two Beauties."] I look at her, she looks at me.... I put on my glasses, she does the same.... Oh, lovely vision! I caught a catarrh of the heart and continued my journey. The weather is devilishly, revoltingly fine. Little Russians, oxen, ravens, white huts, rivers, the line of the Donets railway with one telegraph wire, daughters of landowners and farmers, red dogs, the trees—it all flits by like a dream.... It is hot. The inspector begins to bore me. The rissoles and pies, half of which I have not got through, begin to smell bitter.... I shove them under somebody else's seat, together with the remains of the vodka.

... I arrive at Taganrog.... It gives one the impression of Herculaneum and Pompeii; there are no people, and instead of mummies there are sleepy *drishpaks* [Footnote: Uneducated young men in the jargon of Taganrog.] and melon-shaped heads. All the houses look flattened out, and as though they had long needed replastering, the roofs want painting, the shutters are closed....

At eight o'clock in the evening my uncle, his family, Irina, the dogs, the rats that live in the storeroom, the rabbits were fast asleep. There was nothing for it but to go to bed too. I sleep on the drawing-room sofa. The sofa has not increased in length, and is as short as it was before, and so when I go to bed I have either to stick up my legs in an unseemly way or to let them hang down to the floor. I think of Procrustes and his bed....

April 6.

I wake up at five. The sky is grey. There is a cold, unpleasant wind that reminds one of Moscow. It is dull. I wait for the church bells and go to late Mass. In the cathedral it is all very charming, decorous, and not boring. The choir sings well, not at all in a plebeian style, and the congregation entirely consists of young ladies in olive-green dresses and chocolate-coloured jackets....

April 8, 9, and 10.

Frightfully dull. It is cold and grey.... During all my stay in Taganrog I could only do justice to the following things: remarkably good ring rolls sold at the market, the Santurninsky wine, fresh caviare, excellent crabs and uncle's genuine hospitality. Everything else is poor and not to be envied. The young ladies here are not bad, but it takes some time to get used to them. They are abrupt in their movements, frivolous in their attitude to men, run away from their parents with actors, laugh loudly, easily fall in love, whistle to dogs, drink wine, etc....

On Saturday I continued my journey. At the Moskaya station the air is lovely and fresh, caviare is seventy kopecks a pound. At Rostdov I had two hours to wait, at Taganrog twenty. I spent the night at an acquaintance's. The devil only knows what I haven't spent a night on: on beds with bugs, on sofas, settees, boxes. Last night I spent in a long and narrow parlour on a sofa under a looking-glass....

April 25.

... Yesterday was the wedding—a real Cossack wedding with music, feminine bleating, and revolting drunkenness.... The bride is sixteen. They were married in the cathedral. I acted as best man, and was dressed in somebody else's evening suit with fearfully wide trousers, and not a single stud on my shirt. In Moscow such a best man would have been kicked out, but here I looked smarter than anyone.

I saw many rich and eligible young ladies. The choice is enormous, but I was so drunk all the time that I took bottles for young ladies and young ladies for bottles. Probably owing to my drunken condition the local ladies found me witty and satirical! The young ladies here are regular sheep, if one gets up from her place and walks out of the room all the others follow her. One of them, the boldest and the most brainy, wishing to show that she is not a stranger to social polish and subtlety, kept slapping me on the hand and saying, "Oh, you wretch!" though her face still retained its scared expression. I taught her to say to her partners, "How naive you are!"

The bride and bridegroom, probably because of the local custom of kissing every minute, kissed with such gusto that their lips made a loud smack, and it gave me a taste of sugary raisins in my mouth and a spasm in my left calf. The inflammation of the vein in my left leg got worse through their kisses.

... At Zvyerevo I shall have to wait from nine in the evening till five in the morning. Last time I spent the night there in a second-class railway-carriage on the siding. I went out of the carriage in the night and outside I found veritable marvels: the moon, the limitless steppe, the barrows, the wilderness; deathly stillness, and the carriages and the railway lines sharply standing out from the dusk. It seemed as though the world were dead.... It was a picture one would not forget for ages and ages.

RAGOZINA BALKA,

April 30, 1887.

It is April 30. The evening is warm. There are storm-clouds about, and so one cannot see a thing. The air is close and there is a smell of grass.

I am staying in the Ragozina Balka at K.'s. There is a small house with a thatched roof, and barns made of flat stone. There are three rooms, with earthen floors, crooked ceilings, and windows that lift up and down instead of opening outwards.... The walls are covered with rifles, pistols, sabres and whips. The chest of drawers and the window-sills are littered with cartridges, instruments for mending rifles, tins of gunpowder, and bags of shot. The furniture is lame and the veneer is coming off it. I have to sleep on a consumptive sofa, very hard, and not upholstered ... Ash-trays and all such luxuries are not to be found within a radius of ten versts.... The first necessaries are conspicuous by their absence, and one has in all weathers to slip out to the ravine, and one is warned to make sure there is not a viper or some other creature under the bushes.

The population consists of old K., his wife, Pyotr, a Cossack officer with broad red stripes on his trousers, Alyosha, Hahko (that is, Alexandr), Zoika, Ninka, the shepherd Nikita and the cook Akulina. There are immense numbers of dogs who are furiously spiteful and don't let anyone pass them by day or by night. I have to go about under escort, or there will be one writer less in Russia.... The most cursed of the dogs is Muhtar, an old cur on whose face dirty tow hangs instead of wool. He hates me and rushes at me with a roar every time I go out of the house.

Now about food. In the morning there is tea, eggs, ham and bacon fat. At midday, soup with goose, roast goose with pickled sloes, or a turkey, roast chicken, milk pudding, and sour milk. No vodka or pepper allowed. At five o'clock they make on a camp fire in the wood a porridge of millet and bacon fat. In the evening there is tea, ham, and all that has been left over from dinner.

The entertainments are: shooting bustards, making bonfires, going to Ivanovka, shooting at a mark, setting the dogs at one another, preparing gunpowder paste for fireworks, talking politics, building turrets of stone, etc.

The chief occupation is scientific farming, introduced by the youthful Cossack, who bought five roubles' worth of works on agriculture. The most important part of this farming consists of wholesale slaughter, which does not cease for a single moment in the day. They kill sparrows, swallows, bumblebees, ants, magpies, crows—to prevent them eating bees; to prevent the bees from spoiling the blossom on the fruit-trees they kill bees, and to prevent the fruit-trees from exhausting the ground they cut down the fruit-trees. One gets thus a regular circle which, though somewhat original, is based on the latest data of science.

We retire at nine in the evening. Sleep is disturbed, for Belonozhkas and Muhtars howl in the yard and Tseter furiously barks in answer to them from under my sofa. I am awakened by shooting: my hosts shoot with rifles from the windows at some animal which does damage to their crops. To leave the house at night one has to call the Cossack, for otherwise the dogs would tear one to bits.

The weather is fine. The grass is tall and in blossom. I watch bees and men among whom I feel myself something like a Mikluha-Maklay. Last night there was a beautiful thunderstorm.

... The coal mines are not far off. To-morrow morning early I am going on a one-horse droshky to Ivanovka (twenty-three versts) to fetch my letters from the post.

... We eat turkeys' eggs. Turkeys lay eggs in the wood on last year's leaves. They kill hens, geese, pigs, etc., by shooting here. The shooting is incessant.

TAGANROG,

May 11.

... From K.'s I went to the Holy Mountains.... I came to Slavyansk on a dark evening. The cabmen refuse to take me to the Holy Mountains at night, and advise me to spend the night at Slavyansk, which I did very willingly, for I felt broken and lame with pain.... The town is something like Gogol's *Mirgorod*; there is a hairdresser and a watchmaker, so that one may hope that in another thousand years there will be a telephone. The walls and fences are pasted with the advertisements of a menagerie.... On green and dusty streets walk pigs, cows, and other domestic creatures. The houses look cordial and friendly, rather like kindly grandmothers; the pavements are soft, the streets are wide, there is a smell of lilac and acacia in the air; from the distance come the singing of a nightingale, the croaking of frogs, barking, and sounds of a harmonium, of a woman screeching.... I stopped in Kulikov's hotel, where I took a room for seventy-five kopecks. After sleeping on wooden sofas and washtubs it was a voluptuous sight to see a bed with a mattress, a washstand.... Fragrant breezes came in at the wide-open window and green branches thrust themselves in. It was a glorious morning. It was a holiday (May 6th) and the bells were ringing in the cathedral. People were coming out from mass. I saw police officers, justices of the peace, military superintendents, and other principalities and powers come out of the church. I bought two kopecks' worth of sunflower seeds, and hired for six roubles a carriage on springs to take me to the Holy Mountains and back (in two days' time). I drove out of the town through little streets literally drowned in the green of cherry, apricot, and apple trees. The birds sang unceasingly. Little Russians whom I met took off their caps, taking me probably for Turgenev; my driver jumped every minute off the box to put the harness to rights, or to crack his whip at the boys who ran after the carriage.... There were strings of pilgrims along the road. On all sides there were white hills, big and small. The horizon was bluish-white, the rye was tall, oak copses were met with here and there—the only things lacking were crocodiles and rattlesnakes.

I came to the Holy Mountains at twelve o'clock. It is a remarkably beautiful and unique place. The monastery stands on the bank of the river Donets at the foot of a huge white rock covered with gardens, oaks, and ancient pines crowded together and over-hanging, one above another. It seems as if the trees had not enough room on the rock, and as if some force were driving them upwards.... The pines literally hang in the air and look as though they might fall any minute. Cuckoos and nightingales sing night and day.

The monks, very pleasant people, gave me a very unpleasant room with a pancake-like mattress. I spent two nights at the monastery and gathered a mass of impressions. While I was there some fifteen thousand pilgrims assembled because of St. Nicolas' Day; eight-ninths of them were old women. I did not know before that there were so many old women in the world; had I known, I would have shot myself long ago. About the monks, my acquaintance with them and how I gave medical advice to the monks and the old women, I will write to the *Novoye Vremya* and tell you when we meet. The services are endless: at midnight they ring for matins, at five for early mass, at nine for late mass, at three for the song of praise, at five for vespers, at six for the special prayers. Before every service one hears in the corridors the weeping sound of a bell, and a monk runs along crying in the voice of a creditor who implores his debtor to pay him at least five kopecks for a rouble:

"Lord Jesus Christ, have mercy upon us! Please come to matins!"

It is awkward to stay in one's room, and so one gets up and goes out. I have chosen a spot on the bank of the Donets, where I sit during all the services.

I have bought an ikon for Auntie. [Translator's Note: His mother's sister.] The food is provided gratis by the monastery for all the fifteen thousand: cabbage soup with dried fresh-water fish and porridge. Both are good, and so is the rye bread.

The church bells are wonderful. The choir is not up to much. I took part in a religious procession on boats.

TO V. G. KOROLENKO.

MOSCOW, October 17, 1887.

... I am extremely glad to have met you. I say it sincerely and with all my heart. In the first place, I deeply value and love your talent; it is dear to me for many reasons. In the second, it seems to me that if you and I live in this world another ten or twenty years we shall be bound to find points of contact. Of all the Russians now successfully writing I am the lightest and most frivolous; I am looked upon doubtfully; to speak the language of the poets, I have loved my pure Muse but I have not respected her; I have been unfaithful to her and often took her to places that were not fit for her to go to. But you are serious, strong, and faithful. The difference between us is great, as you see, but nevertheless when I read you, and now when I have met you, I think that we have something in common. I don't know if I am right, but I like to think it.

TO HIS BROTHER ALEXANDR.

MOSCOW, November 20, 1887.

Well, the first performance [Translator's Note: "Ivanov."] is over. I will tell you all about it in detail. To begin with, Korsh promised me ten rehearsals, but gave me only four, of which only two could be called rehearsals, for the other two were tournaments in which *messieurs les artistes* exercised themselves in altercation and abuse. Davydov and Glama were the only two who knew their parts; the others trusted to the prompter and their own inner conviction.

Act One.—I am behind the stage in a small box that looks like a prison cell. My family is in a box of the benoire and is trembling. Contrary to my expectations, I am cool and am conscious of no agitation. The actors are nervous and excited, and cross themselves. The curtain goes up ... the actor whose benefit night it is comes on. His uncertainty, the way that he forgets his part, and the wreath that is presented to him make the play unrecognizable to me from the first sentences. Kiselevsky, of whom I had great hopes, did not deliver a single phrase correctly—literally *not a single one*. He said things of his own composition. In spite of this and of the stage manager's blunders, the first act was a great success. There were many calls.

Act Two.—A lot of people on the stage. Visitors. They don't know their parts, make mistakes, talk nonsense. Every word cuts me like a knife in my back. But—o Muse!—this act, too, was a success. There were calls for all the actors, and I was called before the curtain twice. Congratulations and success.

Act Three.—The acting is not bad. Enormous success. I had to come before the curtain three times, and as I did so Davydov was shaking my hand, and Glama, like Manilov, was pressing my other hand to her heart. The triumph of talent and virtue.

Act Four, Scene One.—It does not go badly. Calls before the curtain again. Then a long, wearisome interval. The audience, not used to leaving their seats and going to the refreshment bar between two scenes, murmur. The curtain goes up. Fine: through the arch one can see the supper table (the wedding). The band plays flourishes. The groomsmen come out: they are drunk, and so you see they think they must behave like clowns and cut capers. The horseplay and pot-house atmosphere reduce me to despair. Then Kiselevsky comes out: it is a poetical, moving passage, but my Kiselevsky does not know his part, is drunk as a cobbler, and a short poetical dialogue is transformed into something tedious and disgusting: the public is perplexed. At the end of the play the hero dies because he cannot get over the insult he has received. The audience, grown cold and tired, does not understand this death (the actors insisted on it; I have another version). There are calls for the actors and for me. During one of the calls I hear sounds of open hissing, drowned by the clapping and stamping.

On the whole I feel tired and annoyed. It was sickening though the play had considerable success....

Theatre-goers say that they had never seen such a ferment in a theatre, such universal clapping and hissing, nor heard such discussions among the audience as they saw and heard at my play. And it has never happened before at Korsh's that the author has been called after the second act.

November 24.

... It has all subsided at last, and I sit as before at my writing-table and compose stories with untroubled spirit. You can't think what it was like! ... I have already told you that at the first performance there was such excitement in the audience and on the stage as the prompter, who has served at the theatre for thirty-two years, had never seen. They made an uproar, shouted, clapped and hissed; at the refreshment bar it almost came to fighting, and in the gallery the students wanted to throw someone out and two persons were removed by the police. The excitement was general....

... The actors were in a state of nervous tension. All that I wrote to you and Maslov about their acting and attitude to their work must not, of course, go any further. There is much one has to excuse and understand....

It turned out that the actress who was doing the chief part in my play had a daughter lying dangerously ill—how could she feel like acting? Kurepin did well to praise the actors.

The next day after the performance there was a review by Pyotr Kitcheyev in the *Moskovsky Listok*. He calls my play impudently cynical and immoral rubbish. The *Moskovskiya Vyedomosti* praised it.

... If you read the play you will not understand the excitement I have described to you; you will find nothing special in it. Nikolay, Shehtel, and Levitan—all of them painters—assure me that on the stage it is so original that it is quite strange to look at. In reading one does not notice it.

TO D. V. GRIGOROVITCH.

MOSCOW, 1887.

I have just read "Karelin's Dream," and I am very much interested to know how far the dream you describe really is a dream. I think your description of the workings of the brain and of the general feeling of a person who is asleep is physiologically correct and remarkably artistic. I remember I read two or three years ago a French story, in which the author described the daughter of a minister., and probably without himself suspecting it, gave a correct medical description of hysteria. I thought at the time that an artist's instinct may sometimes be worth the brains of a scientist, that both have the same purpose, the same nature, and that perhaps in time, as their methods become perfect, they are destined to become one vast prodigious force which now it is difficult even to imagine.... "Karelin's Dream" has suggested to me similar thoughts, and to-day I willingly believe Buckle, who saw in Hamlet's musings on the dust of Alexander the Great, Shakespeare's knowledge of the law of the transmutation of substance—i.e., the power of the artist to run ahead of the men of science.... Sleep is a subjective phenomenon, and the inner aspect of it one can only observe in oneself. But since the process of dreaming is the same in all men, every reader can, I think, judge Karelin by his own standards, and every critic is bound to be subjective. From my own personal experience this is how I can formulate my impression.

In the first place the sensation of cold is given by you with remarkable subtlety. When at night the quilt falls off I begin to dream of huge slippery stones, of cold autumnal water, naked banks—and all this dim, misty, without a patch of blue sky; sad and dejected like one who has lost his way, I look at the stones and feel that for some reason I cannot avoid crossing a deep river; I see then small tugs that drag huge barges, floating beams.... All this is infinitely grey, damp, and dismal. When I run from the river I come across the fallen cemetery gates, funerals, my school-teachers.... And all the time I am cold through and through with that oppressive nightmare-like cold which is impossible in waking life, and which is only felt by those who are asleep. The first pages of "Karelin's Dream" vividly brought it to my memory—especially the first half of page five, where you speak of the cold and loneliness of the grave.

I think that had I been born in Petersburg and constantly lived there, I should always dream of the banks of the Neva, the Senate Square, the massive monuments.

When I feel cold in my sleep I dream of people.... I happened to have read a criticism in which the reviewer blames you for introducing a man who is "almost a minister," and thus spoiling the generally dignified tone of the story. I don't agree with him. What spoils the tone is not the people but your characterization of them, which in some places interrupts the picture of the dream. One does dream of people, and always of unpleasant ones.... I, for instance, when I feel cold, always dream of my teacher of scripture, a learned priest of imposing appearance, who insulted my mother when I was a little boy; I dream of vindictive, implacable, intriguing people, smiling with spiteful glee—such as one can never see in waking life. The laughter at the carriage window is a characteristic symptom of Karelin's nightmare. When in dreams one feels the presence of some evil will, the inevitable ruin brought about by some outside force, one always hears something like such laughter.... One dreams of people one loves, too, but they generally appear to suffer together with the dreamer.

But when my body gets accustomed to the cold, or one of my family covers me up, the sensation of cold, of loneliness, and of an oppressive evil will, gradually disappears.... With the returning warmth I begin to feel that I walk on soft carpets or on grass, I see sunshine, women, children.... The pictures change gradually, but more rapidly than they do in waking life, so that on awaking it is difficult to remember the transitions from one scene to another.... This abruptness is well brought out in your story, and increases the impression of the dream.

Another natural fact you have noticed is also extremely striking: dreamers express their moods in outbursts of an acute kind, with childish genuineness, like Karelin. Everyone knows that people weep and cry out in their sleep much more often than they do in waking life. This is probably due to the lack of inhibition in sleep and of the impulses which make us conceal things.

Forgive me, I so like your story that I am ready to write you a dozen sheets, though I know I can tell you nothing new or good.... I restrain myself and am silent, fearing to bore you and to say something silly.

I will say once more that your story is magnificent. The public finds it "vague," but to a writer who gloats over every line such vagueness is more transparent than holy water.... Hard as I tried I could detect only two small blots, even those are rather farfetched!

(1) I think that at the beginning of the story the feeling of cold is soon blunted in the reader and becomes habitual, owing to the frequent repetition of the word "cold," and (2), the word "glossy" is repeated too often.

There is nothing else I could find, and I feel that as one is always feeling the need of refreshing models, "Karelin's Dream" is a splendid event in my existence as an author. This is why I could not contain myself and ventured to put before you some of my thoughts and impressions.

There is little good I can say about myself. I write not what I want to be writing, and I have not enough energy or solitude to write as you advised me.... There are many good subjects jostling in my head—and that is all. I am sustained by hopes of the future, and watch the present slip fruitlessly away.

Forgive this long letter, and accept the sincere good wishes of your devoted

A. CHEKHOV.

TO V. G. KOROLENKO.

MOSCOW, January 9, 1888.

Following your friendly advice I began writing a story [Footnote: "The Steppe"] for the *Syeverny Vyestnik*. To begin with I have attempted to describe the steppe, the people who live there, and what I have experienced in the steppe. It is a good subject, and I enjoy writing about it, but unfortunately from lack of practice in writing long things, and from fear of making it too rambling, I fall into the opposite extreme: each page turns out a compact whole like a short story, the pictures accumulate, are crowded, and, getting in each other's way, spoil the impression as a whole. As a result one gets, not a picture in which all the details are merged into one whole like stars in the heavens, but a mere diagram, a dry record of impressions. A writer—you, for instance—will understand me, but the reader will be bored and curse.

... Your "Sokolinets" is, I think, the most remarkable novel that has appeared of late. It is written like a good musical composition, in accordance with all the rules which an artist instinctively divines. Altogether in the whole of your book you are such a great artist, such a force, that even your worst failings, which would have been the ruin of any other writer, pass unnoticed. For instance, in the whole of your book there is an obstinate exclusion of women, and I have only just noticed it.

TO A. N. PLESHTCHEYEV.

MOSCOW, February 5, 1888.

... I am longing to read Korolenko's story. He is my favourite of contemporary writers. His colours are rich and vivid, his style is irreproachable, though in places rather elaborate, his images are noble. Leontyev [Footnote: I. L. Shtcheglov.] is good too. He is not so mature and picturesque, but he is warmer than Korolenko, more peaceful and feminine.... But, Allah kerim, why do they both specialize? The first will not part with his convicts, and the second feeds his readers with nothing but officers.... I understand specialization in art such as *genre*, landscape, history, but I cannot admit of such specialties as convicts, officers, priests.... This is not specialization but partiality. In Petersburg you do not care for Korolenko, and here in Moscow we do not read Shtcheglov, but I fully believe in the future of both of them. Ah, if only we had decent critics!

February 9.

... You say you liked Dymov [Translator's Note: One of the characters in "The Steppe."] as a subject. Life creates such characters as the dare-devil Dymov not to be dissenters nor tramps, but downright revolutionaries.... There never will be a revolution in Russia, and Dymov will end by taking to drink or getting into prison. He is a superfluous man.

March 6.

It is devilishly cold, but the poor birds are already flying to Russia! They are driven by homesickness and love for their native land. If poets knew how many millions of birds fall victims to their longing and love for their homes, how many of them freeze on the way, what agonies they endure on getting home in March and at the beginning of April, they would have sung their praises long ago! ... Put yourself in the place of a corncrake who does not fly but walks all the way, or of a wild goose who gives himself up to man to escape being frozen.... Life is hard in this world!

TO I. L. SHTCHEGLOV.

MOSCOW, April 18, 1888.

... In any case I am more often merry than sad, though if one comes to think of it I am bound hand and foot.... You, my dear man, have a flat, but I have a whole house which, though a poor specimen, is still a house, and one of two storeys, too! You have a *wife* who will forgive your having no money, and I have a *whole organization* which will collapse if I don't earn a sufficient number of roubles a month—collapse and fall on my shoulders like a heavy stone.

May 3.

... I have just sent a story [Footnote: "The Lights."] to the *Syeverny Vyestnik*. I feel a little ashamed of it. It is frightfully dull, and there is so much discussion and preaching in it that it is mawkish. I didn't like to send it, but had to, for I need money as I do air....

I have had a letter from Leman. He tells me that "we" (that is all of you Petersburg people) "have agreed to print advertisements about each other's work on our books," invites me to join, and warns me that among the elect may be included only such persons as have a "certain degree of solidarity with us." I wrote to say that I agreed, and asked him how does he know with whom I have solidarity and with whom I have not? How fond of stuffiness you are in Petersburg! Don't you feel stifled with such words as "solidarity," "unity of young writers," "common interests," and so on? Solidarity and all the rest of it I admit on the stock-exchange, in politics, in religious affairs, etc., but solidarity among young writers is impossible and unnecessary.... We cannot feel and think in the same way, our aims are different, or we have no aims whatever, we know each other little or not at all, and so there is nothing on to which this solidarity could be securely hooked.... And is there any need for it? No, in order to help a colleague, to respect his personality and his work, to refrain from gossiping about him, envying him, telling him lies and being hypocritical, one does not need so much to be a young writer as simply a man.... Let us be ordinary people, let us treat everybody alike, and then we shall not need any artificially worked up solidarity. Insistent desire for particular, professional, clique solidarity such as you want, will give rise to unconscious spying on one another, suspiciousness, control, and, without wishing to do so, we shall become something like Jesuits in relation to one another.... I, dear Jean, have no solidarity with you, but I promise you as a literary man perfect freedom so long as you live; that is, you may write where and how you wish, you may think like Koreisha [Footnote: A well-known religious fanatic in Moscow.] if you like, betray your convictions and tendencies a thousand times, etc., etc., and my human relations with you will not alter one jot, and I will always publish advertisements of your books on the wrappers of mine.

TO A. S. SUVORIN.

SUMY, MADAME LINTVARYOV'S ESTATE, May 30, 1888.

... I am staying on the bank of the Psyol, in the lodge of an old signorial estate. I took the place without seeing it, trusting to luck, and have not regretted it so far. The river is wide and deep, with plenty of islands, of fish and of crayfish. The banks are beautiful, well-covered with grass and trees. And best of all, there is so much space that I feel as if for my one hundred roubles I have obtained a right to live on an expanse of which one can see no end. Nature and life here is built on the pattern now so old-fashioned and rejected by magazine editors. Nightingales sing night and day, dogs bark in the distance, there are old neglected gardens, sad and poetical estates shut up and deserted where live the souls of beautiful women; old footmen, relics of serfdom, on the brink of the grave; young ladies longing for the most conventional love. In addition to all these things, not far from me there is even such a hackneyed cliche as a water-mill (with sixteen wheels), with a miller, and his daughter who always sits at the window, apparently waiting for someone. All that I see and hear now seems familiar to me from old novels and fairy-tales. The only thing that has something new about it is a mysterious bird, which sits somewhere far away in the reeds, and night and day makes a noise that sounds partly like a blow on an empty barrel and partly like the mooing of a cow shut up in a barn. Every Little Russian has seen this bird in the course of his life, but everyone describes it differently, which means that no one has seen it.... Every day I row to the mill, and in the evening I go to the islands to fish with fishing maniacs from the Haritovenko factory. Our conversations are sometimes interesting. On the eve of Whit Sunday all the maniacs will spend the night on the islands and fish all night; I, too. There are some splendid types.

My hosts have turned out to be very nice and hospitable people. It is a family worth studying. It consists of six members. The old mother, a very kind, rather flabby woman who has had suffering enough in her life; she reads Schopenhauer and goes to church to hear the Song of Praise; she conscientiously studies every number of the *Vyestnik Evropi* and *Syeverny Vyestnik*, and knows writers I have not dreamed of; attaches much importance to the fact that once the painter Makovsky stayed in her lodge and now a young writer is staying there; talking to Pleshtcheyev she feels a holy thrill all over and rejoices every minute that it has been "vouchsafed" to her to see the great poet.

Her eldest daughter, a woman doctor—the pride of the whole family and "a saint" as the peasants call her—really is remarkable. She has a tumour on the brain, and in consequence of it she is totally blind, has epileptic fits and constant headaches. She knows what awaits her, and stoically with amazing coolness speaks of her approaching death. In the course of my medical practice I have grown used to seeing people who were soon going to die, and I have always felt strange when people whose death was at hand talked, smiled, or wept in my presence; but here, when I see on the verandah this blind woman who laughs, jokes, or hears my stories read to her, what begins to seem strange to me is not that she is dying, but that we do not feel our own death, and write stories as though we were never going to die.

The second daughter, also a woman doctor, is a gentle, shy, infinitely kind creature, loving to everyone. Patients are a regular torture to her, and she is scrupulous to morbidity with them. At consultations we always disagree: I bring good tidings where she sees death, and I double the doses which she prescribes. But where death is obvious and inevitable my lady doctor feels quite in an unprofessional way. I was receiving patients with her one day at a medical centre; a young Little Russian woman came with a malignant tumour of the glands in her neck and at the back of her head.

The tumour had spread so far that no treatment could be thought of. And because the woman was at present feeling no pain, but would in another six months die in terrible agony, the doctor looked at her in such a guilty way as though she were asking forgiveness for being well, and ashamed that medical science was helpless. She takes a zealous part in managing the house and estate, and understands every detail of it. She knows all about horses even. When the side horse does not pull or gets restless, she knows how to help matters and instructs the coachman. I believe she has never hurt anyone, and it seems to me that she has not been happy for a single instant and never will be.

The third daughter, who has finished her studies at Bezstuzhevka, is a vigorous, sunburnt young girl with a loud voice. Her laugh can be heard a mile away. She is a passionate Little Russian patriot. She has built a school on the estate at her own expense, and teaches the children Krylov's fables translated into Little Russian. She goes to Shevtchenko's grave as a Turk goes to Mecca. She does not cut her hair, wears stays and a bustle, looks after the housekeeping, is fond of laughing and singing.

The eldest son is a quiet, modest, intelligent, hardworking young man with no talents; he has no pretensions, and is apparently content with what life has given him. He has been dismissed from the University [Translator's Note: On political grounds, of course, is understood.] just before taking his degree, but he does not boast of it. He speaks little. He loves farming and the land and lives in harmony with the peasants.

The second son is a young man mad over Tchaikovsky's being a genius. He dreams of living according to Tolstoy.

Pleshtcheyev is staying with us. They all look upon him as a demi-god, consider themselves happy if he bestows attention on somebody's junket, bring him flowers, invite him everywhere, and so on.... And he "listens and eats," and smokes his cigars which give his admirers a headache. He is slow to move, with the indolence of old age, but this does not prevent the fair sex from taking him about in boats, driving with him to the neighbouring estates, and singing songs to him. Here he is by way of being the same thing as in Petersburg—i.e., an ikon which is prayed to for being old and for having once hung by the side of the miracle-working ikons. So far as I am concerned I regard him—not to speak of his being a very good, warm-hearted and sincere man—as a vessel full of traditions, interesting memories, and good platitudes.

... What you say about "The Lights" is quite just. You say that neither the conversation about pessimism nor Kisotcha's story in any way help to solve the question of pessimism. It seems to me it is not for writers of fiction to solve such questions as that of God, of pessimism, etc. The writer's business is simply to describe who has been speaking about God or about pessimism, how, and in what circumstances. The artist must be not the judge of his characters and of their conversations, but merely an impartial witness. I have heard a desultory conversation of two Russians about pessimism—a conversation which settles nothing—and I must report that conversation as I heard it; it is for the jury, that is, for the readers, to decide on the value of it. My business is merely to be talented—i.e., to know how to distinguish important statements from unimportant, how to throw light on the characters, and to speak their language. Shtcheglov-Leontyev blames me for finishing the story with the words, "There's no making out anything in this world." He thinks a writer who is a good psychologist ought to be able to make it out—that is what he is a psychologist for. But I don't agree with him. It is time that writers, especially those who are artists, recognized that there is no making out anything in this world, as once Socrates recognized it, and Voltaire, too. The mob thinks it knows and understands everything; and the more stupid it is the wider it imagines its outlook to be. And if a writer whom the mob believes in has the courage to say that he does not understand anything of what he sees, that alone will be something gained in the realm of thought and a great step in advance.

TO A. N. PLESHTCHEYEV.

SUMY, June 28, 1888.

... We have been to the province of Poltava. We went to the Smagins', and to Sorotchintsi. We drove with a four-in-hand, in an ancestral, very comfortable carriage. We had no end of laughter, adventures, misunderstandings, halts, and meetings on the way.... If you had only seen the places where we stayed the night and the villages stretching eight or ten versts through which we drove! ... What weddings we met on the road, what lovely music we heard in the evening stillness, and what a heavy smell of fresh hay there was! Really one might sell one's soul to the devil for the pleasure of looking at the warm evening sky, the pools and the rivulets reflecting the sad, languid sunset....

... The Smagins' estate is "great and fertile," but old, neglected, and dead as last year's cobwebs. The house has sunk, the doors won't shut, the tiles in the stove squeeze one another out and form angles, young suckers of cherries and plums peep up between the cracks of the floors. In the room where I slept a nightingale had made herself a nest between the window and the shutter, and while I was there little naked nightingales, looking like undressed Jew babies, hatched out from the eggs. Sedate storks live on the barn. At the beehouse there is an old grandsire who remembers the King Goroh [Translator's Note: The equivalent of Old King Cole.] and Cleopatra of Egypt.

Everything is crumbling and decrepit, but poetical, sad, and beautiful in the extreme.

TO HIS SISTER.

FEODOSIA, July, 1888.

... The journey from Sumy to Harkov is frightfully dull. Going from Harkov to Simferopol one might well die of boredom. The Crimean steppe is depressing, monotonous, with no horizon, colourless like Ivanenko's stories, and on the whole rather like the tundra.... From Simferopol mountains begin and, with them, beauty. Ravines, mountains, ravines, mountains, poplars stick out from the ravines, vineyards loom dark on the mountains—all this is bathed in moonlight, is new and wild, and sets one's imagination working in harmony with Gogol's "Terrible Vengeance." Particularly fantastic are the alternating precipices and tunnels when you see now depths full of moonlight and now complete sinister darkness. It is rather uncanny and delightful. One feels it is something not Russian, something alien. I reached Sevastopol at night. The town is beautiful in itself and beautiful because it stands by a marvellous sea. The best in the sea is its colour, and that one cannot describe. It is like blue copperas. As to steamers and sailing vessels, piers and harbours, what strikes one most of all is the poverty of the Russians. Except the *"popovkas,"* which look like Moscow merchants' wives, and two or three decent steamers, there is nothing to speak of in the bay.

... In the morning it was deadly dull. Heat, dust, thirst.... In the harbour there was a stench of ropes, and one caught glimpses of faces burnt brick-red, sounds of a pulley, of the splashing of dirty water, knocking, Tatar words, and all sorts of uninteresting nonsense. You go up to a steamer: men in rags, bathed in sweat and almost baked by the sun, dizzy, with tatters on their backs and shoulders, unload Portland cement; you stand and look at them and the whole scene becomes so remote, so alien, that one feels insufferably dull and uninterested. It is entertaining to get on board and set off, but it is rather a bore to sail and talk to a crowd of passengers consisting of elements all of which one knows by heart and is weary of already.... Yalta is a mixture of something European that reminds one of the views of Nice, with something cheap and shoddy. The box-like hotels in which unhappy consumptives are pining, the impudent Tatar faces, the ladies' bustles with their very undisguised expression of something very abominable, the faces of the idle rich, longing for cheap adventures, the smell of perfumery instead of the scent of the cedars and the sea, the miserable dirty pier, the melancholy lights far out at sea, the prattle of young ladies and gentlemen who have crowded here in order to admire nature of which they have no idea—all this taken together produces such a depressing effect and is so overwhelming that one begins to blame oneself for being biassed and unfair.... At five o'clock in the morning I arrived at Feodosia—a greyish-brown, dismal, and dull-looking little town. There is no grass, the trees are wretched, the soil is coarse and hopelessly poor. Everything is burnt up by the sun, and only the sea smiles—the sea which has nothing to do with wretched little towns or tourists. Sea bathing is so nice that when I got into the water I began to laugh for no reason at all....

July 22.

... Yesterday we went to Shah-Mamai Aivazovsky's estate, twenty-five versts from Feodosia. It is a magnificent estate, rather like fairyland; such estates may probably be seen in Persia. Aivazovsky [Translator's Note: The famous marine painter.] himself, a vigorous old man of seventy-five, is a mixture of a good-natured Armenian and an overfed bishop; he is full of dignity, has soft hands, and offers them like a general. He is not very intelligent, but is a complex nature worthy of attention. He combines in himself a general, a bishop, an artist, an Armenian, a naive old peasant, and an Othello. He is married to a young and very beautiful woman whom he rules with a rod of iron. He is friendly with Sultans, Shahs, and Amirs. He collaborated with Glinka in writing "Ruslan and Liudmila." He was a friend of Pushkin, but has never read him. He has not read a single book in his life. When it is suggested to him that he should read something he answers, "Why should I read when I have opinions of my own?" I spent a whole day in his house and had dinner there. The dinner was fearfully long, with endless toasts. By the way, at that dinner I was introduced to the lady doctor, wife of the well-known professor. She is a fat, bulky piece of flesh. If she were undressed and painted green she would look just like a frog. After talking to her I mentally scratched her off the list of women doctors....

TO HIS BROTHER MIHAIL.

July 28, 1888.

On the Seas Black, Caspian, and of Life.

... A wretched little cargo steamer, *Dir*, is racing full steam from Suhum to Poti. It is about midnight. The little cabin—the only one in the steamer—is insufferably hot and stuffy. There is a smell of burning, of rope, of fish and of the sea. One hears the engine going "Boom-boom-boom." ... There are devils creaking up aloft and under the floor. The darkness is swaying in the cabin and the bed rocks up and down.... One's stomach's whole attention is concentrated on the bed, and, as though to find its level, it rolls the Seltzer water I had drunk right up to my throat and then lets it down to my heels. Not to be sick over my clothes in the dark I hastily put on my things and go out.... It is dark. My feet stumble against some invisible iron bars, a rope; wherever you step there are barrels, sacks, rags. There is coal dust under foot. In the dark I knock against a kind of grating: it is a cage with wild goats which I saw in the daytime. They are awake and anxiously listening to the rocking of the boat. By the cage sit two Turks who are not asleep either.... I grope my way up the stairs to the captain's bridge.... A warm but violent and unpleasant wind tries to blow away my cap.... The steamer rocks. The mast in front of the captain's bridge sways regularly and leisurely like a metronome; I try to look away from it, but my eyes will not obey me and, just like my stomach, insist on following moving objects.... The sky and the sea are dark, the shore is not in sight, the deck looks a dark blur ... there is not a single light.

Behind me is a window ... I look into it and see a man who looks attentively at something and turns a wheel with an expression as though he were playing the ninth symphony.... Next to me stands the little stout captain in tan shoes.... He talks to me of Caucasian emigrants, of the heat, of winter storms, and at the same time looks intently into the dark distance in the direction of the shore.

"You seem to be going too much to the left again," he says to someone; or, "There ought to be lights here.... Do you see them?"

"No, sir," someone answers from the dark.

"Climb up and look."

A dark figure appears on the bridge and leisurely climbs up. In a minute we hear:

"Yes, sir."

I look to the left where the lights of the lighthouse are supposed to be, borrow the captain's glasses, but see nothing.... Half an hour passes, then an hour. The mast sways regularly, the devils creak, the wind makes dashes at my cap.... It is not pitch dark, but one feels uneasy.

Suddenly the captain dashes off somewhere to the rear of the ship, crying, "You devil's doll!"

"To the left," he shouts anxiously at the top of his voice. "To the left! ... To the right! A-va-va-a!"

Incomprehensible words of command are heard. The steamer starts, the devils give a creak.... "A-va-va!" shouts the captain; at the bows a bell is rung, on the black deck there are sounds of running, knocking, cries of anxiety.... The *Dir* starts once more, puffs painfully, and apparently tries to move backwards.

"What is it?" I ask, and feel something like a faint terror. There is no answer.

"He'd like a collision, the devil's doll!" I hear the captain's harsh shout. "To the left!"

Red lights appear in front, and suddenly among the uproar is heard the whistling, not of the *Dir*, but of some other steamer.... Now I understand it: there is going to be a collision! The *Dir* puffs, trembles, and does not move, as though waiting for a signal to go down.... But just when I think all is lost, the red lights appear on the left of us, and the dark silhouette of a steamer can be discerned.... A long black body sails past us, guiltily blinks its red eyes, and gives a guilty whistle....

"Oof! What steamer is it?" I ask the captain.

The captain looks at the silhouette through his glasses and replies:

"It is the *Tweedie*."

After a pause we begin to talk of the *Vesta*, which collided with two steamers and went down. Under the influence of this conversation the sea, the night and the wind begin to seem hideous, created on purpose for man's undoing, and I feel sorry as I look at the fat little captain.... Something whispers to me that this poor man, too, will sooner or later sink to the bottom and be choked with salt water. [Footnote: Chekhov's presentiment about the captain was partly fulfilled: that very autumn the *Dir* was wrecked on the shores of Alupka.]

I go back to my cabin.... It is stuffy, and there is a smell of cooking. My travelling companion, Suvorin-*fils*, is asleep already.... I take off all my clothes and go to bed.... The darkness sways to and fro, the bed seems to breathe.... Boom-boom-boom! Bathed in perspiration, breathless, and feeling an oppression all over with the rocking, I ask myself, "What am I here for?"

I wake up. It is no longer dark. Wet all over, with a nasty taste in my mouth, I dress and go out. Everything is covered with dew.... The wild goats look with human eyes through the grating of their cage and seem to be asking "Why are we here?" The captain stands still as before and looks intently into the distance....

A mountainous shore stretches on the left.... Elborus is seen from behind the mountains.

A blurred sun rises in the sky.... One can see the green valley of Rion and the Bay of Poti by the side of it.

TO N. A. LEIKIN.

SUMY, August 12.

... I have been to the Crimea. I spent twelve days at Suvorin's in Feodosia, bathed, idled about; I have been to Aivazovsky's estate. From Feodosia I went by steamer to Batum. On the way I spent half a day at Suhum—a charming little town buried in luxuriant, un-Russian greenery, and one day at the Monastery, at New Athos. It is so lovely there at New Athos that there is no describing it: waterfalls, eucalyptuses, tea-plants, cypresses, olive-trees, and, above all, sea and mountains, mountains, mountains. From Athos and Suhum I went to Poti; the River Rion, renowned for its valley and its sturgeons, is close by. The vegetation is luxuriant. All the streets are planted with poplars. Batum is a big commercial and military, foreign-looking, *cafe'-chantant* sort of town; you feel in it at every step that we have conquered the Turks. There is nothing special about it (except a great number of brothels), but the surrounding country is charming. Particularly fine is the road to Kars and the swift river Tchoraksu.

The road from Batum to Tiflis is poetical and original; you look all the time out of window and exclaim: there are mountains, tunnels, rocks, rivers, waterfalls, big and little. But the road from Tiflis to Baku is the abomination of desolation, a bald plain, covered with sand and created for Persians, tarantulas, and phalangas to live in. There is not a single tree, there is no grass ... dreary as hell.... Baku and the Caspian Sea are such rotten places that I would not agree to live there for a million. There are no roofs, there are no trees either; Persian faces everywhere, fifty degrees Reaumur of heat, a smell of kerosine, the naphtha-soaked mud squelches under one's feet, the drinking water is salt.

... You have seen the Caucasus. I believe you have seen the Georgian Military Road, too. If you have not been there yet, pawn your wives and children and the *Oskolki* [Translator's Note: *Oskolki*, (i.e., "Chips," "Bits") the paper of which Leikin was editor.] and go. I have never in my life seen anything like it. It is not a road, but unbroken poetry, a wonderful, fantastic story written by the Demon in love with Tamara.

TO A. S. SUVORIN.

SUMY, August 29, 1888.

... When as a boy I used to stay at my grandfather's on Count Platov's estate, I had to sit from sunrise to sunset by the thrashing machine and write down the number of *poods* and pounds of corn that had been thrashed; the whistling, the hissing, and the bass note, like the sound of a whirling top, that the machine makes at full speed, the creaking of the wheels, the lazy tread of the oxen, the clouds of dust, the grimy, perspiring faces of some three score of men—all this has stamped itself upon my memory like the Lord's Prayer. And now, too, I have been spending hours at the thrashing and felt intensely happy. When the thrashing engine is at work it looks as though alive; it has a cunning, playful expression, while the men and oxen look like machines. In the district of Mirgorod few have thrashing machines of their own, but everyone can hire one. The engine goes about the whole province drawn by six oxen and offers itself to all who can pay for it.

MOSCOW,

September 11.

... You advise me not to hunt after two hares, and not to think of medical work. I do not know why one should not hunt two hares even in the literal sense.... I feel more confident and more satisfied with myself when I reflect that I have two professions and not one. Medicine is my lawful wife and literature is my mistress. When I get tired of one I spend the night with the other. Though it's disorderly, it's not so dull, and besides neither of them loses anything from my infidelity. If I did not have my medical work I doubt if I could have given my leisure and my spare thoughts to literature. There is no discipline in me.

MOSCOW,

October 27, 1888.

... In conversation with my literary colleagues I always insist that it is not the artist's business to solve problems that require a specialist's knowledge. It is a bad thing if a writer tackles a subject he does not understand. We have specialists for dealing with special questions: it is their business to judge of the commune, of the future of capitalism, of the evils of drunkenness, of boots, of the diseases of women. An artist must only judge of what he understands, his field is just as limited as that of any other specialist—I repeat this and insist on it always. That in his sphere there are no questions, but only answers, can only be maintained by those who have never written and have had no experience of thinking in images. An artist observes, selects, guesses, combines—and this in itself presupposes a problem: unless he had set himself a problem from the very first there would be nothing to conjecture and nothing to select. To put it briefly, I will end by using the language of psychiatry: if one denies that creative work involves problems and purposes, one must admit that an artist creates without premeditation or intention, in a state of aberration; therefore, if an author boasted to me of having written a novel without a preconceived design, under a sudden inspiration, I should call him mad.

You are right in demanding that an artist should take an intelligent attitude to his work, but you confuse two things: *solving a problem* and *stating a problem correctly*. It is only the second that is obligatory for the artist. In "Anna Karenin" and "Evgeny Onyegin" not a single problem is solved, but they satisfy you completely because all the problems are correctly stated in them. It is the business of the judge to put the right questions, but the answers must be given by the jury according to their own lights.

... You say that the hero of my "Party" is a character worth developing. Good Lord! I am not a senseless brute, you know, I understand that. I understand that I cut the throats of my characters and spoil them, and that I waste good material.... To tell you the truth, I would gladly have spent six months over the "Party"; I like taking things easy, and see no attraction in publishing at headlong speed. I would willingly, with pleasure, with feeling, in a leisurely way, describe the *whole* of my hero, describe the state of his mind while his wife was in labour, his trial, the horrid feeling he has after he is acquitted; I would describe the midwife and the doctors having tea in the middle of the night, I would describe the rain.... It would give me nothing but pleasure because I like to rummage about and dawdle. But what am I to do? I begin a story on September 10th with the thought that I must finish it by October 5th at the latest; if I don't I shall fail the editor and be left without money. I let myself go at the beginning and write with an easy mind; but by the time I get to the middle I begin to grow timid and to fear that my story will be too long: I have to remember that the *Syeverny Vyestnik* has not much money, and that I am one of their expensive contributors. This is why the beginning of my stories is always very promising and looks as though I were starting on a novel, the middle is huddled and timid, and the end is, as in a short sketch, like fireworks. And so in planning a story one is bound to think first about its framework: from a crowd of leading or subordinate characters one selects one person only—wife or husband; one puts him on the canvas and paints him alone, making him prominent, while the others one scatters over the canvas like small coin, and the result is something like the vault of heaven: one big moon and a number of very small stars around it. But the moon is not a success because it can only be understood if the stars too are intelligible, and the stars are not worked out. And so what I produce is not literature, but something like the patching of Trishka's coat. What am I to do? I don't know, I don't know. I must trust to time which heals all things.

To tell the truth again, I have not yet begun my literary work, though I have received a literary prize. Subjects for five stories and two novels are languishing in my head. One of the novels was thought of long ago, and some of the characters have grown old without managing to be written. In my head there is a whole army of people asking to be let out and waiting for the word of command. All that I have written so far is rubbish in comparison with what I should like to write and should write with rapture. It is all the same to me whether I write "The Party" or "The Lights," or a vaudeville or a letter to a friend—it is all dull, spiritless, mechanical, and I get annoyed with critics who attach any importance to "The Lights," for instance. I fancy that I deceive him with my work just as I deceive many people with my face, which looks serious or over-cheerful. I don't like being successful; the subjects which sit in my head are annoyed and jealous of what has already been written. I am vexed that the rubbish has been done and the good things lie about in the lumber-room like old books. Of course, in thus lamenting I rather exaggerate, and much of what I say is only my fancy, but there is a part of the truth in it, a good big part of it. What do I call good? The images which seem best to me, which I love and jealously guard lest I spend and spoil them for the sake of some "Party" written against time.... If my love is mistaken, I am wrong, but then it may not be mistaken! I am either a fool and a conceited fellow or I really am an organism capable of being a good writer. All that I now write displeases and bores me, but what sits in my head interests, excites and moves me—from which I conclude that everybody does the wrong thing and I alone know the secret of doing the right one. Most likely all writers think that. But the devil himself would break his neck in these problems.

Money will not help me to decide what I am to do and how I am to act. An extra thousand roubles will not settle matters, and a hundred thousand is a castle in the air. Besides, when I have money—it may be from lack of habit, I don't know—I become extremely careless and idle; the sea seems only knee-deep to me then.... I need time and solitude.

November, 1888.

In the November number of the *Syeverny Vyestnik* there is an article by the poet Merezhkovsky about your humble servant. It is a long article. I commend to your attention the end of it; it is characteristic. Merezhkovsky is still very young, a student—of science I believe. Those who have assimilated the wisdom of the scientific method and learned to think

- 64 -

scientifically experience many alluring temptations. Archimedes wanted to turn the earth round, and the present day hot-heads want by science to conceive the inconceivable, to discover the physical laws of creative art, to detect the laws and the formulae which are instinctively felt by the artist and are followed by him in creating music, novels, pictures, etc. Such formulae probably exist in nature. We know that A, B, C, do, re, mi, fa, sol, are found in nature, and so are curves, straight lines, circles, squares, green, blue, and red.... We know that in certain combinations all this produces a melody, or a poem or a picture, just as simple chemical substances in certain combinations produce a tree, or a stone, or the sea; but all we know is that the combination exists, while the law of it is hidden from us. Those who are masters of the scientific method feel in their souls that a piece of music and a tree have something in common, that both are built up in accordance with equally uniform and simple laws. Hence the question: What are these laws? And hence the temptation to work out a physiology of creative art (like Boborykin), or in the case of younger and more diffident writers, to base their arguments on nature and on the laws of nature (Merezhkovsky). There probably is such a thing as the physiology of creative art, but we must nip in the bud our dreams of discovering it. If the critics take up a scientific attitude no good will come of it: they will waste a dozen years, write a lot of rubbish, make the subject more obscure than ever—and nothing more. It is always a good thing to think scientifically, but the trouble is that scientific thinking about creative art will be bound to degenerate in the end into searching for the "cells" or the "centres" which control the creative faculty. Some stolid German will discover these cells somewhere in the occipital lobes, another German will agree with him, a third will disagree, and a Russian will glance through the article about the cells and reel off an essay about it to the *Syeverny Vyestnik*. The *Vyestnik Evropi* will criticize the essay, and for three years there will be in Russia an epidemic of nonsense which will give money and popularity to blockheads and do nothing but irritate intelligent people.

For those who are obsessed with the scientific method and to whom God has given the rare talent of thinking scientifically, there is to my mind only one way out—the philosophy of creative art. One might collect together all the best works of art that have been produced throughout the ages and, with the help of the scientific method, discover the common element in them which makes them like one another and conditions their value. That common element will be the law. There is a great deal that works which are called immortal have in common; if this common element were excluded from each of them, a work would lose its charm and its value. So that this universal something is necessary, and is *the conditio sine qua non* of every work that claims to be immortal. It is of more use to young people to write critical articles than poetry. Merezhkovsky writes smoothly and youthfully, but at every page he loses heart, makes reservations and concessions, and this means that he is not clear upon the subject. He calls me a poet, he styles my stories "novelli" and my heroes "failures"—that is, he follows the beaten track. It is time to give up these "failures," superfluous people, etc., and to think of something original. Merezhkovsky calls my monk [Translator's Note: "Easter Eve."] who composes the songs of praise a failure. But how is he a failure? God grant us all a life like his: he believed in God, and he had enough to eat and he had the gift of composing poetry.... To divide men into the successful and the unsuccessful is to look at human nature from a narrow, preconceived point of view. Are you a success or not? Am I? Was Napoleon? Is your servant Vassily? What is the criterion? One must be a god to be able to tell successes from failures without making a mistake.

MOSCOW,

November 7, 1888.

... It is not the public that is to blame for our theatres being so wretched. The public is always and everywhere the same: intelligent and stupid, sympathetic and pitiless according to mood. It has always been a flock which needs good shepherds and dogs, and it has always gone in the direction in which the shepherds and the dogs drove it. You are indignant that it laughs at flat witticisms and applauds sounding phrases; but then the very same stupid public fills the house to hear "Othello," and, listening to the opera "Evgeny Onyegin," weeps when Tatyana writes her letter.

... The water-carrier has stolen from somewhere a Siberian kitten with long white fur and black eyes, and brought it to us. This kitten takes people for mice: when it sees anyone it lies flat on its stomach, stalks one's feet and rushes at them. This morning as I was pacing up and down the room it several times stalked me, and *a la tigre* pounced at my boots. I imagine the thought of being more terrible than anyone in the house affords it the greatest delight.

November 11, 1888.

I finished to-day the story [Footnote: "A Nervous Breakdown."] for the Garshin *sbornik*: it is such a load off my mind. In this story I have told my own opinion—which is of no interest to anyone—of such rare men as Garshin. I have run to almost 2,000 lines. I speak at length about prostitution, but settle nothing. Why do they write nothing about prostitution in your paper? It is the most fearful evil, you know. Our Sobolev street is a regular slave-market.

November 15, 1888.

My "Party" has pleased the ladies. They sing my praises wherever I go. It really isn't bad to be a doctor and to understand what one is writing about. The ladies say the description of the confinement is *true*. In the story for the Garshin *sbornik* I have described spiritual agony.

(No date), 1888.

... You say that writers are God's elect. I will not contradict you. Shtcheglov calls me the Potyomkin of literature, and so it is not for me to speak of the thorny path, of disappointments, and so on. I do not know whether I have ever suffered more than shoemakers, mathematicians, or railway guards do; I do not know who speaks through my lips—God or someone worse. I will allow myself to mention only one little drawback which I have experienced and you probably know from experience also. It is this. You and I are fond of ordinary people; but other people are fond of us because they think we are not ordinary. Me, for instance, they invite everywhere and regale me with food and drink like a general at a wedding. My sister is indignant that people on all sides invite her simply because she is a writer's sister. No one wants to love the ordinary people in us. Hence it follows that if in the eyes of our friends we should appear to-morrow as ordinary mortals, they will leave off loving us, and will only pity us. And that is horrid. It is horrid, too, that they like the very things in us which we often dislike and despise in ourselves. It is horrid that I was right when I wrote the story "The First-Class Passenger," in which an engineer and a professor talk about fame.

I am going away into the country. Hang them all! You have Feodosia. By the way, about Feodosia and the Tatars. The Tatars have been robbed of their land, but no one thinks of their welfare. There ought to be Tatar schools. Write and suggest that the money which is being spent on the sausage Dorpat University, where useless Germans are studying, should be devoted to schools for Tatars, who are of use to Russia. I would write about it myself, but I don't know how to.

December 23, 1888.

... There are moments when I completely lose heart. For whom and for what do I write? For the public? But I don't see it, and believe in it less than I do in spooks: it is uneducated, badly brought up, and its best elements are unfair and insincere to us. I cannot make out whether this public wants me or not. Burenin says that it does not, and that I waste my time on trifles; the Academy has given me a prize. The devil himself could not make head or tail of it. Write for the sake of money? But I never have any money, and not being used to having it I am almost indifferent to it. For the sake of money I work apathetically. Write for the sake of praise? But praise merely irritates me. Literary society, students, Pleshtcheyev, young ladies, etc., were enthusiastic in their praises of my "Nervous Breakdown," but Grigorovitch is the only one who has noticed the description of the first snow. And so on, and so on. If we had critics I should know that I provide material, whether good or bad does not matter—that to men who devote themselves to the study of life I am as necessary as a star is to an astronomer. And then I would take trouble over my work and should know what I was working for. But as it is you, I, Muravlin, and the rest are like lunatics who write books and plays to please themselves. To please oneself is, of course, an excellent thing; one feels the pleasure while one is writing, but afterwards? But ... I will shut up. In short, I am sorry for Tatyana Repin, [Translator's Note: Suvorin's play.] not because she poisoned herself, but because she lived her life, died in agony, and was described absolutely to no purpose, without any good to anyone. A number of tribes, religions, languages, civilizations, have vanished without a trace—vanished because there were no historians or biologists. In the same way a number of lives and works of art disappear before our very eyes owing to the complete absence of criticism. It may be objected that critics would have nothing to do because all modern works are poor and insignificant. But this is a narrow way of looking at things. Life must be studied not from the pluses alone, but from the minuses too. The conviction that the "eighties" have not produced a single writer may in itself provide material for five volumes.

... I settled down last night to write a story for the *Novoye Vremya*, but a woman appeared and dragged me to see the poet Palmin who, when he was drunk, had fallen and cut his forehead to the bone. I was busy over the drunken fellow for nearly two hours, was tired out, began to smell of iodoform all over, felt cross, and came home exhausted.... Altogether my life is a dreary one, and I begin to get fits of hating people which used never to happen to me before. Long stupid conversations, visitors, people asking for help, and helping them to the extent of one or two or three roubles, spending money on cabs for the sake of patients who do not pay me a penny—altogether it is such a hotch-potch that I feel like running away from home. People borrow money from me and don't pay it back, they take my books, they waste my time.... Blighted love is the one thing that is missing.

December 26, 1888.

... You say that from compassion women fall in love, from compassion they get married.... And what about men? I don't like realistic writers to slander women, but I don't like it either when people put women on a pedestal and attempt to prove that even if they are worse than men, anyway they are angels and men scoundrels. Neither men nor women are worth a brass farthing, but men are more just and more intelligent.

December 30, 1888.

... This is how I understand my characters. [Translator's Note: In the play "Ivanov."] Ivanov is a gentleman, a University man, and not remarkable in any way. He is excitable, hotheaded, easily carried away, honest and straightforward like most people of his class. He has lived on his estate and served on the Zemstvo. What he has been doing and how he has behaved, what he has been interested in and enthusiastic over, can be seen from the following words of his, addressed to the doctor (Act I., Scene 5): "Don't marry Jewesses or neurotic women or blue-stockings ... don't fight with thousands single-handed, don't wage war on windmills, don't batter your head against the wall ... God preserve you from scientific farming, wonderful schools, enthusiastic speeches...." This is what he has in his past. Sarra, who has seen his scientific farming and other crazes, says about him to the doctor: "He is a remarkable man, doctor, and I am sorry you did not meet him two or three years ago. Now he is depressed and melancholy, he doesn't talk or do anything, but in old days ... how charming he was!" (Act I., Scene 7). His past is beautiful, as is generally the case with educated Russians. There is not, or there hardly is, a single Russian gentleman or University man who does not boast of his past. The present is always worse than the past. Why? Because Russian excitability has one specific characteristic: it is quickly followed by exhaustion. A man has scarcely left the class-room before he rushes to take up a burden beyond his strength; he tackles at once the schools, the peasants, scientific farming, and the *Vyestnik Evropi*, he makes speeches, writes to the minister, combats evil, applauds good, falls in love, not in an ordinary, simple way, but selects either a blue-stocking or a neurotic or a Jewess, or even a prostitute whom he tries to save, and so on, and so on. But by the time he is thirty or thirty-five he begins to feel tired and bored. He has not got decent moustaches yet, but he already says with authority:

"Don't marry, my dear fellow.... Trust my experience," or, "After all, what does Liberalism come to? Between ourselves Katkov was often right...." He is ready to reject the Zemstvo and scientific farming, and science and love. My Ivanov says to the doctor (Act I., Scene 5): "You took your degree only last year, my dear friend, you are still young and vigorous, while I am thirty-five. I have a right to advise you...." That is how these prematurely exhausted people talk. Further down, sighing authoritatively, he advises: "Don't you marry in this or that way (see above), but choose something commonplace, grey, with no vivid colours or superfluous flourishes. Altogether build your life according to the conventional pattern. The greyer and more monotonous the background the better.... The life that I have led—how tiring it is! Ah, how tiring!"

Conscious of physical exhaustion and boredom, he does not understand what is the matter with him, and what has happened. Horrified, he says to the doctor (Act I., Scene 3): "Here you tell me she is soon going to die and I feel neither love nor pity, but a sort of emptiness and weariness.... If one looks at me from outside it must be horrible. I don't understand what is happening to my soul." Finding themselves in such a position, narrow and unconscientious people generally throw the whole blame on their environment, or write themselves down as Hamlets and superfluous people, and are satisfied with that. But Ivanov, a straightforward man, openly says to the doctor and to the public that he does not understand his own mind. "I don't understand! I don't understand!" That he really doesn't understand can be seen from his long monologue in Act III., where, *tete-a-tete* with the public, he opens his heart to it and even weeps.

The change that has taken place in him offends his sense of what is fitting. He looks for the causes outside himself and fails to find them; he begins to look for them inside and finds only an indefinite feeling of guilt. It is a Russian feeling. Whether there is a death or illness in his family, whether he owes money or lends it, a Russian always feels guilty. Ivanov talks all the time about being to blame in some way, and the feeling of guilt increases in him at every juncture. In Act I. he says: "Suppose I am terribly to blame, yet my thoughts are in a tangle, my soul is in bondage to a sort of sloth, and I am incapable of understanding myself...." In Act II. he says to Sasha: "My conscience aches day and night, I feel that I am profoundly to blame, but in what exactly I have done wrong I cannot make out."

To exhaustion, boredom, and the feeling of guilt add one more enemy: loneliness. Were Ivanov an official, an actor, a priest, a professor, he would have grown used to his position. But he lives on his estate. He is in the country. His neighbours are either drunkards or fond of cards, or are of the same type as the doctor. None of them care about his feelings or the change that has taken place in him. He is lonely. Long winters, long evenings, an empty garden, empty rooms, the grumbling Count, the ailing wife.... He has nowhere to go. This is why he is every minute tortured by the question: what is he to do with himself?

Now about his fifth enemy. Ivanov is tired and does not understand himself, but life has nothing to do with that! It makes its legitimate demands upon him, and whether he will or no, he must settle problems. His sick wife is a problem, his numerous debts are a problem, Sasha flinging herself on his neck is a problem. The way in which he settles all these problems must be evident from his monologue in Act III., and from the contents of the last two acts. Men like Ivanov do not solve difficulties but collapse under their weight. They lose their heads, gesticulate, become nervous, complain, do silly things, and finally, giving rein to their flabby, undisciplined nerves, lose the ground under their feet and enter the class of the "broken down" and "misunderstood."

Disappointment, apathy, nervous limpness and exhaustion are the inevitable consequence of extreme excitability, and such excitability is extremely characteristic of our young people. Take literature. Take the present time.... Socialism is one of the forms of this excitement. But where is socialism? You see it in Tihomirov's letter to the Tsar. The socialists are married and are criticizing the Zemstvo. Where is Liberalism? Mihailovsky himself says that all the labels have been mixed up now. And what are all the Russian enthusiasms worth? The war has wearied us, Bulgaria has wearied us till we can only be ironical about it. Zucchi has wearied us and so has the comic opera.

Exhaustion (Dr. Bertensen will confirm this) finds expression not only in complaining or the sensation of boredom. The life of an over-tired man cannot be represented like this:

[Transcriber's note: The line graph in the print version depicts a wavy horizontal "line" with minimal variation in the vertical direction. The ASCII diagram below gives a rough approximation.]

~~~~~~~~~~~~~~~~~~~~~~~~~~~~

It is very unequal. Over-tired people never lose the capacity for becoming extremely excited, but cannot keep it up for long, and each excitement is followed by still greater apathy.... Graphically, it could be represented like this:

[Transcriber's note: The line graph in the print version depicts a series of wavy horizontal segments punctuated by sharp "dips," each horizontal segment a little lower than the one before. The ASCII illustration below gives a rough approximation.]

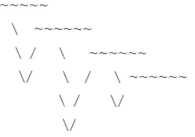

```
      ~~~~~~~
   \    ~~~~~~
   \ /   \    ~~~~~~~
   \/    \ /   \ ~~~~~~~
         \ /   \/
         \/
```

The fall, as you see, is not continuous but broken. Sasha declares her love and Ivanov cries out in ecstasy, "A new life!"—and next morning he believes in this new life as little as he does in spooks (the monologue in Act III.); his wife insults him, and, fearfully worked up and beside himself with anger, he flings a cruel insult at her. He is called a scoundrel. This is either fatal to his tottering brain, or stimulates him to a fresh paroxysm and he pronounces sentence on himself.

Not to tire you out altogether I pass now to Dr. Lvov. He is the type of an honest, straightforward, hotheaded, but narrow and uncompromising man. Clever people say of such men: "He is stupid but his heart is in the right place." Anything like width of outlook or unreflecting feeling is foreign to Lvov. He is the embodiment of a programme, a walking tendency. He looks through a narrow frame at every person and event, he judges everything according to preconceived notions. Those who shout, "Make way for honest labour!" are an object of worship to him; those who do not shout it are scoundrels and exploiters. There is no middle. He has been brought up on Mihailov's [Translator's Note: The author of second-rate works inculcating civic virtue with a revolutionary bias.] novels; at the theatre he has seen on the stage "new men," i.e., the exploiters and sons of our age, painted by the modern playwrights. He has stored it all up, and so much so, that when he reads "Rudin" he is sure to be asking himself, "Is Rudin a scoundrel or not?" Literature and the stage have so educated him that he approaches every character in real life and in fiction with this question.... It is not enough for him that all men are sinners. He wants saints and villains!

He was prejudiced before he came to the district. He at once classed all the rich peasants as exploiters, and Ivanov, whom he could not understand, as a scoundrel. Why, the man has a sick wife and he goes to see a rich lady neighbour—of course he is a scoundrel! It is obvious that he is killing his wife in order to marry an heiress.

Lvov is honest and straightforward, and he blurts out the truth without sparing himself. If necessary, he will throw a bomb at a carriage, give a school inspector a blow in the face, or call a man a scoundrel. He will not stop at anything. He never feels remorse—it is his mission as "an honest worker" to fight "the powers of darkness"!

Such people are useful, and are for the most part attractive. To caricature them, even in the interests of the play, is unfair and, indeed, unnecessary. True, a caricature is more striking, and therefore easier to understand, but it is better to put your colour on too faint than too strong.

Now about the women. What do they love Ivanov for? Sarra loves him because he is a fine man, because he has enthusiasm, because he is brilliant and speaks with as much heat as Lvov does (Act I., Scene 7). She loves him so long as he is excited and interesting; but when he begins to grow misty in her eyes, and to lose definiteness of outline, she ceases to understand him, and at the end of Act III. speaks out plainly and sharply.

Sasha is a young woman of the newest type. She is well-educated, intelligent, honest, and so on. In the realm of the blind a one-eyed man is king, and so she favours Ivanov in spite of his being thirty-five. He is better than anyone else. She knew him when she was a child and saw his work close at hand, at the period before he was exhausted. He is a friend of her father's.

She is a female who is not won by the vivid plumage of the male, not by their courage and dexterity, but by their complaints, whinings and failures. She is the sort of girl who loves a man when he is going downhill. The moment Ivanov loses heart the young lady is on the spot! That's just what she was waiting for. Just think of it, she now has such a holy, such a grateful task before her! She will raise up the fallen one, set him on his feet, make him happy.... It is not Ivanov she loves, but this task. Argenton in Daudet's book says, "Life is not a novel." Sasha does not know this. She does not know that for Ivanov love is only a fresh complication, an extra stab in the back. And what comes of it? She struggles with him for a whole year and, instead of being raised, he sinks lower and lower.

... In my description of Ivanov there often occurs the word "Russian." Don't be cross about it. When I was writing the play I had in mind only the things that really matter—that is, only the typical Russian characteristics. Thus the extreme excitability, the feeling of guilt, the liability to become exhausted are purely Russian. Germans are never excited, and that is why Germany knows nothing of disappointed, superfluous, or over-tired people.... The excitability of the French is always maintained at one and the same level, and makes no sudden bounds or falls, and so a Frenchman is normally excited down to a decrepit old age. In other words, the French do not have to waste their strength in over-excitement; they spend their powers sensibly, and do not go bankrupt.

... Ivanov and Lvov appear to my imagination to be living people. I tell you honestly, in all conscience, these men were born in my head, not by accident, not out of sea foam, or preconceived "intellectual" ideas. They are the result of observing and studying life. They stand in my brain, and I feel that I have not falsified the truth nor exaggerated it a jot. If on paper they have not come out clear and living, the fault is not in them but in me, for not being able to express my thoughts. It shows it is too early for me to begin writing plays.

January 7, 1889.

... I have been cherishing the bold dream of summing up all that has hitherto been written about whining, miserable people, and with my Ivanov saying the last word. It seemed to me that all Russian novelists and playwrights were drawn to depict despondent men, but that they all wrote instinctively, having no definite image or views on the subject. As far as my design goes I was on the right track, but the execution is good for nothing. I ought to have waited! I am glad I did not listen to Grigorovitch two or three years ago, and write a novel! I can just imagine what a lot of good material I should have spoiled. He says: "Talent and freshness overcome everything." It is more true to say that talent and freshness can spoil a great deal. In addition to plenty of material and talent, one wants something else which is no less important. One wants to be mature—that is one thing; and for another the *feeling of personal freedom* is essential, and that feeling has only recently begun to develop in me. I used not to have it before; its place was successfully filled by my frivolity, carelessness, and lack of respect for my work.

What writers belonging to the upper class have received from nature for nothing, plebeians acquire at the cost of their youth. Write a story of how a young man, the son of a serf, who has served in a shop, sung in a choir, been at a high school and a university, who has been brought up to respect everyone of higher rank and position, to kiss priests' hands, to reverence other people's ideas, to be thankful for every morsel of bread, who has been many times whipped, who has trudged from one pupil to another without goloshes, who has been used to fighting, and tormenting animals, who has liked dining with his rich relations, and been hypocritical before God and men from the mere consciousness of his own insignificance— write how this young man squeezes the slave out of himself, drop by drop, and how waking one beautiful morning he feels that he has no longer a slave's blood in his veins but a real man's....

March 5, 1889.

... Last night I drove out of town and listened to the gypsies. They sing well, the wild creatures. Their singing reminds me of a train falling off a high bank in a violent snow-storm: there is a lot of turmoil, screeching and banging.

... I bought Dostoevsky in your shop and am now reading him. It is fine, but very long and indiscreet. It is over-pretentious.

SUMY,

LINTVARYOVS' ESTATE, May, 1889.

... Among other things I am reading Gontcharov and wondering. I wonder how I could have considered Gontcharov a first-rate writer. His "Oblomov" is not really good. Oblomov himself is exaggerated and is not so striking as to make it worth while to write a whole book about him. A flabby sluggard like so many, a commonplace, petty nature without any complexity in it: to raise this person to the rank of a social type is to make too much of him. I ask myself, what would Oblomov be if he had not been a sluggard? And I answer that he would not have been anything. And if so, let him snore in peace. The other characters are trivial, with a flavour of Leikin about them; they are taken at random, and are half unreal. They are not characteristic of the epoch and give one nothing new. Stoltz does not inspire me with any confidence. The author says he is a splendid fellow, but I don't believe him. He is a sly brute, who thinks very well of himself and is very complacent. He is half unreal, and three-quarters on stilts. Olga is unreal and is dragged in by the tail. And the chief trouble is that the whole novel is cold, cold, cold. I scratch out Gontcharov from the list of my demi-gods.

But how direct, how powerful is Gogol, and what an artist he is! His "Marriage" alone is worth two hundred thousand roubles. It is simply delicious, and that is all about it. He is the greatest of Russian writers. In "The Inspector General" the first act is the best, in "The Marriage" the third act is the worst. I am going to read it aloud to my people.

May 4, 1889.

... Nature is an excellent sedative. It pacifies—that is, it makes one indifferent. And it is essential in this world to be indifferent. Only those who are indifferent are able to see things clearly, to be just and to work. Of course, I am only speaking of intelligent people of fine natures; the empty and selfish are indifferent enough any way.

You say that I have grown lazy. That does not mean that I am now lazier than I used to be. I work now as much as I did three or five years ago. To work and to look as though I were working from nine in the morning till dinner, and from evening tea till bedtime has become a habit with me, and in that respect I am just like a government clerk. And if my work does not produce two novels a month or an income of ten thousand, it is not my laziness that is at fault, but my fundamental, psychological peculiarities. I do not care enough for money to succeed in medicine, and for literature I have not enough passion and therefore not enough talent. The fire burns in me slowly and evenly, without suddenly spluttering and flaring up, and this is why it does not happen to me to write three or four signatures a night, or to be so carried away by work as to prevent myself from going to bed if I am sleepy; this is why I commit no particular follies nor do anything particularly wise.

I am afraid that in this respect I resemble Gontcharov, whom I don't like, who is ten heads taller than I am in talent. I have not enough passion; add to that this sort of lunacy: for the last two years I have for no reason at all ceased to care about seeing my work in print, have become indifferent to reviews, to literary conversations, to gossip, to success and failure, to good pay—in short, I have gone downright silly. There is a sort of stagnation in my soul. I explain it by the stagnation in my personal life. I am not disappointed, I am not tired, I am not depressed, but simply everything has suddenly become less interesting. I must do something to rouse myself.

May 7.

I have read Bourget's "Disciple" in the Russian translation. This is how it strikes me. Bourget is a gifted, very intelligent and cultured man. He is as thoroughly acquainted with the method of the natural sciences, and as imbued with it as though he had taken a good degree in science or medicine. He is not a stranger in the domain he proposes to deal with—a merit absent in Russian writers both new and old.

... The novel is interesting. I have read it and understand why you were so absorbed by it. It is clever, interesting, in places witty, somewhat fantastic. As to its defects, the chief of them is his pretentious crusade against materialism. Forgive me, but I can't understand such crusades. They never lead to anything and only bring needless confusion into people's thoughts. Whom is the crusade against, and what is its object? Where is the enemy and what is there dangerous about him? In the first place, the materialistic movement is not a school or tendency in the narrow journalistic sense; it is not something passing or accidental; it is necessary, inevitable, and beyond the power of man. All that lives on earth is bound to be materialistic. In animals, in savages, in Moscow merchants, all that is higher and non-animal is conditioned by an unconscious instinct, while all the rest is material, and they of course cannot help it. Beings of a higher order, thinking men, are also bound to be materialists. They seek for truth in matter, for there is nowhere else to seek for it, since they see, hear, and sense matter alone. Of necessity they can only seek for truth where their microscopes, lancets, and knives are of use to them. To forbid a man to follow the materialistic line of thought is equivalent to forbidding him to seek truth. Outside matter there is neither knowledge nor experience, and consequently there is no truth....

I think that when dissecting a corpse, the most inveterate spiritualist will be bound to ask himself, "Where is the soul here?" And if one knows how great is the likeness between bodily and mental diseases, and that both are treated by the same remedies, one cannot help refusing to separate the soul from the body.

... To speak of the danger and harm of materialism, and even more to fight against it, is, to say the least, premature. We have not enough data to draw up an indictment. There are many theories and suppositions, but no facts.... The priests complain of unbelief, immorality, and so on. There is no unbelief. People believe in something, whatever it may be....

As to immorality, it is not people like Mendeleyev but poets, abbots, and personages regularly attending Embassy churches, who have the reputation of being perverted debauchees, libertines, and drunkards.

In short, I cannot understand Bourget's crusade. If, in starting upon it, he had at the same time taken the trouble to point out to the materialists an incorporeal God in the sky, and to point to Him in such a way that they should see Him, that would be another matter, and I should understand what he is driving at.

May 14, 1889.

... You want to know if the lady doctor hates you as before. Alas! she has grown stouter and much more resigned, which I do not like at all. There are not many women doctors left on earth. They are disappearing and dying out like the branches in the Byelovyezhsky forest. Some die of consumption, others become mystics, some marry widowed squadron-commanders, some still try to stand firm, but are obviously losing heart. Probably the first tailors and the first astrologers also died out rapidly. Life is hard on those who have the temerity first to enter upon an unknown path. The vanguard always has a bad time of it.

May 15, 1889.

If you have not gone abroad yet, I will answer your letter about Bourget.... You are speaking of the "right to live" of this or that branch of knowledge; I am speaking of peace, not of rights. I want people not to see war where there is none. Different branches of knowledge have always lived together in peace. Anatomy and belles-lettres are of equally noble descent; they have the same purpose and the same enemy—the devil—and there is absolutely nothing for them to fight about. There is no struggle for existence between them. If a man knows about the circulation of the blood, he is rich; if he also learns the history of religion and the song "I remember a marvellous moment," he becomes richer, not poorer—that is to say, we are concerned with pluses alone. This is why geniuses have never fought, and in Goethe the poet lived amicably side by side with the scientist.

It is not branches of knowledge such as poetry and anatomy, but errors—that is to say, men—that fight with one another. When a man fails to understand something he is conscious of a discord, and seeks for the cause of it not in himself, as he should, but outside himself—hence the war with what he does not understand. In the middle ages alchemy was gradually in a natural, peaceful way changing into chemistry, and astrology into astronomy; the monks did not understand, saw a conflict and fought against it. Just such a belligerent Spanish monk was our Pisarev in the sixties.

Bourget, too, is fighting. You say he is not, and I say he is. Imagine his novel falling into the hands of a man whose children are studying in the faculty of science, or of a bishop who is looking for a subject for his Sunday sermon. Will the effect be anything like peace? It will not. Or imagine the novel catching the eye of an anatomist or a physiologist, or any such. It will not breathe peace into anyone's soul; it will irritate those who know and give false ideas to those who don't.

TO A. N. PLESHTCHEYEV.

MOSCOW, September 30, 1889.

... I do not think I ought to change the title of the story. [Footnote: "A Dreary Story."] The wags who will, as you foretell, make jokes about "A Dreary Story," are so dull that one need not fear them; and if someone makes a good joke I shall be glad to have given him the occasion for it. The professor could not write about Katya's husband because he did not know him, and Katya does not say anything about him; besides, one of my hero's chief characteristics is that he cares far too little about the inner life of those who surround him, and while people around him are weeping, making mistakes, telling lies, he calmly talks about the theatre or literature. Were he a different sort of man, Liza and Katya might not have come to grief.

October, 1889.

I am afraid of those who look for a tendency between the lines, and who are determined to regard me either as a liberal or as a conservative. I am not a liberal, not a conservative, not a believer in gradual progress, not a monk, not an indifferentist. I should like to be a free artist and nothing more, and I regret that God has not given me the power to be one. I hate lying and violence in all their forms, and am equally repelled by the secretaries of consistories and by Notovitch and Gradovsky. Pharisaism, stupidity and despotism reign not in merchants' houses and prisons alone. I see them in science, in literature, in the younger generation.... That is why I have no preference either for gendarmes, or for butchers, or for scientists, or for writers, or for the younger generation. I regard trade-marks and labels as a superstition. My holy of holies is the human body, health, intelligence, talent, inspiration, love, and the most absolute freedom—freedom from violence and lying, whatever forms they may take. This is the programme I would follow if I were a great artist.

MOSCOW,

February 15, 1890.

I answer you, dear Alexey Nikolaevitch, at once on receiving your letter. It was your name-day, and I forgot it!! Forgive me, dear friend, and accept my belated congratulations.

Did you really not like the "Kreutzer Sonata"? I don't say it is a work of genius for all time, of that I am no judge; but to my thinking, among the mass of all that is written now, here and abroad, one scarcely could find anything else as powerful both in the gravity of its conception and the beauty of its execution. To say nothing of its artistic merits, which in places are striking, one must be grateful to the novel, if only because it is keenly stimulating to thought. As one reads it, one can scarcely refrain from crying out: "That's true," or "That's absurd." It is true it has some very annoying defects. Apart from all those you enumerate, it has one for which one cannot readily forgive the author—that is, the audacity with which Tolstoy holds forth about what he doesn't know and is too obstinate to care to understand. Thus his statements about syphilis, foundling hospitals, the aversion of women for the sexual relation, and so on, are not merely open to dispute, but show him up as an ignoramus who has not, in the course of his long life, taken the trouble to read two or three books written by specialists. But yet these defects fly away like feathers in the wind; one simply does not notice them in face of the real worth of the story, or, if one notices them, it is only with a little vexation that the story has not escaped the fate of all the works of man, all imperfect and never free from blemish.

My Petersburg friends and acquaintances are angry with me? What for? For my not having bored them enough with my presence, which has for so long been a bore to myself! Soothe their minds. Tell them that in Petersburg I ate a great many dinners and a great many suppers, but did not fascinate one lady; that every day I was confident of leaving by the evening train, that I was detained by my friends and by *The Marine Almanack*, the whole of which I had to look through from the year 1852. While I was in Petersburg, I got through in one month more than my young friends would in a year. Let them be angry, though!

I sit all day long reading and making extracts. I have nothing in my head or on paper except Sahalin. Mental obsession. Mania Sachalinosa.

Not long ago I dined with Madame Yermolov. [Translator's Note: The celebrated actress.] A wild-flower thrust into the same nosegay with the carnation was the more fragrant for the good company it had kept. So I, after dining with the star, was aware of a halo round my head for two days afterwards ...

Good-bye, my dear friend; come and see us....

TO A. S. SUVORIN.

MOSCOW, February 23, 1890.

... My brother Alexandr is a slow-witted creature; he is enthusiastic over Ornatsky's missionary speech, in which he says that the natives do not become Christians because they are waiting for a special ukaz (that is, command) from the Tsar on the subject and are waiting for their chiefs to be baptized ... (by force—be it understood). This eloquent pontifex says, too, that the native priests ought, in view of their ascetic manner of life, to be removed from the natives and put into special institutions somewhat after the fashion of monasteries. A nice set of people and no mistake! They have wasted two million roubles, they send out every year from the academy dozens of missionaries who cost the treasury and the people large sums, yet they cannot convert the natives, and what is more, want the police and the military to help them with fire and sword....

If you have Madame Tsebrikov's article, do not trouble to send it. Such articles give no information and only waste time; I want facts. Indeed, in Russia there is a terrible poverty of facts, and a terrible abundance of reflections of all sorts.

February 28.

... To-morrow is spring, and within ten to fifteen days the larks will come back. But alas!—the coming spring seems strange to me, for I am going away from it.

In Sahalin there is very good fish, but there are no hot drinks....

Our geologists, ichthyologists, zoologists and so on, are fearfully uneducated people. They write such a vile jargon that it not only bores one to read it, but one actually has at times to remodel the sentences before one can understand them; on the other hand, they have solemnity and earnestness enough and to spare. It's really beastly....

March 4.

I have sent you to-day two stories: Filippov's (he was here yesterday) and Yezhov's. I have not had time to read the latter, and I think it is as well to say, once for all, that I am not responsible for what I send you. My handwriting on the address does not mean that I like the story.

Poor Yezhov has been to see me; he sat near the table crying: his young wife is in consumption. He must take her at once to the south. To my question whether he had money he answered that he had.... It's vile catch-cold weather; the sky itself is sneezing. I can't bear to look at it.... I have already begun writing of Sahalin. I have written five pages. It reads all right, as though written with intelligence and authority ... I quote foreign authors second-hand, but minutely and in a tone as though I could speak every foreign language perfectly. It's regular swindling.

Yezhov has upset me with his tears. He reminded me of something, and I was sorry for him too.

Don't forget us sinners.

TO N. M. LINTVARYOV.

MOSCOW, March 5, 1890.

... As for me, I have a cough too, but I am alive and I believe I'm well. I shan't be with you this summer, as I am going in April, on affairs of my own, to the island of Sahalin, and shall not be back till December. I am going across Siberia (eleven thousand versts) and shall come back by sea. I believe Misha wrote to you as though someone were commissioning me to go, but that's nonsense. I am commissioning myself to go, on my own account. There are lots of bears and escaped convicts in Sahalin, so that in case *messieurs* the wild beasts dine off me or some tramp cuts my throat, I beg you not to remember evil against me.

Of course if I have the time and the skill to write what I want to about Sahalin, I shall send you the book immediately that it comes into the world; it will be dull, a specialist's book consisting of nothing but figures, but let me count upon your indulgence: you will suppress your yawns as you read it....

TO A. S. SUVORIN.

MOSCOW, March 9.

About Sahalin we are both mistaken, but you probably more than I. I am going in the full conviction that my visit will furnish no contribution of value either to literature or science: I have neither the knowledge, nor the time, nor the ambition for that. I have neither the plans of a Humboldt nor of a Kennan. I want to write some 100 to 200 pages, and so do something, however little, for medical science, which, as you are aware, I have neglected shockingly. Possibly I shall not succeed in writing anything, but still the expedition does not lose its charm for me: reading, looking about me, and listening, I shall learn a great deal and gain experience. I have not yet travelled, but thanks to the books which I have been compelled to read, I have learned a great deal which anyone ought to be flogged for not knowing, and which I was so ignorant as not to have known before. Moreover, I imagine the journey will be six months of incessant hard work, physical and mental, and that is essential for me, for I am a Little Russian and have already begun to be lazy. I must take myself in hand. My expedition may be nonsense, obstinacy, a craze, but think a moment and tell me what I am losing if I go. Time? Money? Shall I suffer hardships? My time is worth nothing; money I never have anyway; as for hardships, I shall travel with horses, twenty-five to thirty days, not more, all the rest of the time I shall be sitting on the deck of a steamer or in a room, and shall be continually bombarding you with letters.

Suppose the expedition gives me nothing, yet surely there will be 2 or 3 days out of the whole journey which I shall remember all my life with ecstasy or bitterness, etc., etc.... So that's how it is, sir. All that is unconvincing, but you know you write just as unconvincingly. For instance, you say that Sahalin is of no use and no interest to anyone. Can that be true? Sahalin can be useless and uninteresting only to a society which does not exile thousands of people to it and does not spend millions of roubles on it. Except Australia in the past and Cayenne, Sahalin is the only place where one can study colonization by convicts; all Europe is interested in it, and is it no use to us? Not more than 25 to 30 years ago our Russians exploring Sahalin performed amazing feats which exalt them above humanity, and that's no use to us: we don't know what those men were, and simply sit within four walls and complain that God has made man amiss. Sahalin is a place of the most unbearable sufferings of which man, free and captive, is capable. Those who work near it and upon it have solved fearful, responsible problems, and are still solving them. I am not sentimental, or I would say that we ought to go to places like Sahalin to worship as the Turks go to Mecca, and that sailors and gaolers ought to think of the prison in Sahalin as military men think of Sevastopol. From the books I have read and am reading, it is evident that we have sent *millions* of men to rot in prison, have destroyed them—casually, without thinking, barbarously; we have driven men in fetters through the cold ten thousand versts, have infected them with syphilis, have depraved them, have multiplied criminals, and the blame for all this we have thrown upon the gaolers and red-nosed superintendents. Now all educated Europe knows that it is not the superintendents that are to blame, but all of us; yet that has nothing to do with us, it is not interesting. The vaunted sixties did *nothing* for the sick and for prisoners, so breaking the chief commandment of Christian civilization. In our day something is being done for the sick, nothing for prisoners; prison management is entirely without interest for our jurists. No, I assure you that Sahalin is of use and of interest to us, and the only thing to regret is that I am going there, and not someone else who knows more about it and would be more able to rouse public interest. Nothing much will come of my going there.

There have been disturbances among the students on a grand scale here. It began with the Petrovsky Academy, where the authorities forbade the students to take young ladies to their rooms, suspecting the ladies of politics as well as of prostitution. From the Academy it spread to the University, where now the students, surrounded by fully armed and mounted Hectors and Achilleses with lances, make the following demands:

1. Complete autonomy for the universities.

2. Complete freedom of teaching.

3. Free right of entrance to the university without distinction of religious denomination, nationality, sex, and social position.

4. Right of entrance to the university for the Jews without restriction, and equal rights for them with the other students.

5. Freedom of meeting and recognition of the students' associations.

6. The establishment of a university and students' tribunal.

7. The abolition of the police duties of the inspectors.

8. Lowering of the fees for instruction.

This I copied from a manifesto, with some abbreviations.

TO I. L. SHTCHEGLOV.

MOSCOW, March 22, 1890.

My greetings, dear Jean! Thanks for your long letter and for the good will of which it is full from beginning to end. I shall be delighted to read your military story. Will it come out in the Easter number? It is a long time since I read anything of yours or my own. You say that you want to give me a harsh scolding "especially on the score of morality and art," you speak vaguely of my crimes as deserving friendly censure, and threaten me with "an influential newspaper criticism." If you scratch out the word "art," the whole phrase in quotation marks becomes clearer, but gains a significance which, to tell the truth, perplexes me not a little. Jean, what is it? How is one to understand it? Can I really be different in my ideas of morality from people like you, and so much so as to deserve censure and even an influential article? I cannot take it that you mean some subtle higher morality, as there are no lower, higher, or medium moralities, but only one which Jesus Christ gave us, and which now prevents you and me and Barantsevitch from stealing, insulting, lying, and so on. If I can trust the ease of my conscience, I have never by word or deed, in thought, or in my stories, or in my farces, coveted my neighbour's wife, nor his man, nor his ox, nor any of his cattle, I have not stolen, nor been a hypocrite, I have not flattered the great nor sought their favour, I have not blackmailed, nor lived at other people's expense. It is true I have waxed wanton and slothful, have laughed heedlessly, have eaten too much and drunk too much and been profligate. But all that is a personal matter, and all that does not deprive me of the right to think that, as far as morals are concerned, I am nothing out of the ordinary, one way or the other. Nothing heroic and nothing scoundrelly—I am just like everyone else; I have many sins, but I am quits with morality, as I pay for those sins with interest in the discomforts they bring with them. If you want to abuse me cruelly because I am not a hero, you'd better throw your cruelty out of the window, and instead of abuse, let me hear your charming tragic laugh—that's better.

But of the word "art" I am terrified, as merchants' wives are terrified of "brimstone." When people talk to me of what is artistic and inartistic, of what is dramatic and not dramatic, of tendency, realism, and so on, I am bewildered, hesitatingly assent, and answer with banal half-truths not worth a brass farthing. I divide all works into two classes: those I like and those I don't. I have no other criterion, and if you ask me why I like Shakespeare and don't like Zlatovratsky, I don't venture to answer. Perhaps in time and as I grow wiser I may work out some criterion, but meanwhile all conversations about what is "artistic" only weary me, and seem to me like a continuation of the scholastic disputations with which people wearied themselves in the middle ages.

If criticism, on the authority of which you rely, knows what you and I don't know, why has it up till now not spoken? why does it not reveal the truth and the immutable laws? If it knew, believe me, it would long ago have shown us the true path and we should have known what to do, and Fofanov would not have been in a madhouse, Garshin would have been alive to-day, Barantsevitch would not have been so depressed and we should not be so dull and ill at ease as we are, and you would not feel drawn to the theatre and I to Sahalin. But criticism maintains a dignified silence or gets out of it with idle trashy babble. If it seems to you authoritative it is because it is stupid, conceited, impudent, and clamorous; because it is an empty barrel one cannot help hearing.

But let us have done with that and sing something out of a different opera. Please don't build any literary hopes on my Sahalin trip. I am not going for the sake of impressions or observations, but simply for the sake of living for six months differently from how I have lived hitherto. Don't rely on me, old man; if I am successful and clever enough to do something, so much the better; if not, don't blame me. I am going after Easter. I will send you in due time my Sahalin address and minute instructions....

TO A. S. SUVORIN.

MOSCOW, March 22, 1890.

... Yesterday a young lady told me that Professor Storozhenko had related to her the following anecdote. The Sovereign liked the *Kreutzer Sonata*. Pobyedonostsev, Lubimov, and the other cherubim and seraphim, hastened to justify their attitude to Tolstoy by showing his Majesty "Nikolay Palkin." After reading it, his Majesty was so furious that he ordered measures to be taken. Prince Dolgorukov was informed. And so one fine day an adjutant from Dolgorukov comes to Tolstoy and invites him to go at once to the prince. The latter replies: "Tell the prince that I only visit the houses of my acquaintances." The adjutant, overcome with confusion, rides away, and next day brings Tolstoy the official notice demanding from him an explanation in regard to his "Nikolay Palkin." Tolstoy reads the document and says:

"Tell his excellency that I have not for a long time past written anything for publication; I write only for my friends, and if my friends spread my writings abroad, they are responsible and not I. Tell him that!"

"But I can't tell him that," cried the adjutant in horror, "the prince will not believe me!"

"The prince will not believe his subordinates? That's bad."

Two days later the adjutant comes again with a fresh document, and learns that Tolstoy has gone away to Yasnaya Polyana. That is the end of the anecdote.

Now about the new movements. They flog in our police stations; a rate has been fixed; from a peasant they take ten kopecks for a beating, from a workman twenty—that's for the rods and the trouble. Peasant women are flogged too. Not long ago, in their enthusiasm for beating in a police station, they thrashed a couple of budding lawyers, an incident upon which *Russkiya Vyedomosti* has a vague paragraph to-day; an investigation has begun.

Another sign of the times: the cabmen approve of the students' disturbances.

"They are making a riot for the poor to be taken in to study," they explain, "learning is not only for the rich." It is said that when a crowd of students were being taken by night to the prison the populace fell upon the gendarmes to rescue the students from them. The populace is said to have shouted: "You have set up flogging for us, but they stand up for us."

March 29.

... Fatigue is a relative matter. You say you used to work twenty hours out of the twenty-four and were not exhausted. But you know one may be exhausted lying all day long on the sofa. You used to write for twenty hours, but you know you were in perfect health all that time, you were stimulated by success, defiance, a sense of your talent; you liked your work, or you wouldn't have written. Your heir-apparent sits up late, not because he has a talent for journalism or a love for his work, but simply because his father is an editor of a newspaper. The difference is vast. He ought to have been a doctor or a lawyer, to have had an income of two thousand roubles a year, and published his articles not in *Novoye Vremya* and not in the spirit of *Novoye Vremya*. Only those young people can be accepted as healthy who refuse to be reconciled with the old order and foolishly or wisely struggle against it—such is the will of nature and it is the foundation of progress, while your son began by absorbing the old order. In our most intimate talks he has never once abused Tatistchev or Burenin, and that's a bad sign. You are a hundred times as liberal as he is, and it ought to be the other way. He utters a listless and indolent protest, he soon drops his voice and soon agrees, and altogether one has the impression that he has no interest whatever in the contest; that is, he looks on at the cock-fight like a spectator and has no cock of his own. And one ought to have one's own cock, else life is without interest. The unfortunate thing, too, is that he is intelligent, and great intelligence with little interest in life is like a great machine which produces nothing, yet requires a great deal of fuel and exhausts the owner....

April 1.

You abuse me for objectivity, calling it indifference to good and evil, lack of ideals and ideas, and so on. You would have me, when I describe horse-stealers, say: "Stealing horses is an evil." But that has been known for ages without my saying so. Let the jury judge them, it's my job simply to show what sort of people they are. I write: you are dealing with horse-stealers, so let me tell you that they are not beggars but well-fed people, that they are people of a special cult, and that horse-stealing is not simply theft but a passion. Of course it would be pleasant to combine art with a sermon, but for me personally it is extremely difficult and almost impossible, owing to the conditions of technique. You see, to depict horse-stealers in seven hundred lines I must all the time speak and think in their tone and feel in their spirit, otherwise, if I introduce subjectivity, the image becomes blurred and the story will not be as compact as all short stories ought to be. When I write I reckon entirely upon the reader to add for himself the subjective elements that are lacking in the story.

April 11.

Madame N. who used at one time to live in your family is here now. She married the artist N., a nice but tedious man who wants at all costs to travel with me to Sahalin to sketch. To refuse him my company I haven't the courage, but to travel with him would be simple misery. He is going to Petersburg in a day or two to sell his pictures, and at his wife's request will call on you to *ask your advice*. With a view to this his wife came to ask me for a letter of introduction to you. Be my benefactor, tell N. that I am a drunkard, a swindler, a nihilist, a rowdy character, and that it is out of the question to travel with me, and that a journey in my company will do nothing but upset him. Tell him he will be wasting his time. Of course it would be very nice to have my book illustrated, but when I learned that N. was hoping to get not less than a thousand roubles for it, I lost all appetite for illustrations. My dear fellow, advise him against it!!! Why it is your advice he wants, the devil only knows.

April 15.

And so, my dear friend, I am setting off on Wednesday or Thursday at latest. Good-bye till December. Good luck in my absence. I received the money, thank you very much, though fifteen hundred roubles is a great deal; I don't know where to put it.... I feel as though I were preparing for the battlefield, though I see no dangers before me but toothache, which I am sure to have on the journey. As I am provided with nothing in the way of papers but a passport, I may have unpleasant encounters with the authorities, but that is a passing trouble. If they refuse to show me something, I shall simply write in my book that they wouldn't show it me, and that's all, and I won't worry. In case I am drowned or anything of that sort, you might keep it in mind that all I have or may have in the future belongs to my sister; she will pay my debts.

I am taking my mother with me and putting her down at the Troitsky Monastery; I am taking my sister too, and leaving her at Kostroma. I am telling them I shall be back in September.

I shall go over the university in Tomsk. As the only faculty there is medicine I shall not show myself an ignoramus.

I have bought myself a fur coat, an officer's waterproof leather coat, big boots, and a big knife for cutting sausage and hunting tigers. I am equipped from head to foot.

TO HIS SISTER.

STEAMER "ALEXANDR NEVSKY 23," April, 1890, early in the morning.

My dear Tunguses!

Did you have rain when Ivan was coming back from the monastery? In Yaroslavl there was such a downpour that I had to swathe myself in my leather chiton. My first impression of the Volga was poisoned by the rain, by the tear-stained windows of the cabin, and the wet nose of G., who came to meet me at the station. In the rain Yaroslavl looks like Zvenigorod, and its churches remind me of Perervinsky Monastery; there are lots of illiterate signboards, it's muddy, jackdaws with big heads strut about the pavement.

In the steamer I made it my first duty to indulge my talent—that is, to sleep. When I woke I beheld the sun. The Volga is not bad; water meadows, monasteries bathed in sunshine, white churches; the wide expanse is marvellous, wherever one looks it would be a nice place to sit down and begin fishing. Class ladies [Translator's Note: I.e., School chaperons, whose duty it is to sit in the classroom while the girls are receiving instruction from a master.] wander about on the banks, nipping at the green grass. The shepherd's horn can be heard now and then. White gulls, looking like the younger Drishka, hover over the water.

The steamer is not up to much....

Kundasova is travelling with me. Where she is going and with what object I don't know. When I question her about it, she launches off into extremely misty allusions about someone who has appointed a tryst with her in a ravine near Kineshma, then goes off into a wild giggle and begins stamping her feet or prodding with her elbow whatever comes first. We have passed both Kineshma and the ravine, but she still goes on in the steamer, at which of course I am very much pleased; by the way, yesterday for the first time in my life I saw her eating. She eats no less than other people, but she eats mechanically, as though she were munching oats.

Kostroma is a nice town. I saw the stretch of river on which the languid Levitan used to live. I saw Kineshma, where I walked along the boulevard and watched the local *beaus*. Here I went into the chemist's shop to buy some Bertholet salts for my tongue, which was like leather after the medicine I had taken. The chemist, on seeing Olga Petrovna, was overcome with delight and confusion; she was the same. They were evidently old acquaintances, and judging from the conversation between them they had walked more than once about the ravines near Kineshma.

... It's rather cold and rather dull, but interesting on the whole. The steamer whistles every minute; its whistle is midway between the bray of an ass and an Aeolian harp. In five or six hours we shall be in Nizhni. The sun is rising. I slept last night artistically. My money is safe; that is because I am constantly pressing my hands on my stomach.

Very beautiful are the steam-tugs, dragging after them four or five barges each; they look like some fine young intellectual trying to run away while a plebeian wife, mother-in-law, sister-in-law, and wife's grandmother hold on to his coat-tails.

The sun is hiding behind the clouds, the sky is overcast, and the broad Volga looks gloomy. Levitan ought not to live on the Volga. It lays a weight of gloom on the soul. Though it would not be bad to have an estate on its banks.

If the waiter would wake I should ask him for some coffee; as it is, I have to drink water without any relish for it. My greetings to Maryushka and Olga. [Footnote: The Chekhovs' servants.]

Well, keep well and take care of yourselves. I will write regularly.

Your bored Volga-travelling

Homo Sachaliensis,

A. CHEKHOV.

FROM THE STEAMER,

Evening, April 24, 1890.

MY DEAR TUNGUSES!

I am floating on the Kama, but I can't fix the exact locality; I believe we are near Tchistopol. I cannot extol the beauties of the scenery either, as it is hellishly cold; the birches are not yet out, there are still patches of snow here and there, bits of ice float by—in short, the picturesque has gone to the dogs. I sit in the cabin, where people of all sorts and conditions sit at the table, and listen to the conversation, wondering whether it is not time for me to have tea. If I had my way I should do nothing all day but eat; as I haven't the money to be eating all day long I sleep and sleep. I don't go up on deck, it's cold. By night it rains and by day there is an unpleasant wind.

Oh, the caviare! I eat it and eat and never have enough.

... It is a pity I did not think to get myself a little bag for tea and sugar. I have to order it a glass at a time, which is tiresome and expensive. I meant to buy some tea and sugar to-day at Kazan, but I over-slept myself.

Rejoice, O mother! I believe I stop twenty-four hours at Ekaterinburg, and shall see the relations. Perhaps their hearts may be softened and they will give me three roubles and an ounce of tea.

From the conversation I am listening to at this moment, I gather that the members of a judicial tribunal are travelling with me. They are not gifted persons. The merchants, who put in their word from time to time seem, however, intelligent. One comes across fearfully rich people.

Sterlets are cheaper than mushrooms; you soon get sick of them. What more is there for me to write about? There is nothing.... There is a General, though, and a lean fair man. The former keeps dashing from his cabin to the deck and back again, and sending his photograph off somewhere; the latter is got up to look like Nadson, and tries thereby to give one to know that he is a writer. Today he was mendaciously telling a lady that he had a book published by Suvorin; I, of course, put on an expression of awe.

My money is all safe, except what I have eaten. They won't feed me for nothing, the scoundrels.

I am neither gay nor bored, but there is a sort of numbness in my soul. I like to sit without moving or speaking. To-day, for instance, I have scarcely uttered five words. That's not true, though: I talked to a priest on deck.

We begin to come across natives; there are lots of Tatars: they are a respectable and well-behaved people.

I beg Father and Mother not to worry, and not to imagine dangers which do not exist.

Excuse me for writing about nothing but food. If I did not write about food I should have to write about cold, for I have no other subjects.

April 29, 1890.

MY DEAR TUNGUSES!

The Kama is a very dull river. To realise its beauties one would have to be a native sitting motionless on a barge beside a barrel of naphtha, or a sack of dried fish, continually taking a pull at the bottle. The river banks are bare, the trees are bare, the earth is a dull brown, there are patches of snow, and there is such a wind that the devil himself could not blow as keenly and hatefully. When a cold wind blows and ruffles up the water, which now after the floods is the colour of coffee slops, one feels cold and bored and miserable; the strains of a concertina on the bank sound dejected, figures in tattered sheepskins standing motionless on the barges that meet us look as though they were petrified by some unending grief. The towns on the Kama are grey; one would think the inhabitants were employed in the manufacture of clouds, boredom, soaking fences and mud in the streets, as their sole occupation. The stopping-places are thronged with inhabitants of the educated class, for whom the arrival of a steamer is an event....

... To judge from appearances not one of them earns more than thirty-five roubles, and all of them are ailing in some way.

I have told you already there are some legal gentlemen in the steamer: the president of the court, one of the judges, and the prosecutor. The president is a hale and hearty old German who has embraced Orthodoxy, is pious, a homoeopath, and evidently a devotee of the sex. The judge is an old man such as dear Nikolay used to draw; he walks bent double, coughs, and is fond of facetious subjects. The prosecutor is a man of forty-three, dissatisfied with life, a liberal, a sceptic, and a very good-natured fellow. All the journey these gentlemen have been occupied in eating, settling mighty questions and eating, reading and eating. There is a library on the steamer, and I saw the prosecutor reading my "In the Twilight." They began talking about me. Mamin-Sibiryak, who has described the Urals, is the author most liked in these parts. He is more talked of than Tolstoy.

I have been two and a half years sailing to Perm, so it seems to me. We reached there at two o'clock in the night. The train went at six o'clock in the evening. I had to wait. It rained. Rain, cold, mud ... brrr! The Uralsky line is a good one.... That is due to the abundance of business-like people here, factories, mines, and so on, for whom time is precious.

Waking yesterday morning and looking out of the carriage window I felt an aversion for nature: the earth was white, trees covered with hoar-frost, and a regular blizzard pursuing the train. Now isn't it revolting? Isn't it disgusting? ... I have no goloshes, I pulled on my big boots, and on my way to the refreshment-room for coffee I made the whole Ural region smell of tar. And when we got to Ekaterinburg there was rain, snow, and hail. I put on my leather coat. The cabs are something inconceivable, wretched, dirty, drenched, without springs, the horse's four legs straddling, huge hoofs, gaunt spines ... the droshkies here are a clumsy parody of our britchkas. A tattered top is put on to a britchka, that is all. And the more exactly I describe the cabman here and his vehicle, the more it will seem like a caricature. They drive not on the middle of the road where it is jolting, but near the gutter where it is muddy and soft. All the cabmen are like Dobrolyubov.

In Russia all the towns are alike. Ekaterinburg is exactly the same as Perm or Tula. The note of the bells is magnificent, velvety. I stopped at the American Hotel (not at all bad), and at once sent word of my arrival to A. M. S., telling him I meant to stay in my hotel room for two days.

The people here inspire the newcomer with a feeling akin to horror. They are big-browed, big-jawed, broad-shouldered fellows with huge fists and tiny eyes. They are born in the local iron foundries, and at their birth a mechanic officiates instead of an accoucheur. A specimen comes into your room with a samovar or a bottle of water, and you expect him every minute to murder you. I stand aside. This morning just such a one came in, big-browed, big-jawed, huge, towering up to the ceiling, seven feet across the shoulders and wearing a fur coat too.

Well, I thought, this one will certainly murder me. It appeared that this was our relation A. M. S. We began to talk. He is a member of the local Zemstvo and manager of his cousin's mill, which is lighted by electric light; he is editor of the *Ekaterinburg Week* which is under the censorship of the police-master Baron Taube, is married and has two children, is growing rich and getting fat and elderly, and lives in a "substantial way." He says he has no time to be bored. He advised me to visit the museum, the factories, and the mines; I thanked him for his advice. He invited me to tea to-morrow evening; I invited him to dine with me. He did not invite me to dinner, and altogether did not press me very much to visit him. From this mother may conclude that the relations' heart is not softened.... Relations are a race in which I take no interest.

There is snow in the street, and I have purposely let down the blind over the windows so as not to see the Asiatic sight. I am sitting here waiting for an answer from Tyumen to my telegram. I telegraphed: "Tyumen. Kurbatov steamer line. Reply paid. Inform me when the passenger steamer starts Tomsk." It depends on the answer whether I go by steamer or gallop fifteen hundred versts in the slush of the thaw.

All night long they beat on sheets of iron at every corner here. You need a head of iron not to go crazy from the incessant clanging. To-day I tried to make myself coffee. The result was a horrid mess. I just drank it with a shrug. I looked at five sheets, handled them, and did not take one. I am going to-day to buy rubber overshoes.

Shall I find a letter from you at Irkutsk?

Ask Lika not to leave such big margins in her letters.

Your Homo Sachaliensis,

A. CHEKHOV.

TO MADAME KISELYOV.

THE BANK OF THE IRTYSH, May 7, 1890.

My greetings, honoured Marya Vladimirovna! I meant to write you a farewell letter from Moscow, but I had not time; I write to you now sitting in a hut on the bank of the Irtysh.

It is night. This is how I have come to be here. I am driving across the plain of Siberia. I have already driven 715 versts; I have been transformed from head to foot into a great martyr. This morning a keen cold wind began blowing, and it began drizzling with the most detestable rain. I must observe that there is no spring yet in Siberia. The earth is brown, the trees are bare, and there are white patches of snow wherever one looks; I wear my fur coat and felt overboots day and night.... Well, the wind has been blowing since early morning.... Heavy leaden clouds, dull brown earth, mud, rain, wind.... Brrr! I drive on and on.... I drive on endlessly, and the weather does not improve. Towards evening I am told at the station I can't go on further, as everything is under water, the bridges have been carried away, and so on. Knowing how fond these drivers are of frightening one with the elements so as to keep the traveller for the night (it is to their interest), I did not believe them, and ordered them to harness the three horses; and now— alas for me!—I had not driven more than five versts when I saw the land on the bank of the Irtysh all covered with great lakes, the road disappeared under water, and the bridges on the road really had been swept away or had decayed. I was prevented from turning back partly by obstinacy and partly by the desire to get out of these dreary parts as quickly as possible. We began driving through the lakes.... My God, I have never experienced anything like it in my life! The cutting wind, the cold, the loathsome rain, and one had to get out of the chaise (not a covered one), if you please, and hold the horses: at each little bridge one could only lead the horses over one at a time.... What had I come to? Where was I? All around, desert, dreariness; the bare sullen bank of the Irtysh in sight.... We drive into the very biggest lake. Now I should be glad to turn back, but it is not easy.... We drive on a long strip of land ... the strip comes to an end—we go splash! Again a strip of land, again a splash.... My hands were numb, and the wild ducks seemed jeering at us and floated in huge flocks over our heads.... It got dark. The driver said nothing—he was bewildered. But at last we reached the last strip that separated the Irtysh from the lake.... The sloping bank of the Irtysh was nearly three feet above the level; it was of clay, bare, hollowed out, and looked slippery. The water was muddy.... White waves splashed on the clay, but the Irtysh itself made no roar or din, but gave forth a strange sound as though someone were nailing up a coffin under the water.... The further bank was a flat, disconsolate plain.... You often dream of the Bozharovsky pool; in the same way now I shall dream of the Irtysh....

But behold a ferry. We must be ferried across to the other side. A peasant shrinking from the rain comes out of a hut, and tells us that the ferry cannot cross now as it is too windy.... (The ferries are worked by oars). He advises us to wait for calm weather....

And so I am sitting at night in a hut on a lake at the very edge of the Irtysh. I feel a penetrating dampness to the very marrow of my bones, and a loneliness in my soul; I hear my Irtysh banging on the coffins and the wind howling, and wonder where I am, why I am here.

In the next room the peasants who work the ferry and my driver are asleep. They are good-natured people. But if they were bad people they could perfectly well rob me and drown me in the Irtysh. The hut is the only one on the river bank; there would be no witnesses.

The road to Tomsk is absolutely free from danger as far as brigands are concerned. It isn't the fashion even to talk of robbery. There is no stealing even from travellers. When you go into a hut you can leave your things outside and they will all be safe.

But they very nearly did kill me all the same. Imagine the night just before dawn.... I was driving along in a chaise, thinking and thinking.... All at once I see coming flying towards us at full gallop a post-cart with three horses; my driver had hardly time to turn to the right, the three horses dashed by, and I noticed in it the driver who had to take it back.... Behind it came another, also at full speed; we had turned to the right, it turned to the left. "We shall smash into each other," flashed into my mind ... one instant, and—there was a crash, the horses were mixed up in a black mass, my chaise was rearing in the air, and I was rolling on the ground with all my bags and boxes on the top of me. I leap up and see—a third troika dashing upon us....

My mother must have been praying for me that night, I suppose. If I had been asleep, or if the third troika had come immediately after the second, I should have been crushed to death or maimed. It appeared the foremost driver lashed on the horses, while the drivers in the second and the third carts were asleep and did not see us. The collision was followed by the blankest amazement on both sides, then a storm of ferocious abuse. The traces were torn, the shafts were broken, the yokes were lying about on the road.... Ah, how the drivers swore! At night, in that swearing turbulent crew, I felt in utter solitude such as I have never felt before in my life....

But my paper is running out.

TO HIS SISTER.

THE VILLAGE OF YAR, 45 VERSTS FROM TOMSK, May 14, 1890.

My glorious mother, my splendid Masha, my sweet Misha, and all my household! At Ekaterinburg I got my reply telegram from Tyumen. "The first steamer to Tomsk goes on the 18th May." This meant that, whether I liked it or not, I must do the journey with horses. So I did. I drove out of Tyumen on the third of May after spending in Ekaterinburg two or three days, which I devoted to the repair of my coughing and haemorrhoidal person. Besides the public posting service, one can get private drivers that take one across Siberia. I chose the latter: it is just the same. They put me, the servant of God, into a basketwork chaise and drove me with two horses; one sits in the basket like a goldfinch, looking at God's world and thinking of nothing.... The plain of Siberia begins, I think, from Ekaterinburg, and ends goodness knows where; I should say it is very like our South Russian Steppe, except for the little birch copses here and there and the cold wind that stings one's cheeks. Spring has not begun yet. There is no green at all, the woods are bare, the snow has not thawed everywhere. There is opaque ice on the lakes. On the ninth of May there was a hard frost, and to-day, the fourteenth, snow has fallen to the depth of three or four inches. No one speaks of spring but the ducks. Ah, what masses of ducks! Never in my life have I seen such abundance. They fly over one's head, they fly up close to the chaise, swim on the lakes and in the pools—in short, with the poorest sort of gun I could have shot a thousand in one day. One can hear the wild geese calling.... There are lots of them here too. One often comes upon a string of cranes or swans.... Snipe and woodcock flutter about in the birch copses. The hares which are not eaten or shot here, stand on their hindlegs, and, pricking up their ears, watch the passer-by with an inquisitive stare without the slightest misgiving. They are so often running across the road that to see them doing so is not considered a bad omen.

It's cold driving ...; I have my fur coat on. My body is all right, but my feet are freezing. I wrap them in the leather overcoat-but it is no use.... I have two pairs of breeches on. Well, one drives on and on.... Telegraph poles, pools, birch copses flash by. Here we overtake some emigrants, then an etape.... We meet tramps with pots on their back; these gentry promenade all over the plain of Siberia without hindrance. One time they will murder some poor old woman to take her petticoat for their leg-wrappers; at another they will strip from the verst post the metal plate with the number on it—it might be useful; at another will smash the head of some beggar or knock out the eyes of some brother exile; but they never touch travellers. Altogether, travelling here is absolutely safe as far as brigands are concerned. Neither the post-drivers nor the private ones from Tyumen to Tomsk remember an instance of any things being stolen from a traveller. When you reach a station you leave your things outside; if you ask whether they won't be stolen, they merely smile in answer. It is not the thing even to speak of robbery and murder on the road. I believe, if I were to lose my money in the station or in the chaise, the driver would certainly give it me if he found it, and would not boast of having done so. Altogether the people here are good and kindly, and have excellent traditions. Their rooms are simply furnished but clean, with claims to luxury; the beds are soft, all feather mattresses and big pillows. The floors are painted or covered with home-made linen rugs. The explanation of this, of course, is their prosperity, the fact that a family has sixteen dessyatins [Footnote: I.e., about 48 acres.] of black earth, and that excellent wheat grows in this black earth. (Wheaten flour costs thirty kopecks a *pood* here. [Footnote: i.e., about 7-1/2d. for 36 lb.]) But it cannot all be put down to prosperity and being well fed. One must give some of the credit to their manner of life. When you go at night into a room where people are asleep, the nose is not aware of any stuffiness or "Russian smell." It is true one old woman when she handed me a teaspoon wiped it on the back of her skirt; but they don't set you down to drink tea without a tablecloth, and they don't search in each other's heads in your presence, they don't put their fingers inside the glass when they hand you milk or water; the crockery is clean, the kvass is transparent as beer—in fact, there is a cleanliness of which our Little Russians can only dream, yet the Little Russians are far and away cleaner than the Great Russians! They make the most delicious bread here—I over-ate myself with it at first. The pies and pancakes and fritters and the fancy rolls, which remind one of the spongy Little Russian ring rolls, are very good too.... But all the rest is not for the European stomach. For instance, I am regaled everywhere with "duck broth." It's perfectly disgusting, a muddy-looking liquid with bits of wild duck and uncooked onion floating in it.... I once asked them to make me some soup from meat and to fry me some perch. They gave me soup too salt, dirty, with hard bits of skin instead of meat; and the perch was cooked with the scales on it. They make their cabbage soup from salt meat; they roast it too. They have just served me some salt meat roasted: it's most repulsive; I chewed at it and gave it up. They drink brick tea. It is a decoction of sage and beetles—that's what it is like in taste and appearance.

By the way, I brought from Ekaterinburg a quarter of a pound of tea, five pounds of sugar, and three lemons. It was not enough tea and there is nowhere to buy any. In these scurvy little towns even the government officials drink brick tea, and even the best shops don't keep tea at more than one rouble fifty kopecks a pound. I have to drink the sage brew.

The distance apart of the posting stations depends on the distance of the nearest villages from each other—that is, 20 to 40 versts. The villages here are large, there are no little hamlets. There are churches and schools everywhere, the huts are of wood and there are some with two storeys.

Towards the evening the road and the puddles begin to freeze, and at night there is a regular frost, one wants an extra fur coat ... Brrr! It's jolting, for the mud is transformed into hard lumps. One's soul is shaken inside out.... Towards daybreak one is fearfully exhausted by the cold, by the jolting and the jingle of the bells: one has a passionate longing for warmth and a bed. While they change horses one curls up in some corner and at once drops asleep, and a minute later the driver pulls at one's sleeve and says: "Get up, friend, it is time to start." On the second night I had acute toothache in my heels. It was unbearably painful. I wondered whether they were frostbitten.

I can't write more though. The "president," that is the district police inspector, has come. We have made acquaintance and are beginning to talk. Goodbye till to-morrow.

TOMSK,

May 16.

It seems my strong boots were the cause, being too tight at the back. My sweet Misha, if you ever have any children, which I have no doubt you will, the advice I bequeath to them is not to run after cheap goods. Cheapness in Russian goods is the label of worthlessness. To my mind it is better to go barefoot than to wear cheap boots. Picture my agony! I keep getting out of the chaise, sitting down on damp ground and taking off my boots to rest my heels. So comfortable in the frost! I had to buy felt over-boots in Ishim.... So I drove in felt boots till they collapsed from the mud and the damp.

In the morning between five and six o'clock one drinks tea at a hut. Tea on a journey is a great blessing. I know its value now, and drink it with the fury of a Yanov. It warms one through and drives away sleep; one eats a lot of bread with it, and in the absence of other nourishment, bread has to be eaten in great quantities; that is why peasants eat so much bread and farinaceous food. One drinks tea and talks with the peasant women, who are sensible, tenderhearted, industrious, as well as being devoted mothers and more free than in European Russia; their husbands don't abuse or beat them, because they are as tall, as strong, and as clever as their lords and masters are. They act as drivers when their husbands are away from home; they like making jokes. They are not severe with their children, they spoil them. The children sleep on soft beds and lie as long as they like, drink tea and eat with the men, and scold the latter when they laugh at them affectionately. There is no diphtheria. Malignant smallpox is prevalent here, but strange to say, it is less contagious than in other parts of the world; two or three catch it and die and that is the end of the epidemic. There are no hospitals or doctors. The doctoring is done by feldshers. Bleeding and cupping are done on a grandiose, brutal scale. I examined a Jew with cancer in the liver. The Jew was exhausted, hardly breathing, but that did not prevent the feldsher from cupping him twelve times. Apropos of the Jews. Here they till the land, work as drivers and ferry-men, trade and are called Krestyany, [Translator's Note: I.e., Peasants, literally "Christians."] because they are de jure and de facto Krestyany. They enjoy universal respect, and according to the "president" they are not infrequently chosen as village elders. I saw a tall thin Jew who scowled with disgust and spat when the "president" told indecent stories: a chaste soul; his wife makes splendid fish-soup. The wife of the Jew who had cancer regaled me with pike caviare and with most delicious white bread. One hears nothing of exploitation by the Jews. And, by the way, about the Poles. There are a few exiles here, sent from Poland in 1864. They are good, hospitable, and very refined people. Some of them live in a very wealthy way; others are very poor, and serve as clerks at the stations. Upon the amnesty the former went back to their own country, but soon returned to Siberia again—here they are better off; the latter dream of their native land, though they are old and infirm. At Ishim a wealthy Pole, Pan Zalyessky, who has a daughter like Sasha Kiselyov, for a rouble gave me an excellent dinner and a room to sleep in; he keeps an inn and has become a money-grubber to the marrow of his bones; he fleeces everyone, but yet one feels the Polish gentleman in his manner, in the way the meals are served, in everything. He does not go back to Poland through greed, and through greed endures snow till St. Nikolay's day; when he dies his daughter, who was born at Ishim, will remain here for ever and so will multiply the black eyes and soft features in Siberia! This casual intermixture of blood is to the good, for the Siberian people are not beautiful. There are no dark-haired people. Perhaps you would like me to write about the Tatars? Certainly. There are very few of them here. They are good people. In the province of Kazan everyone speaks well of them, even the priests, and in Siberia they are "better than the Russians" as the "president" said to me in the presence of Russians, who assented to this by their silence. My God, how rich Russia is in good people! If it were not for the cold which deprives Siberia of the summer, and if it were not for the officials who corrupt the peasants and the exiles, Siberia would be the richest and happiest of lands.

I have nothing for dinner. Sensible people usually take twenty pounds of provisions when they go to Tomsk. It seems I was a fool and so I have fed for a fortnight on nothing but milk and eggs, which are boiled so that the yolk is hard and the white is soft. One is sick of such fare in two days. I have only twice had dinner during the whole journey, not counting the Jewess's fish-soup, which I swallowed after I had had enough to eat with my tea. I have not had any vodka: the Siberian vodka is disgusting, and indeed, I got out of the habit of taking it while I was on the way to Ekaterinburg. One ought to drink vodka: it stimulates the brain, dull and apathetic from travelling, which makes one stupid and feeble.

Stop! I can't write: the editor of the *Sibirsky Vyestnik*, N., a local Nozdryov, a drunkard and a rake, has come to make my acquaintance.

N. has drunk some beer and gone away. I continue.

For the first three days of my journey my collarbones, my shoulders and my vertebrae ached from the shaking and jolting. I couldn't stand or sit or lie.... But on the other hand, all pains in my head and chest have vanished, my appetite has developed incredibly, and my haemorrhoids have subsided completely. The overstrain, the constant worry with luggage and so on, and perhaps the farewell drinking parties in Moscow, had brought on spitting of blood in the mornings, which induced something like depression, arousing gloomy thoughts, but towards the end of the journey it has left off; now I haven't even a cough. It is a long time since I have coughed so little as now, after being for a fortnight in the open air. After the first three days of travelling my body grew used to the jolting, and in time I did not notice the coming of midday and then of evening and night. The time flew by rapidly as it does in serious illness. You think it is scarcely midday when the peasants say—"You ought to put up for the night, sir, or we may lose our way in the dark"; you look at your watch, and it is actually eight o'clock.

They drive quickly, but the speed is nothing remarkable. Probably I have come upon the roads in bad condition, and in winter travelling would have been quicker. They dash uphill at a gallop, and before setting off and before the driver gets on the box, the horses need two or three men to hold them. The horses remind me of the fire brigade horses in Moscow. One day we nearly ran over an old woman, and another time almost dashed into an etape. Now, would you like an adventure for which I am indebted to Siberian driving? Only I beg mother not to wail and lament, for it all ended well. On the 6th of May towards daybreak I was being driven with two horses by a very nice old man. It was a little chaise, I was drowsy, and, to while away the time, watched the gleaming of zigzagging lights in the fields and birch copses—it was last year's grass on fire; it is their habit here to burn it. Suddenly I hear the swift rattle of wheels, a post-cart at full speed comes flying towards us like a bird, my old man hastens to move to the right, the three horses dash by, and I see in the dusk a huge heavy post-cart with a driver for the return journey in it. It was followed by a second cart also going at full speed. We made haste to move aside to the right. To my great amazement and alarm the approaching cart moved not to its right, but its left ... I hardly had time to think, "Good heavens! we shall run into each other," when there was a desperate crash, the horses were mixed up in a dark blur, the yokes fell off, my chaise reared up into the air, and I flew to the ground, and my luggage on the top of me. But that was not all ... A third cart was dashing upon us. This really ought to have smashed me and my luggage to atoms but, thank God! I was not asleep, I broke no bones in the fall, and managed to jump up so quickly that I was able to get out of the way. "Stop," I bawled to the third cart, "Stop!" The third dashed up to the second and stopped. Of course if I were able to sleep in a chaise, or if the third cart had followed instantly on the second, I should certainly have come back a cripple or a headless horseman. The results of the collision were broken shafts, torn traces, yokes and luggage scattered on the ground, the horses scared and harassed, and the alarming feeling that we had just been in danger. It turned out that the first driver had lashed up the horses; while in the other two carts the drivers were asleep, and the horses followed the first team with no one controlling them. On recovering from the shock, my old man and the other three men fell to abusing each other ferociously. Oh, how they swore! I thought it would end in a fight. You can't imagine the feeling of isolation in the middle of that savage swearing crew in the open country, just before dawn, in sight of the fires far and near consuming the grass, but not warming the cold night air! Oh, how heavy my heart was! One listened to the swearing, looked at the broken shafts and at one's tormented luggage, and it seemed as though one were cast away in another world, as though one would be crushed in a moment.... After an hour's abuse my old man began splicing together the shafts with cord and tying up the traces; my straps were forced into the service too. We got to the station somehow, crawling along and stopping from time to time.

After five or six days rain with high winds began. It rained day and night. The leather overcoat came to the rescue and kept me safe from rain and wind. It's a wonderful coat. The mud was almost impassable, the drivers began to be unwilling to go on at night. But what was worst of all, and what I shall never forget, was crossing the rivers. One reaches a river at night.... One begins shouting and so does the driver.... Rain, wind, pieces of ice glide down the river, there is a sound of splashing.... And to add to our gaiety there is the cry of a heron. Herons live on the Siberian rivers, so it seems they don't consider the climate but the geographical position.... Well, an hour later, in the darkness, a huge ferry-boat of the shape of a barge comes into sight with huge oars that look like the pincers of a crab. The ferry-men are a rowdy set, for the most part exiles banished here by the verdict of society for their vicious life. They use insufferably bad language, shout, and ask for money for vodka.... The ferrying across takes a long, long time ... an agonizingly long time. The ferryboat crawls. Again the feeling of loneliness, and the heron seems calling on purpose, as though he means to say: "Don't be frightened, old man, I am here, the Lintvaryovs have sent me here from the Psyol."

On the 7th of May when I asked for horses the driver said the Irtysh had overflowed its banks and flooded the meadows, that Kuzma had set off the day before and had difficulty in getting back, and that I could not go, but must wait.... I asked: "Wait till when?" Answer: "The Lord only knows!" That was vague. Besides, I had taken a vow to get rid on the journey of two of my vices which were a source of considerable expense, trouble, and inconvenience; I mean my readiness to give in, and be overpersuaded. I am quick to agree, and so I have had to travel anyhow, sometimes to pay double and to wait for hours at a time. I had taken to refusing to agree and to believe—and my sides have ached less. For instance, they bring out not a proper carriage but a common, jolting cart. I refuse to travel in the jolting cart, I insist, and the carriage is sure to appear, though they may have declared that there was no such thing in the whole village, and so on. Well, I suspected that the Irtysh floods were invented simply to avoid driving me by night through the mud. I protested and told them to start. The peasant who had heard of the floods from Kuzma, and had not himself seen them, scratched himself and consented; the old men encouraged him, saying that when they were young and used to drive, they were afraid of nothing. We set off. Much rain, a vicious wind, cold ... and felt boots on my feet. Do you know what felt boots are like when they are soaked? They are like boots of jelly. We drive on and on, and behold, there lies stretched before my eyes an immense lake from which the earth appears in patches here and there, and bushes stand out: these are the flooded meadows. In the distance stretches the steep bank of the Irtysh, on which there are white streaks of snow.... We begin driving through the lake. We might have turned back, but obstinacy prevented me, and an incomprehensible impulse of defiance mastered me—that impulse which made me bathe from the yacht in the middle of the Black Sea and has impelled me to not a few acts of folly ... I suppose it is a special neurosis. We drive on and make for the little islands and strips of land. The direction is indicated by bridges and planks; they have been washed away. To cross by them we had to unharness the horses and lead them over one by one.... The driver unharnesses the horses, I jump out into the water in my felt boots and hold them.... A pleasant diversion! And the rain and wind.... Queen of Heaven! At last we get to a little island where there stands a hut without a roof.... Wet horses are wandering about in the wet dung. A peasant with a long stick comes out of the hut and undertakes to guide us. He measures the depth of the water with his stick, and tries the ground. He led us out—God bless him for it!— on to a long strip of ground which he called "the ridge." He instructs us that we must keep to the right—or perhaps it was to the left, I don't remember—and get on to another ridge. This we do. My felt boots are soaking and squelching, my socks are snuffling. The driver says nothing and clicks dejectedly to his horses. He would gladly turn back, but by now it was late, it was dark.... At last—oh, joy!—we reach the Irtysh.... The further bank is steep but the near bank is sloping. The near one is hollowed out, looks slippery, hateful, not a trace of vegetation.... The turbid water splashes upon it with crests of white foam, and dashes back again as though disgusted at touching the uncouth slippery bank on which it seems that none but toads and the souls of murderers could live.... The Irtysh makes no loud or roaring sound, but it sounds as though it were hammering on coffins in its depths.... A damnable impression! The further bank is steep, dark brown, desolate....

There is a hut; the ferry-men live in it. One of them comes out and announces that it is impossible to work the ferry as a storm has come up. The river, they said, was wide, and the wind was strong. And so I had to stay the night at the hut.... I remember the night. The snoring of the ferry-men and my driver, the roar of the wind, the patter of the rain, the mutterings of the Irtysh.... Before going to sleep I wrote a letter to Marya Vladimirovna; I was reminded of the Bozharovsky pool.

In the morning they were unwilling to ferry me across: there was a high wind. We had to row across in the boat. I am rowed across the river, while the rain comes lashing down, the wind blows, my luggage is drenched and my felt boots, which had been dried overnight in the oven, become jelly again. Oh, the darling leather coat! If I did not catch cold I owe it entirely to that. When I come back you must reward it with an anointing of tallow or castor-oil. On the bank I sat for a whole hour on my portmanteau waiting for horses to come from the village. I remember it was very slippery clambering up the bank. In the village I warmed myself and had some tea. Some exiles came to beg for alms. Every family makes forty pounds of wheaten flour into bread for them every day. It's a kind of forced tribute.

The exiles take the bread and sell it for drink at the tavern. One exile, a tattered, closely shaven old man, whose eyes had been knocked out in the tavern by his fellow-exiles, hearing that there was a traveller in the room and taking me for a merchant, began singing and repeating the prayers. He recited the prayer for health and for the rest of the soul, and sang the Easter hymn, "Let the Lord arise," and "With thy Saints, O Lord"— goodness knows what he didn't sing! Then he began telling lies, saying that he was a Moscow merchant. I noticed how this drunken creature despised the peasants upon whom he was living.

On the 11th I drove with posting horses. I read the books of complaints at the posting station in my boredom.

... On the 12th of May they would not give me horses, saying that I could not drive, because the River Ob had overflowed its banks and flooded all the meadows. They advised me to turn off the track as far as Krasny Yar; then go by boat twelve versts to Dubrovin, and at Dubrovin you can get posting horses.... I drove with private horses as far as Krasny Yar. I arrive in the morning; I am told there is a boat, but that I must wait a little as the grandfather had sent the workman to row the president's secretary to Dubrovin in it. Very well, we will wait.... An hour passes, a second, a third.... Midday arrives, then evening.... Allah kerim, what a lot of tea I drank, what a lot of bread I ate, what a lot of thoughts I thought! And what a lot I slept! Night came on and still no boat.... Early morning came.... At last at nine o'clock the workmen returned.... Thank heaven, we are afloat at last! And how pleasant it is! The air is still, the oarsmen are good, the islands are beautiful.... The floods caught men and cattle unawares and I see peasant women rowing in boats to the islands to milk the cows. And the cows are lean and dejected. There is absolutely no grass for them, owing to the cold. I was rowed twelve versts. At the station of Dubrovin I had tea, and for tea they gave me, can you imagine! waffles.... I suppose the woman of the house was an exile or the wife of an exile. At the next station an old clerk, a Pole, to whom I gave some antipyrin for his headache, complained of his poverty, and said Count Sapyega, a Pole who was a gentleman-in-waiting at the Austrian Court, and who assisted his fellow-countrymen, had lately arrived there on his way to Siberia, "He stayed near the station," said the clerk, "and I didn't know it! Holy Mother! He would have helped me! I wrote to him at Vienna, but I got no answer, ..." and so on. Why am I not a Sapyega? I would send this poor fellow to his own country.

On the 14th of May again they would not give me horses. The Tom was flooded. How vexatious! It meant not mere vexation but despair! Fifty versts from Tomsk and how unexpected! A woman in my place would have sobbed. Some kind-hearted people found a solution for me. "Drive on, sir, as far as the Tom, it is only six versts from here; there they will row you across to Yar, and Ilya Markovitch will take you on from there to Tomsk." I hired a horse and drove to the Tom, to the place where the boat was to be. I drove—there was no boat. They told me it had just set off with the post, and was hardly likely to return as there was such a wind. I began waiting.... The ground was covered with snow, it rained and hailed and the wind blew.... One hour passed, a second, and no boat. Fate was laughing at me. I returned to the station. There the driver of the mail with three posting horses was just setting off for the Tom. I told him there was no boat. He stayed. Fate rewarded me; the clerk in response to my hesitating inquiry whether there was anything to eat told me the woman of the house had some cabbage soup. Oh, rapture! Oh, radiant day! And the daughter of the house did in fact give me some excellent cabbage soup, with some capital meat with roast potatoes and cucumbers. I have not had such a dinner since I was at Pan Zalyessky's. After the potatoes I let myself go, and made myself some coffee.

Towards evening the mail driver, an elderly man who had evidently endured a good deal in his day, and who did not venture to sit down in my presence, began preparing to set off to the Tom. I did the same. We drove off. As soon as we reached the river the boat came into sight—a long boat: I have never dreamed of a boat so long. While the post was being loaded on to the boat I witnessed a strange phenomenon—there was a peal of thunder, a queer thing in a cold wind, with snow on the ground. They loaded up and rowed off. My sweet Misha, forgive me for being so rejoiced that I did not bring you with me! How sensible it was of me not to take anyone with me! At first our boat floated over a meadow near willow-bushes.... As is common before a storm or during a storm, a violent wind suddenly sprang up on the water and stirred up the waves. The boatman who was sitting at the helm advised our waiting in the willow-bushes till the storm was over. They answered him that if the storm grew worse, they might stay in the willow-bushes till night and be drowned all the same. They proceeded to settle it by *majority of votes*, and decided to row on. An evil mocking fate is mine. Oh, why these jests? We rowed on in silence, concentrating our thoughts.... I remember the figure of the mail-driver, a man of varied experiences. I remember the little soldier who suddenly became as crimson as cherry juice. I thought, if the boat upsets I will fling off my fur coat and my leather coat ... then my felt boots, then ... and so on.... But the bank came nearer and nearer, one's soul felt easier and easier, one's heart throbbed with joy, one heaved deep sighs as though one could breathe freely at last, and leapt on the wet slippery bank.... Thank God!

At Ilya Markovitch's, the converted Jew's, I was told that I could not drive at night; the road was bad; that I must remain till next day. Very good, I stayed. After tea I sat down to write you this letter, interrupted by the visit of the "president." The president is a rich mixture of Nozdryov, Hlestakov and a cur. A drunkard, a rake, a liar, a singer, a story-teller, and with all that a good-natured man. He had brought with him a big trunk stuffed full of business papers, a bedstead and mattress, a gun, and a secretary. The secretary is an excellent, well-educated man, a protesting liberal who has studied in Petersburg, and is free in his ideas; I don't know how he came to Siberia, he is infected to the marrow of his bones with every sort of disease, and is taking to drink, thanks to his principal, who calls him Kolya. The representative of authority sends for a cordial. "Doctor," he bawls, "drink another glass, I beseech you humbly!" Of course, I drink it. The representative of authority drinks soundly, lies outrageously, uses shameless language. We go to bed. In the morning a cordial is sent for again. They swill the cordial till ten o'clock and at last they go. The converted Jew, Ilya Markovitch, whom the peasants here idolize—so I was told—gave me horses to drive to Tomsk.

The "president," the secretary and I got into the same conveyance. All the way the "president" told lies, drank out of the bottle, boasted that he did not take bribes, raved about the scenery, and shook his fist at the tramps that he met. We drove fifteen versts, then halt! The village of Brovkino.... We stop near a Jew's shop and go to take "rest and refreshment." The Jew runs to fetch us a cordial while his wife makes us some fish-soup, of which I have written to you already. The "president" gave orders that the *sotsky*, the *desyatsky*, and the road contractor should come to him, and in his drunkenness began reproving them, not the least restrained by my presence. He swore like a Tatar.

I soon parted from the "president," and on the evening of the 15th of May by an appalling road reached Tomsk. During the last two days I have only done seventy versts; you can imagine what the roads are like!

In Tomsk the mud was almost impassable. Of the town and the manner of living here I will write in a day or two, but good-bye for now—I am tired of writing.

There are no poplars. The Kuvshinnikov General was lying. I have seen no nightingales. There are magpies and cuckoos.

I received a telegram of eighty words from Suvorin to-day.

Excuse this letter's being like a hotch-potch. It's incoherent, but I can't help it. Sitting in an hotel room one can't write better. Excuse its being long, It's not my fault. My pen ran away with me—besides, I wanted to go on talking to you. It's three o'clock in the night. My hand is tired. The wick of the candle wants snuffing, I can hardly see. Write to me at Sahalin every four or five days. It seems that the post goes there, not only by sea but across Siberia, so I shall get letters frequently.

All the Tomsk people tell me that there has not been a spring so cold and rainy as this one since 1842. Half Tomsk is under water. My luck!

I am eating sweets.

I shall have to stay at Tomsk till the rains are over. They say the road to Irkutsk is awful.

TOMSK,

May 20.

It is Trinity Sunday with you, while with us even the willow has not yet come out, and there is still snow on the banks of the Tom. To-morrow I am starting for Irkutsk. I am rested. There is no need for hurry, as steam navigation on Lake Baikal does not begin till the 10th of June; but I shall go all the same.

I am alive and well, my money is safe; I have a slight pain in my right eye. It aches.

... Everyone advises me to go back across America, as they say one may die of boredom in the Volunteer Fleet; it's all military discipline and red tape regulations, and they don't often touch at a port.

To fill up my time I have been writing some impressions of my journey and sending them to *Novoye Vremya*; you will read them soon after the 10th of June. I write a little about everything, chit-chat. I don't write for glory but from a financial point of view, and in consideration of the money I have had in advance.

Tomsk is a very dull town. To judge from the drunkards whose acquaintance I have made, and from the intellectual people who have come to the hotel to pay their respects to me, the inhabitants are very dull too.

In two and a half days I shall be in Krasnoyarsk, and in seven or eight in Irkutsk. It's fifteen hundred versts to Irkutsk. I have made myself coffee and am just going to drink it.

... After Tomsk the Taiga begins. We shall see it.

My greeting to all the Lintvaryovs and to our old Maryushka. I beg mother not to worry and not to put faith in bad dreams. Have the radishes succeeded? There are none here at all.

Keep well, don't worry about money—there will be plenty; don't try to spend less and spoil the summer for yourselves.

TO A. S. SUVORIN.

TOMSK, May 20, 1890.

Greetings to you at last from Siberia, dear Alexey Sergeyevitch! I have missed you and our correspondence terribly.

I will begin from the beginning, however. At Tyumen I was told the first steamer to Tomsk went on the 18th of May. I had to do the journey with horses. For the first three days every joint and sinew ached, but afterwards I got used to the jolting and felt no more aches. Only the lack of sleep, the continual worry over the luggage, the jolting and the fasting brought on spitting of blood when I coughed, and this depressed my spirits, which were none too grand before. For the first few days it was bearable but then a cold wind began to blow, the windows of heaven were opened, the rivers flooded the meadows and roads, I was continually having to change my chaise for a boat. You'll read of my struggles with the floods and the mud in the article I enclose. I did not mention in it that my big high boots were tight, and that I waded through the mud and the water in my felt boots, and that my felt boots were soaked to jelly. The road was so abominable that during the last two days of my journey I only did seventy versts.

When I set off I promised to send you notes of my journey after Tomsk, since the road between Tyumen and Tomsk has been described a thousand times already. But in your telegram you have expressed the desire to get my impressions of Siberia as quickly as possible, and have even had the cruelty, sir, to reproach me with lapse of memory, as though I had forgotten you. It was absolutely impossible to write on the road. I kept a brief diary in pencil and can offer you now only what is written in that diary. To avoid writing at great length and getting mixed up, I divided all my impressions into chapters. I am sending you six chapters. They are written *for you personally*. I wrote for you only, and so have not been afraid of being too subjective, and have not been afraid of there being more of Chekhov's feelings and thoughts than of Siberia in them. If you find some lines interesting and worth printing, give them a profitable publicity, signing them with my name and printing them in separate chapters, a tablespoonful once an hour. The general title can be *From Siberia*, then *From Trans-Baikalia*, then *From the Amur*, and so on.

You shall have another helping from Irkutsk, for which I am starting to-morrow. I shall not be less than ten days on the journey—the road is bad. I shall send you a few chapters again, and shall send them whether you intend to print them or not. Read them and when you are tired of them telegraph to me "Shut up!"

I have been as hungry as a dog the whole way. I stuffed myself with bread so as not to dream of turbot, asparagus, and suchlike. I even dreamed of buckwheat porridge. I have dreamed of it for hours at a time.

At Tyumen I bought some sausage for the journey, but what sausage! When you take a bit in your mouth there's a sniff as though you had gone into a stable at the very moment when the coachmen were taking off their leg-wrappers; when you begin chewing it, you feel as though you had fastened your teeth into a dog's tail defiled with pitch. Tfoo! I ate some once or twice, and threw it away.

I have had one telegram and the letter from you in which you write that you want to bring out an encyclopaedic dictionary. I don't know why, but the news of that dictionary rejoiced me greatly. Do, my dear friend! If I am any use for working on it, I will devote November and December to you, and will spend those months in Petersburg. I will sit at it from morning till night.

I made a fair copy of my notes at Tomsk in horrid hotel surroundings, but I took trouble about it and was not without a desire to please you. I thought, he must be bored and hot in Feodosia, let him read about the cold. These notes will come to you instead of a letter which has been taking shape in my head during the whole journey. In return you must send to me at Sahalin all your critical reviews except the first two, which I have read; have Peshel's "Ethnology" sent me there too, except the first two instalments, which I have already.

The post to Sahalin goes both by sea and across Siberia, so if people write to me I shall get letters often. Don't lose my address—*Island of Sahalin, Alexandrovsky Post.*

Oh, the expense! *Gewalt!* Thanks to the floods, I had to pay the drivers double and almost treble, for it has been fiendishly hard work. My trunk, a very charming article, has turned out unsuitable for the journey; it takes a lot of room, pokes one in the ribs, and rattles, and worst of all threatens to burst open. "Don't take boxes on long journeys!" good people said to me, but I remembered this advice only when I had gone half-way. Well, I am leaving my trunk to reside permanently at Tomsk, and am buying instead of it a sort of leather carcase, which has the advantage that it can be tied so as to form two halves at the bottom of the chaise as one likes. I paid sixteen roubles for it. Next point. To travel to the Amur, changing one's conveyance at every station, is torture. You shatter both yourself and all your luggage. I was advised to buy a trap. I bought one to-day for one hundred and thirty roubles. If I don't succeed in selling it at Sryetensk, where my horse journey ends, I shall be in a fix and shall howl aloud. To-day I dined with the editor of the *Sibirsky Vyestnik*, a local Nozdryov, a broad nature.... He drank to the tune of six roubles.

Stop! They announce that the deputy police master wants to see me. What can it be?!?

My alarm was unnecessary. The police officer turns out to be devoted to literature and himself an author; he has come to pay his respects to me. He went home to fetch his play, and I believe intends to regale me with it. He is just coming again and preventing me from writing to you....

... My greetings to Nastyusha and Boris. I should be genuinely delighted for their satisfaction to fling myself into the jaws of a tiger and call them to my aid, but, alas! I haven't reached the tigers here: the only furry animals I have seen so far in Siberia are many hares and one mouse.

Stop! The police officer has returned. He has not read me his drama though he brought it, but regaled me with a story. It's not bad, only too local. He showed me a nugget of gold. He asked for some vodka. I don't remember a single educated Siberian who has not asked for vodka on coming to see me. He told me he had a mistress, a married woman; he gave me a petition to the Tsar about divorce to read....

How glad I am when I am forced to stop somewhere for the night! I no sooner roll into bed than I am asleep. Here, travelling and not sleeping at night, one prizes sleep above everything. There is no greater enjoyment in life than sleep when one is sleepy. In Moscow, in Russia generally, I never was sleepy as I understand the word now. I went to bed simply because one had to. But now! Another observation. On a journey one has no desire for spirits. I can't drink. I smoke a great deal. One's mind does not work well. I cannot put my thoughts together. Time flies rapidly, so that one scarcely notices it, from ten o'clock in the morning to seven o'clock in the evening. Evening comes quickly after morning. It's just the same when one is seriously ill. The wind and the rain have made my face all scaly, and when I look in the looking-glass I don't recognize my once noble features.

I am not going to describe Tomsk. All the towns are alike in Russia. Tomsk is a dull and intemperate town. There are absolutely no good-looking women, and the disregard for justice is Asiatic. The town is remarkable for the fact that governors die in it.

If my letters are short, careless, or dry, don't be cross, for one cannot always be oneself on a journey and write as one wants to. The ink is bad, and there is always a hair or a splodge on one's pen.

TO HIS SISTER.

KRASNOYARSK, May 28, 1890.

What a deadly road! It was all we could do to crawl to Krasnoyarsk and my trap had to be repaired twice. The first thing to be broken was the vertical piece of iron connecting the front of the carriage with the axle; then the so-called circle under the front broke. I have never in all my life seen such a road—such impassable mud and such an utterly neglected road. I am going to write about its horrors to the *Novoye Vremya*, and so won't talk about it now.

The last three stations have been splendid; as one comes down to Krasnoyarsk one seems to be getting into a different world. You come out of the forest into a plain which is like our Donets steppe, but here the mountain ridges are grander. The sun shines its very best and the birch-trees are out, though three stations back the buds were not even bursting. Thank God, I have at last reached a summer in which there is neither rain nor a cold wind. Krasnoyarsk is a picturesque, cultured town; compared with it, Tomsk is "a pig in a skull-cap and the acme of *mauvais ton.*" The streets are clean and paved, the houses are of stone and large, the churches are elegant.

I am alive and perfectly well. My money is all right, and so are my things; I lost my woollen stockings but soon found them again.

Apart from my trap, everything so far has been satisfactory and I have nothing to complain of. Only I am spending an awful lot of money. Incompetence in the practical affairs of life is never felt so much as on a journey. I pay more than I need to, I do the wrong thing, and I say the wrong thing, and I am always expecting what does not happen.

... I shall be in Irkutsk in five or six days, shall spend as many days there, then drive on to Sryetensk—and that will be the end of my journey on land. For more than a fortnight I have been driving without a break, I think about nothing else, I live for nothing else; every morning I see the sunrise from beginning to end. I've grown so used to it that it seems as though all my life I had been driving and struggling with the muddy roads. When it does not rain, and there are no pits of mud on the road, one feels queer and even a little bored. And how filthy I am, what a rapscallion I look! What a state my luckless clothes are in!

... For mother's information: I have still a jar and a half of coffee; I feed on locusts and wild honey; I shall dine to-day at Irkutsk. The further east one gets the dearer everything is. Rye flour is seventy kopecks a *pood*, while on the other side of Tomsk it was twenty-five and twenty-seven kopecks per *pood*, and wheaten flour thirty kopecks. The tobacco sold in Siberia is vile and loathsome; I tremble because mine is nearly done.

... I am travelling with two lieutenants and an army doctor who are all on their way to the Amur. So my revolver is after all quite superfluous. In such company hell would have no terrors. We are just having tea at the station, and after tea we are going to have a look at the town.

I should have no objection to living in Krasnoyarsk. I can't think why this is a favourite place for sending exiles to.

Your Homo Sachaliensis,

A. CHEKHOV.

TO HIS BROTHER ALEXANDR.

IRKUTSK, June 5, 1890.

MY EUROPEAN BROTHER,

It is, of course, unpleasant to live in Siberia; but better to live in Siberia and feel oneself a man of moral worth, than to live in Petersburg with the reputation of a drunkard and a scoundrel. No reference to present company.

Siberia is a cold and long country. I drive on and on and see no end to it. I see little that is new or of interest, but I feel and experience a great deal. I have contended with flooded rivers, with cold, with impassable mud, hunger and sleepiness: such sensations as you could not get for a million in Moscow! You ought to come to Siberia. Ask the authorities to exile you.

The best of all Siberian towns is Irkutsk. Tomskis not worth a brass farthing, and the district towns are no better than the Kryepkaya in which you were so heedlessly born. What is most provoking, there is nothing to eat in the district towns, and oh dear, how conscious one is of that on the journey! You get to a town and feel ready to eat a mountain; you arrive and—alack!—no sausage, no cheese, no meat, no herring even, but the same insipid eggs and milk as in the villages.

On the whole I am satisfied with my expedition, and don't regret having come. The travelling is hard, but the resting after it is delightful. I rest with enjoyment.

From Irkutsk I shall make for Baikal, which I shall cross by steamer; it's a thousand versts from the Baikal to the Amur, and thence I shall go by steamer to the Pacific, where the first thing I shall do is to have a bath and eat oysters.

I got here yesterday and went first of all to have a bath, then to bed. Oh, how I slept! I never understood what sleep meant till now.

I bless you with both hands.

Your Asiatic brother,

A. CHEKHOV.

TO A. N. PLESHTCHEYEV.

IRKUTSK, June 5, 1890.

A thousand greetings to you, dear Alexey Nikolaevitch. At last I have vanquished the most difficult three thousand versts; I am sitting in a decent hotel and can write. I have rigged myself out all in new things and, as far as possible, smart ones, for you cannot imagine how sick I was of my big muddy boots, of my sheepskin smelling of tar, of my overcoat covered with bits of hay, of dust and crumbs in my pockets, and of my extremely dirty linen. I looked such a ragamuffin on the journey that even the tramps eyed me askance; and then, as ill luck would have it, the cold winds and rain chapped my face and made it scaly like a fish. Now at last I am a European again, and I am conscious of it all over.

Well, what am I to write to you? It's all so long and so vast that one doesn't know where to begin. All my experiences in Siberia I divide into three periods. (1) From Tyumen to Tomsk, fifteen hundred versts, terrible cold, day and night, sheepskin, felt boots, cold rains, winds and a desperate life-and-death struggle with the flooded rivers. The rivers had flooded the meadows and roads, and I was constantly exchanging my trap for a boat and floating like a Venetian on a gondola; the boats, the waiting on the bank for them, the rowing across, etc., all that took up so much time that during the last two days before reaching Tomsk, in spite of all my efforts, I only did seventy versts instead of four or five hundred. There were, moreover, some very uneasy and unpleasant moments, especially when the wind rose and began to buffet the boat. (2) From Tomsk to Krasnoyarsk, five hundred versts, impassable mud, my chaise and I stuck in the mud like flies in thick jam. How many times I broke my chaise (it's my own property!) how many versts I walked! how bespattered my countenance and my clothes were! It was not driving but wading through mud. How I swore at it all! My brain would not work, I could do nothing but swear. I was utterly exhausted, and was very glad to reach the posting station at Krasnoyarsk. (3) From Krasnoyarsk to Irkutsk, fifteen hundred and sixty-six versts, heat, smoke from the burning woods, and dust—dust in one's mouth, in one's nose, in one's pockets; when you look at yourself in the glass, you think your face has been painted. When, on reaching Irkutsk, I washed at the baths, the soapsuds off my head were not white but of an ashen brown colour, as though I were washing a horse.

When I get home I will tell you about the Yenissey and the Taiga—very interesting and curious, for it is something quite new to a European; everything else is ordinary and monotonous. Roughly speaking, the scenery of Siberia is not very different from that of European Russia; there are differences, but they are not very noticeable. Travelling is perfectly safe.

Robbers and highwaymen are all nonsense and fairy tales. A revolver is utterly unnecessary, and you are as safe at night in the forest as you are by day on the Nevsky Prospect. It's different for anyone travelling on foot....

TO N. A. LEIKIN.

IRKUTSK, June 5, 1890.

Greetings, dear Nikolay Alexandrovitch!

I send you heartfelt good wishes from Irkutsk, from the depths of Siberia. I reached Irkutsk last night and was very glad to have arrived, as I was exhausted by the journey and missed friends and relations, to whom I had not written for ages. Well, what is there of interest to write to you? I will begin by telling you that the journey is extraordinarily long. From Tyumen to Irkutsk I have driven more than three thousand versts. From Tyumen to Tomsk I had cold and flooded rivers to contend with. The cold was awful; on Ascension Day there was frost and snow, so that I could not take off my sheepskin and felt boots until I reached the hotel at Tomsk. As for the floods, they were a veritable plague of Egypt. The rivers rose above their banks and overflowed the meadows, and with them the roads, for dozens of versts around. I was continually having to exchange my chaise for a boat, and one could not get a boat for nothing—for a good boat one had to pay with one's heart's blood, for one had to sit waiting on the bank for twenty-four hours at a stretch in the cold wind and the rain.... From Tomsk to Krasnoyarsk was a desperate struggle through impassable mud. My goodness, it frightens me to think of it! How often I had to mend my chaise, to walk, to swear, to get out of my chaise and get into it again, and so on! It sometimes happened that I was from six to ten hours getting from one station to another, and every time the chaise had to be mended it took from ten to fifteen hours. From Krasnoyarsk to Irkutsk was fearfully hot and dusty. Add to all that hunger, dust in one's nose, one's eyes glued together with sleep, the continual dread that something would get broken in the chaise (it is my own), and boredom.... Nevertheless I am well content, and I thank God that He has given me the strength and opportunity to make this journey. I have seen and experienced a great deal, and it has all been very new and interesting to me not as a literary man, but as a human being. The Yenissey, the Taiga, the stations, the drivers, the wild scenery, the wild life, the physical agonies caused by the discomforts of the journey, the enjoyment I got from rest—all taken together is so delightful that I can't describe it. The mere fact that I have been for more than a month in the open air is interesting and healthy; every day for a month I have seen the sunrise....

TO HIS SISTER.

IRKUTSK, June 6, 1890.

Greetings to you, dear mother, Ivan, Masha and Misha, and all of you!

In my last long letter I wrote to you that the mountains near Krasnoyarsk are like the Donets Ridge, but that's not true; when I looked at them from the street I saw they were like high walls surrounding the city, and I was vividly reminded of the Caucasus. And when towards evening I left the town and was crossing the Yenissey, I saw on the other bank mountains that were exactly like the Caucasus, as misty and dreamy. The Yenissey is a broad, swift, winding river, beautiful, finer than the Volga. And the ferry across it is wonderful, ingeniously constructed, moving against the current; I will tell you when I am home about the construction of it. And so the mountains and the Yenissey are the first things original and new that I have met in Siberia. The mountains and the Yenissey have given me sensations which have made up to me a hundredfold for all the trials and troubles of the journey, and which have made me call Levitan a fool for being so stupid as not to come with me.

The Taiga stretches unbroken from Krasnoyarsk to Irkutsk. The trees are not bigger than in Sokolniki, but not one driver knows how far it goes. There is no end to be seen to it. It stretches for hundreds of versts. No one knows who or what is in the Taiga, and it only happens in winter that people come through the Taiga from the far north with reindeer for bread. When you get to the top of a mountain and look down, you see a mountain before you, then another, mountains at the sides too—and all thickly covered with forest. It makes one feel almost frightened. That's the second thing original and new.

From Krasnoyarsk it began to be hot and dusty. The heat was terrible. My sheepskin and cap lie buried away. The dust is in my mouth, in my nose, down my neck—tfoo! We were approaching Irkutsk—we had to cross the Angara by ferry. As though to mock us a high wind sprang up. My military companions and I, after dreaming for ten days of a bath, dinner, and sleep, stood on the bank and turned pale at the thought that we should have to spend the night not at Irkutsk, but in the village. The ferry could not succeed in reaching the bank. We stood an hour, a second, and—oh Heavens!—the ferry made an effort and reached the bank. Bravo, we shall have a bath, we shall have supper and sleep! Oh, how sweet to steam oneself, to eat, to sleep!

Irkutsk is a fine town. Quite a cultured town. There is a theatre, a museum, a town garden with a band, a good hotel.... No hideous fences, no absurd shop-signs, and no waste places with warming placards. There is a tavern called "Taganrog"; sugar costs twenty-four kopecks a pound, pine kernels six kopecks a pound.

I am quite well. My money is safe. I am saving up my coffee for Sahalin. I have splendid tea here, after which I am aware of an agreeable excitement. I see Chinamen. They are a good-natured and intelligent people. At the Siberian bank they gave me money at once, received me cordially, regaled me with cigarettes, and invited me to their summer villa. There is a magnificent confectioner's but everything is fiendishly dear. The pavements are of wood.

Last night I drove with the officers about the town. We heard someone cry "help" six times. It must have been someone being murdered. We went to look, but could not find anyone.

The cabs in Irkutsk have springs. It is a better town than Ekaterinburg or Tomsk. Quite European.

Have a Mass celebrated on June 17th, [Footnote: The anniversary of the death of his brother Nikolay.] and keep the 29th [Footnote: His father's name-day.] as festively as you can; I shall be with you in thought and you must drink my health.

Everything I have is crumpled, dirty, torn! I look like a pickpocket.

I shall not bring you any furs most likely. I do not know where they are sold, and I am too lazy to ask.

One must take at least two big pillows for a journey and dark pillow cases are essential.

What is Ivan doing? Where has he been? Has he been to the south? I am going from Irkutsk to Baikal. My companions are preparing for sea-sickness.

My big boots have grown looser with wearing, and don't hurt my heels now.

I have ordered buckwheat porridge for to-morrow. On the journey here I thought of curds and began having them with milk at the stations.

Did you get my postcards from the little towns? Keep them: I shall be able to judge from them how long the post takes. The post here is in no hurry.

IRKUTSK,

June 7, 1890.

... The steamer from Sryetensk leaves on June 20th. Good Christians, what am I to do till the 20th? How am I to dispose of myself? The journey to Sryetensk will only take five or six days. I have greatly altered the route of my journey. From Habarovsk (look at the map [Footnote: Chekhov's family had, during his absence, a map of Siberia on the wall by means of which they followed his progress.]) I am going not to Nikolaevsk, but by the Ussuri to Vladivostok, and from there to Sahalin. I must have a look at the Ussuri region. At Vladivostok I shall bathe in the sea and eat oysters.

It was cold till I reached Kansk; from Kansk (see map) I began to go down to the south. Everything is as green as with you, even the oaks are out. The birches here are darker than in Russia, the green is not so sentimental. There are masses of the Russian white service-tree, which here takes the place of both the lilac and the cherry. They say they make an excellent jam from the service-tree. I tasted some of the fruit pickled; it was not bad.

Two lieutenants and an army doctor are travelling with me. They have received their travelling expenses three times over, but have spent all the money, though they are travelling in one carriage. They are sitting without a farthing, waiting for the pay department to send them some money. They are nice fellows. They have had from fifteen hundred to two thousand roubles each for travelling expenses, and the journey will cost them next to nothing (excluding, of course, the cost of the stopping places). They do nothing but pitch into everybody at hotels and stations so that people are positively afraid to present their bills. In their company I pay less than usual.... To-day for the first time in my life I saw a Siberian cat. It has long soft fur, and a gentle disposition.

... I felt homesick and sent you a telegram today asking you to subscribe together and send me a long telegram. It would be nothing to all of you, inhabitants of Luka, to fling away five roubles.

... With whom is Mishka in love? To what happy woman is Ivanenko telling stories of his uncle? ... I must be in love with *Jamais* as I dreamed of her yesterday. In comparison with all the "jeunes Siberiennes" with their Yakut-Buriat physiognomies, who do not know how to dress, to sing, and to laugh, our *Jamais*, Drishka, and Gundassiha are simply queens. The Siberian girls and women are like frozen fish; one would have to be a walrus or a seal to get up a flirtation with them.

I am tired of my companions. It is much nicer travelling alone. I like silence better than anything on the journey and my companions talk and sing without stopping, and they talk of nothing but women. They borrowed a hundred and thirty-six roubles from me till to-morrow and have already spent it. They are regular sieves.

... The stations are sometimes thirty to thirty-five versts apart. You drive by night, you drive and drive, till you feel silly and light-headed, and if you venture to ask the driver how far it is to the next station, he will never say less than seventeen versts. That's particularly agonizing when you have to go at a walking pace along a muddy road full of holes, and when you are thirsty. I have learned to do without sleep; I don't mind a bit when they wake me. As a rule one does not sleep for one day and night, and then the next day at dinner-time there is a strained feeling in one's eyelids; in the evening and in the night towards daybreak of the third day, one dozes in the chaise and sometimes falls asleep for a minute as one sits; at dinner and after dinner at the stations, while the horses are being harnessed, one lolls on the sofa, and the real torture only begins at night. In the evening, after drinking five glasses of tea, one's face begins to burn, one's body feels limp all over and longs to bend backwards; one's eyes close, one's feet ache in one's big boots, one's brain is in a tangle. If I allow myself to put up for the night I fall into a dead sleep at once; if I have strength of will to go on, I drop asleep in the chaise, however violent the jolting may be; at the stations the drivers wake one up, as one has to get out of the chaise and pay for the journey. They wake one not so much by shouting and tugging at one's sleeve, as by the stink of garlic that issues from their lips; they smell of garlic and onion till they make me sick. I only learned to sleep in the chaise after Krasnoyarsk. On the way to Irkutsk I slept for fifty-eight versts, and was only once woken up. But the sleep one gets as one drives makes one feel no better. It's not real sleep, but a sort of unconscious condition, after which one's head is muddled and there's a bad taste in one's mouth.

Chinamen are like those decrepit old gentlemen dear Nikolay [Footnote: Chekhov's brother.] used to like drawing. Some of them have splendid pigtails.

The police came to see me at Tomsk. Towards eleven o'clock the waiter suddenly announced to me that the assistant police-master wanted to see me. What was this for? Could it be politics? Could they suspect me of being a Voltairian? I said to the waiter, "Ask him in." A gentleman with long moustaches walks in and introduces himself. It appears he is devoted to literature, writes himself, and has come to me in my hotel room as though to Mahomed at Mecca to worship. I'll tell you why I thought of him. Late in the autumn he is going to Petersburg, and I have foisted my trunk upon him and asked him to leave it at the *Novoye Vremya* office. You might keep that in mind in case any one of us or our friends goes to Petersburg.

You might, by the way, look out for a place in the country. When I get back to Russia I shall take five years' rest—that is, stay in one place and twiddle my thumbs. A place in the country will come in very handy. I think the money will be found, for things don't look bad. If I work off the money I have had in advance (half of it is worked off already) I shall certainly borrow two or three thousand in the spring, to be paid off over a period of five years. That will not be against my conscience, as I have already let the publishing department of the *Novoye Vremya* make two or three thousand out of my books, and I shall let them make more.

I think I shall not begin on any serious work till I am five and thirty.... I want to try personal life, of which I have had some before, but have not noticed it owing to various circumstances.

To-day I rubbed my leather coat with grease. It's a splendid coat. It has saved me from catching cold. My sheepskin is a capital thing, too: it serves me as a coat and a mattress, both. One is as warm in it as on a stove. It's wretched without pillows. Hay does not take the place of them, and with the continual friction there's a lot of dust from it which tickles one's face and prevents one from dozing. I haven't a single sheet. That's horrid too. And I ought to have taken some more trousers. The more luggage one has the better—there's less jolting and more comfort.

Good-bye, though. I have got nothing more to write about. My greetings to all.

STATION LISTVENITCHNAYA,

ON LAKE BAIKAL, June 13.

I am having an idiotic time. On the evening of the 11th of June, the day before yesterday, we set off from Irkutsk, in the fond hope of catching the Baikal steamer, which leaves at four o'clock in the morning. From Irkutsk to Baikal there are only three stations. At the first station they informed us that all the horses were exhausted and that it was therefore impossible to go. We had to put up for the night. Yesterday morning we set off from that station, and by midday we reached Baikal. We went to the harbour, and in answer to our inquiries were told that the steamer did not go till Friday the fifteenth. This meant that we should have to sit on the bank and look at the water and wait. As there is nothing that does not end in time, I have no objection to waiting, and always wait patiently; but the point is the steamer leaves Sryetensk on the 20th and sails down the Amur: if we don't catch it we must wait for the next steamer, which does not go till the 30th. Merciful Heavens, when shall I get to Sahalin!

We drove to Baikal along the bank of the Angara, which rises out of Lake Baikal and flows into the Yenissey. Look at the map. The banks are picturesque. Mountains and mountains, and dense forests on the mountains. The weather was exquisite still, sunny and warm; as I drove I felt I was exceptionally well; I felt so happy that I cannot describe it. It was perhaps the contrast after the stay at Irkutsk, and because the scenery on the Angara is like Switzerland. It is something new and original. We drove along the river bank, came to the mouth of the river, and turned to the left; then we came upon the bank of Lake Baikal, which in Siberia is called the sea. It is like a mirror. The other side, of course, is out of sight; it is ninety versts away. The banks are high, steep, stony, and covered with forest, to right and to left there are promontories which jut into the sea like Au-dag or the Tohtebel at Feodosia. It's like the Crimea. The station of Listvenitchnaya lies at the water's edge, and is strikingly like Yalta: if the houses were white it would be exactly like Yalta. Only there are no buildings on the mountains, as they are too overhanging and it is impossible to build on them.

We have taken a little barn of a lodging that reminds one of any of the Kraskovsky summer villas. Just outside the window, two or three yards from the wall, is Lake Baikal. We pay a rouble a day. The mountains, the forests, the mirror-like Baikal are all poisoned for me by the thought that we shall have to stay here till the fifteenth. What are we to do here? What is more, we don't know what there is for us to eat. The inhabitants feed upon nothing but garlic. There is neither meat nor fish. They have given us no milk, but have promised it. For a little white loaf they demanded sixteen kopecks. I bought some buckwheat and a piece of smoked pork, and asked them to make a thin porridge of it: it was not nice, but there was nothing to be done, I had to eat it. All the evening we hunted about the village to find someone who would sell us a hen, and found no one.... But there is vodka. The Russian is a great pig. If you ask him why he doesn't eat meat and fish he justifies himself by the absence of transport, ways and communications, and so on, and yet vodka is to be found in the remotest villages and as much of it as you please. And yet one would have supposed that it would have been much easier to obtain meat and fish than vodka, which is more expensive and more difficult to transport.... Yes, drinking vodka must be much more interesting than fishing in Lake Baikal or rearing cattle.

At midnight a little steamer arrived; we went to look at it, and seized the opportunity to ask if there was anything to eat. We were told that to-morrow we should be able to get dinner, but that now it was late, the kitchen fire was out, and so on. We thanked them for "to-morrow"—it was something to look forward to anyway! But alas! the captain came in and told us that at four o'clock in the morning the steamer was setting off for Kultuk. We thanked him. In the refreshment bar, where there was not room to turn round, we drank a bottle of sour beer (thirty-five kopecks), and saw on a plate some amber beads—it was salmon caviare. We returned home, and to sleep. I am sick of sleeping. Every day one has to put down one's sheepskin with the wool upwards, under one's head one puts a folded greatcoat and a pillow, and one sleeps on this heap in one's waistcoat and trousers.... Civilization, where art thou?

To-day there is rain and Lake Baikal is plunged in mist. "Interesting," Semaskho would say. It's dull. One ought to sit down and write, but one can never work in bad weather. One has a foreboding of merciless boredom; if I were alone I should not mind but there are two lieutenants and an army doctor with me, who are fond of talking and arguing. They don't understand much but they talk about everything. One of the lieutenants, moreover, is a bit of a Hlestakov and a braggart. When one is travelling one absolutely must be alone. To sit in a chaise or in a room alone with one's thoughts is much more interesting than being with people.

Congratulate me: I sold my own carriage at Irkutsk. How much I gained on it I won't say, or mother would fall into a faint and not sleep for five nights.

Your Homo Sachaliensis,

A. CHEKHOV.

TO HIS MOTHER.

STEAMER "YERMAK," June 20, 1890.

Greeting, dear ones at home!

At last I can take off my heavy muddy boots, my shabby breeches, and my blue shirt which is shiny with dust and sweat; I can wash and dress like a human being. I am not sitting in a chaise but in a first-class cabin of the steamer *Yermak*. This change took place ten days ago, and this is how it happened. I wrote to you from Listvenitchnaya that I was late for the Baikal steamer, that I had to cross Lake Baikal on Friday instead of Tuesday, and that owing to this I should only be able to catch the Amur steamer on the 30th. But fate is capricious, and often plays us tricks we do not expect. On Thursday morning I went out for a walk on the shores of Lake Baikal; behold—the funnel of one of the little steamers is smoking. I inquire where the steamer is going. They tell me, "Across the sea" to Klyuevo; some merchant had hired it to take his waggons of goods across the Lake. We, too, wanted to cross "the sea" and to go to Boyarskaya station. I inquire how many versts from Klyuevo to Boyarskaya. They tell me twenty-seven. I run back to my companions and beg them to take the risk of going to Klyuevo. I say the "risk" because, going to Klyuevo where there is nothing but a harbour and a watchman's hut, we ran the risk of not finding horses, having to stay on at Klyuevo, and being late for Friday's steamer, which for us would be worse than Igor's death, as we should have to wait till Tuesday. My companions consented. We gathered together our belongings, with cheerful legs stepped on to the steamer and straight to the refreshment bar: soup, for the love of God! Half my kingdom for a plate of soup! The refreshment bar was very nasty and cramped; but the cook, Grigory Ivanitch, who had been a house-serf at Voronezh, turned out to be at the tip-top of his profession. He fed us magnificently. The weather was still and sunny. The water of Lake Baikal is the colour of turquoise, more transparent than the Black Sea. They say that in deep places you can see the bottom over a verst below; and I myself have seen to such a depth, with rocks and mountains plunged in the turquoise-blue, that it sent a shiver all over me. Our journey over Lake Baikal was wonderful. I shall never forget it as long as I live. But I will tell you what was not nice. We travelled third class, and the whole deck was occupied by the waggon-horses, which were wild as mad things. These horses gave a special character to our crossing: it seemed as though we were in a brigand's steamer. At Klyuevo the watchman undertook to convey our luggage to the station; he drove the cart while we walked along the very picturesque shore. Levitan was an ass not to come with me. The way was through woods: on the right, woods running uphill; on the left, woods running down to the Lake. Such ravines, such crags! The colouring of Lake Baikal is soft and warm. It was, by the way, very warm. After walking eight versts we reached the station of Myskan, where a Kyahtan official, who was also on his travels, regaled us with excellent tea, and where we got the horses for Boyarskaya; and so we set off on Thursday instead of Friday; what is more, we got twenty-four hours in advance of the post, which usually takes all the horses at the station. We began driving as fast as we could, cherishing a faint hope of reaching Sryetensk by the 20th. I will tell you when we meet about my journey along the bank of the Selenga and across Transbaikalia. Now I will only say that Selenga is one continuous loneliness, and in Transbaikalia I found everything I wanted: the Caucasus, and the valley of the Psyol, and the Zvenigorod district, and the Don. By day you gallop through the Caucasus, at night along the steppe of the Don; in the morning, rousing yourself from slumber, behold the province of Poltava—and so for the whole thousand versts. Verhneudinsk is a nice little town. Tchita is a wretched place, in the style of Sumy. I need hardly say that we had no time to think of sleep or dinner. One gallops on thinking of nothing but the chance that at the next station we might not get horses, and might be kept five or six hours. We did two hundred versts in twenty-four hours—one can't do more than that in the summer. We were stupefied. The heat was fearful by day, while at night it was so cold that I had to put on my leather coat over my cloth one. One night I even wore my sheepskin. Well, we drove on and on, and reached Sryetensk this morning just an hour before the steamer left, giving the drivers from the last two stations a rouble each for themselves.

And so my horse-journey is over. It has lasted two months (I set out on the 21st of April). If we exclude the time spent on the railway and the steamer, the three days spent in Ekaterinburg, the week in Tomsk, the day in Krasnoyarsk, the week in Irkutsk, the two days on the shores of Lake Baikal, and the days wasted in waiting for boats to cross the floods, you can judge of the rate at which I have driven. My journey has been most successful, I wish nothing better for anyone. I have not once been ill, and of the mass of things I had with me I have lost nothing but a penknife, the strap off my trunk, and a little jar of carbolic ointment. My money is safe. It is not often that anyone succeeds in travelling a thousand versts so well.

I have grown so used to driving that now I don't feel like myself, and cannot believe that I am not in a chaise and that I don't hear the rattling and the jingling of the bells. It seems strange that when I go to bed I can stretch out my legs full length, and that my face is not covered with dust. But what is stranger still is that the bottle of brandy Kuvshinnikov gave me has not been broken, and that the brandy is still in it, every drop of it. I have vowed not to uncork it except on the shore of the Pacific.

I am sailing down the Shilka, which runs into the Amur at the Pokrovskaya Stanitsa. The river is not broader than the Psyol, it is even narrower. The shores are stony: there are crags and forests. It is absolutely wild.... We tack about to avoid foundering on a sandbank, or running our helm into the banks: steamers and barges often do so in the rapids. It's stifling. We have just stopped at Ust-Kara, where we have landed five or six convicts. There are mines here and a convict prison.

Yesterday we were at Nertchinsk. The little town is nothing to boast of, but one could live there.

And how are you, messieurs and mesdames? I know positively nothing about you. You might subscribe twopence each and send me a full telegram.

The steamer will stay the night at Gorbitsa. The nights here are foggy, sailing is dangerous, I shall send off this letter at Gorbitsa.

... I am going first class because my companions are in the second. I have got away from them. We have driven together (three in one chaise), we have slept together and are sick of each other, especially I of them.

My handwriting is very bad, shaky. That is because the steamer rocks. It's difficult to write.

I broke off here. I went to my lieutenants and had tea. They have both had a long sleep and were in a very cordial mood. One of them, Lieutenant N. (the surname jars upon my ear), is in the infantry; he is a tall, well-fed, loud-voiced Courlander, a great braggart and Hlestakov, who sings songs from every opera, but has no more ear than a smoked herring, an unlucky fellow who has squandered all the money for his travelling expenses, knows all Mickiewicz by heart, is ill-bred, far too unreserved, and babbles till it makes you sick. Like me, he is fond of talking about his uncles and aunts. The other lieutenant, M., a geographer, is a quiet, modest, thoroughly well-educated fellow. If it were not for N., I could travel with the other for a million versts without being bored. But with N., who intrudes into every conversation, the other bores me too.... I believe we are reaching Gorbitsa.

To-morrow I will make up the form of a telegram which you must send me to Sahalin. I will try to put all I want to know in thirty words, and you must try and keep strictly to the pattern.

The gad-flies bite.

TO N. A. LEIKIN.

GORBITSA, June 20, 1890.

Greetings, dear Nikolay Alexandrovitch!

I wrote you this as I approached Gorbitsa, one of the Cossack settlements on the banks of the Shilka, a tributary of the Amur. This is where I have got to. I am sailing down the Amur.

I sent you a letter from Irkutsk. Did you get it? Since then more than a week has passed, in the course of which I have crossed Lake Baikal and driven through Transbaikalia. Lake Baikal is wonderful, and the Siberians may well call it a sea instead of a lake. The water is extraordinarily transparent, so that one can see through it as through air; the colour is a soft turquoise very agreeable to the eye. The banks are mountainous, and covered with forests; it is all impenetrable wildness without a break anywhere.

There are great numbers of bears, wild goats, and wild creatures of all sorts, who spend their time living in the Taiga and eating one another. I spent two days and nights on the shore of Lake Baikal.

It was still and hot when I was sailing.

Transbaikalia is splendid. It is a mixture of Switzerland, the Don, and Finland.

I have driven with horses more than four thousand versts. My journey was entirely successful. I was in good health all the time, and lost nothing of my luggage but a penknife. I can wish no one a better journey. The journey is absolutely free from danger, and all the tales of escaped convicts, of night attacks, and so on are nothing but legends, traditions of the remote past. A revolver is an entirely superfluous article. Now I am sitting in a first-class cabin, and feel as though I were in Europe. I feel in the mood one is in after passing an examination. A whistle!—that's Gorbitsa.

The banks of the Shilka are picturesque like stage scenes but, alas! there is something oppressive in this complete absence of human beings. It is like a cage without a bird.

TO HIS SISTER.

June 21, 1890.

6 o'clock in the evening, not far from the Stanitsa Pokrovskaya.

We ran upon a rock, stove a hole in the steamer, and are now undergoing repairs. We are aground on a sandbank and pumping out water. On the left is the Russian bank, on the right the Chinese. If I were back at home now I should have the right to boast: "Though I have not been in China I have seen China only twenty feet off." We are to stay the night in Pokrovskaya. We shall make up a party to see the place.

If I were a millionaire I should certainly have a steamer of my own on the Amur. It is a fine, interesting country. I advise Yegor Mihailovitch not to go to Tuapse but here; there are here by the way neither tarantulas nor phalangas. On the Chinese side there is a sentry post—a small hut; sacks of flour are piled up on the bank, ragged Chinamen are dragging the sacks on barrows to the hut. And beyond is the dense, endless forest.

Some schoolgirls are travelling with us from Irkutsk—Russian faces, but not good-looking.

POKROVSKAYA STANITSA,

June 23, 1890.

I have told you already we are aground on a sandbank. At Ust-Stryelka, where the Shilka joins the Argun (see map), the steamer went aground in two and a half feet of water, struck a rock, and stove in several holes in its side and, the hold filling with water, the steamer sank to the bottom. They began pumping out water and putting on patches; a naked sailor crawled into the hold, stood up to his neck in water, and tried the holes with his heels. Each hole was covered on the inside with cloth smeared with grease: they lay a board on the top, and stuck a support upon the latter which pressed against the ceiling like a column. Such is the repairing. They were pumping from five o'clock in the evening till night, but still the water did not abate: they had to put off the work till morning. In the morning they discovered some more holes, and began patching and pumping again. The sailors pump while we, the general public, pace up and down the decks, criticize, eat, drink, and sleep; the captain and his mate do the same as the general public, and seem in no hurry. On the right is the Chinese bank, on the left is the stanitsa, Pokrovskaya, with the Cossacks of the Amur; if one likes one can stay in Russia, if one likes one can go into China, there is nothing to hinder one. It is insufferably hot in the daytime, so that one has to put on a silk shirt. They give us dinner at twelve o'clock, supper at seven.

Unluckily the steamer *Vyestnik* coming the other way with a crowd of passengers is approaching the stanitsa. The *Vyestnik* cannot go on either, and both steamers stay stock-still. There is a military band on the *Vyestnik*, consequently there has been a regular festival. All yesterday the band was playing on deck to the entertainment of the captain and sailors, and consequently to the delay of the repairing. The feminine half of the public were highly delighted; a band, officers, naval men ... oh! The schoolgirls were particularly pleased. Yesterday evening we walked about the Cossack settlement, where the same band, hired by the Cossacks, was playing. Today we are continuing the repairs.

The captain promises that we shall start after dinner, but he promises it listlessly, gazing away into space—obviously he does not mean it. We are in no haste. When I asked a passenger, "Whenever are we going on?" he asked, "Why, aren't you all right here!"

And that's true. Why not stay, as long as we are not bored?

The captain, his mate, and his agent are the acme of politeness. The Chinese in the third class are good-natured and funny. Yesterday a Chinaman sat on the deck and sang something very mournful in a falsetto voice; as he did so his profile was funnier than any caricature. Everybody looked at him and laughed, while he took not the slightest notice. He sang falsetto and then began singing tenor. My God, what a voice! It was like the bleat of a sheep or a calf. The Chinese remind me of good-natured tame animals, their pigtails are long and black like Natalya Mihailovna's. Apropos of tame animals, there's a tame fox cub living in the toilet-room. It sits and looks on as one washes. If it sees no one for a long time it begins to whine.

What strange conversations one hears! They talk of nothing but gold, the mines, the Volunteer Fleet and Japan. In Pokrovskaya all the peasants and even the priests mine for gold. The exiles follow the same occupation and grow rich as quickly as they grow poor. There are people who look like artizans and who never drink anything but champagne, and walk to the tavern on red baize which is laid down from their hut to the tavern.

The Amur country is exceedingly interesting. Highly original. The life here is such as people have no conception of in Europe. It reminds me of American stories. The shores of the Amur are so wild, original, and luxuriant that one longs to live there all one's life. I am writing these last few lines on the 25th of June. The steamer rocks and prevents my writing properly. We are moving again. I have come a thousand versts down the Amur already, and have seen a million gorgeous landscapes; I feel giddy with ecstasy.... It's marvellous scenery, and how hot! What warm nights! There is a mist in the mornings but it is warm.

I look through an opera-glass at the shore and see a prodigious number of ducks, geese, grebes, herons and all sorts of creatures with long beaks. This would be the place to take a summer villa in! At a little place called Reinov a goldminer asked me to see his sick wife. As I was leaving him he thrust into my hands a roll of notes. I felt ashamed. I was beginning to refuse and thrust it back, saying that I was very rich myself; we talked together for a long time trying to persuade each other, and yet in the end fifteen roubles remained in my hands. Yesterday a goldminer with the face of Petya Polevaev dined in my cabin; at dinner he drank champagne instead of water, and treated us to it.

The villages here are like those on the Don. There is a difference in the buildings but nothing to speak of. The inhabitants don't keep the fasts, and eat meat even in Holy Week; the girls smoke cigarettes, and old women smoke pipes—it is the correct thing. It's strange to see peasants with cigarettes! And what liberalism! Oh, what liberalism!

The air on the steamer is positively red-hot with the talk that goes on. People are not afraid to talk aloud here. There's no one to arrest them and nowhere to exile them to, so you can be as liberal as you like. The people for the most part are independent, self-reliant, and logical. If there is any misunderstanding at Ust-Kara, where the convicts work (among them many politicals who don't work), all the Amur region is in revolt. It is not the thing to tell tales. An escaped convict can travel freely on the steamer to the ocean, without any fear of the captain's giving him up. This is partly due to the absolute indifference to everything that is done in Russia. Everybody says: "What is it to do with me?"

I forgot to tell you that in Transbaikalia the drivers are not Russians but Buriats. A funny people! Their horses are regular vipers; they could never be harnessed without trouble—more furious than fire-brigade horses. While the trace-horse is being harnessed, its legs are hobbled; as soon as they are set free the chaise goes flying to the devil, so that one holds one's breath. If one does not hobble a horse while it is being harnessed, it kicks, knocks bits out of the shaft with its hoofs, tears the harness, and behaves like a young devil that has been caught by the horns.

June 26.

We are getting near Blagoveshtchensk. Be well and merry, and don't get used to being without me. No doubt you have already? Respectful greetings to all, and a friendly kiss.

I am perfectly well.

TO A. S. SUVORIN.

BLAGOVESHTCHENSK, June 27, 1890.

The Amur is a very fine river; I have gained more from it than I could have expected, and I have been wishing for a long time to share my transports with you, but the rascally steamer has been rocking all the seven days I have been on it, and prevents me writing properly. Moreover, I am quite incapable of describing anything so beautiful as the shores of the Amur; I am at a complete loss before them, and recognise my bankruptcy. How is one to describe them? ... Rocks, crags, forests, thousands of ducks, herons and all sorts of beaked gentry, and absolute wilderness. On the left the Russian shore, on the right the Chinese. I can look at Russia or China as I please. China is as deserted and wild as Russia: villages and sentinels' huts are rare. Everything in my head is muddled; and no wonder, your Excellency! I have come more than a thousand versts down the Amur and seen a million landscapes, and you know before the Amur there was Lake Baikal, Transbaikalia.... Truly I have seen such riches and had so much enjoyment that death would have no terrors now. The people on the Amur are original, their life is interesting, unlike ours. They talk of gold, gold, gold, and nothing else. I am in a stupid state, I feel no inclination to write, and I write shortly, piggishly; to-day I sent you four papers about Yenissey and the Taiga, later on I will send you something about Lake Baikal, Transbaikalia, and the Amur. Don't throw away these sheets; I will collect them, and they will serve as notes from which I can tell you what I don't know how to put on paper.

To-day I changed into the steamer *Muravyov*, which they say does not rock; maybe I shall write.

I am in love with the Amur; I should be glad to spend a couple of years on it. There is beauty, space, freedom and warmth. Switzerland and France have never known such freedom. The lowest convict breathes more freely on the Amur than the highest general in Russia. If you lived here, you would write a great deal of good stuff and delight the public, but I am not equal to it.

One begins to meet Chinamen at Irkutsk, and here they are common as flies. They are the most good-natured people. If Nastya and Borya made the acquaintance of the Chinese, they would leave donkeys alone, and transfer their affection to the Chinese. They are charming tame animals.

... When I invited a Chinaman to the refreshment bar to treat him to vodka, before drinking it he held out the glass to me, the bar-keeper, the waiters, and said: "Taste." That's the Chinese ceremonial. He did not drink it off as we do, but drank it in sips, eating something between each sip, and then, to express his gratitude, gave me several Chinese coins. An awfully polite people. They are dressed poorly, but beautifully; they eat daintily, with ceremony....

TO HIS SISTER.

THE STEAMER "MURAVYOV," June 29, 1890.

Meteors are flying in my cabin—these are luminous beetles that look like electric sparks. Wild goats swim across the Amur in the day-time. The flies here are huge. I am sharing my cabin with a Chinaman—Son-Luli—who is constantly telling me how in China for the merest trifle it is "off with his head." Last night he got drunk with opium, and was talking in his sleep all night and preventing me from sleeping. On the 27th I walked about the Chinese town Aigun. Little by little I seem gradually to be stepping into a fantastic world. The steamer rocks, it is hard to write.

To-morrow I shall reach Habarovsk. The Chinaman began to sing from music written on his fan.

TELEGRAM TO HIS MOTHER.

SAHALIN, July 11, 1890.

Arrived well, telegraph Sahalin.—CHEKHOV.

TELEGRAM TO HIS MOTHER.

SAHALIN, September 27, 1890.

Well. Shall arrive shortly.—CHEKHOV.

TO A. S. SUVORIN.

THE STEAMER "BAIKAL," September 11, 1890.

Greetings! I am sailing on the Gulf of Tartary from the north of Sahalin to the south. I am writing; and don't know when this letter will reach you. I am well, though I see on all sides glaring at me the green eyes of cholera which has laid a trap for me. In Vladivostok, in Japan, in Shanghai, Tchifu, Suez, and even in the moon, I fancy—everywhere there is cholera, everywhere quarantine and terror.... They expect the cholera in Sahalin and keep all vessels in quarantine. In short, it is a bad lookout. Europeans are dying at Vladivostok, among others the wife of a general has died.

I have spent just two months in the north of Sahalin. I was received by the local administration very amicably, though Galkin had not written a single word about me. Neither Galkin nor the Baroness V., nor any of the other genii I was so foolish as to appeal to for help, turned out of the slightest use to me; I had to act on my own initiative.

The Sahalin general, Kononovitch, is a cultivated and gentlemanly man. We soon got on together, and everything went off well. I am bringing some papers with me from which you will see that I was put on the most agreeable footing from the first. I have seen *everything*, so that the question is not now *what* I have seen, but how I have seen it.

I don't know what will come of it, but I have done a good deal. I have got enough material for three dissertations. I got up every morning at five o'clock and went to bed late; and all day long was on the strain from the thought that there was still so much I hadn't done; and now that I have done with the convict system, I have the feeling that I have seen everything but have not noticed the elephants.

By the way, I had the patience to make a census of the whole Sahalin population. I made the round of all the settlements, went into every hut and talked to everyone; I made use of the card system in making the census, and I have already registered about ten thousand convicts and settlers. In other words, there is not in Sahalin one convict or settler who has not talked with me. I was particularly successful with the census of the children, on which I am building great hopes.

I dined at Landsberg's; I sat in the kitchen of the former Baroness Gembruk.... I visited all the celebrities. I was present at a flogging, after which I dreamed for three or four nights of the executioner and the revolting accessories. I have talked to men who were chained to trucks. Once when I was drinking tea in a mine, Borodavkin, once a Petersburg merchant who was convicted of arson, took a teaspoon out of his pocket and gave it to me, and the long and the short of it is that I have upset my nerves and have vowed not to come to Sahalin again.

I should write more to you, but there is a lady in the cabin who giggles and chatters unceasingly. I haven't the strength to write. She has been laughing and cackling ever since yesterday evening.

This letter will go across America, but I shall go probably not across America. Everyone says that the American way is duller and more expensive.

To-morrow I shall see Japan, the Island of Matsmai. Now it is twelve o'clock at night. It is dark on the sea, the wind is blowing. I don't understand how the steamer can go on and find its direction when one can't see a thing, and above all in such wild, little-known waters as those in the Gulf of Tartary.

When I remember that I am ten thousand versts away from my world I am overcome with apathy. It seems I shall not be home for a hundred years.... God give you health and all blessings. I feel dreary.

TO HIS MOTHER.

SAHALIN, October 6, 1890.

My greetings, dear mother!

I write you this letter almost on the eve of my departure for Russia. Every day we expect a steamer of the Volunteer Fleet, and cherish hopes that it will not come later than the 10th of October. I send this letter to Japan, whence it will go by Shanghai or America. I am living at the station of Korsakovo, where there is neither telegraph nor post, and which is not visited by ships oftener than once a fortnight. Yesterday a steamer arrived and brought me from the north a pile of letters and telegrams. From the letters I learn that Masha likes the Crimea, I believe she will like the Caucasus better still....

———————————

Strange, with you it has been cold and rainy, while in Sahalin from the day of my arrival till to-day it has been bright warm weather: there is slight cold with hoar-frost in the mornings, the snow is white on one of the mountains, but the earth is still green, the leaves have not fallen, and all the vegetation is still as flourishing as at a summer villa in May. There you have Sahalin!

———————————

At midnight yesterday I heard the roar of a steamer. Everybody jumped out of bed: hurrah! the steamer has arrived! We dressed and went out with lanterns to the harbour; we gazed into the distance; there really was a steamer.... The majority of voices decided that it was the *Petersburg*, on which I am to go to Russia. I was overjoyed. We got into a boat and rowed to the steamer. We went on and on, till at last we saw in the mist the dark hulk of a steamer. One of us shouted in a hoarse voice asking the name of the vessel. And we received the answer "the *Baikal*." Tfoo! anathema! what a disappointment! I am I homesick, and weary of Sahalin. Here for the last three months I have seen no one but convicts or people who can talk of nothing but penal servitude, the lash, and the convicts. A depressing existence. One longs to get quickly to Japan and from there to India.

I am quite well, except for flashes in my eye from which I often suffer now, after which I always have a bad headache. I had the flashes in my eye yesterday and to-day, and so I am writing this with a headache and heaviness all over.

At the station the Japanese General Kuse-San lives with his two secretaries, good friends of mine. They live like Europeans. To-day the local authorities visited them in state to present decorations that had been conferred on them; and I, too, went with my headache and had to drink champagne.

Since I have been in the south I have three times driven to Nay Race where the real ocean waves break. Look at the map and you will see at once on the south coast that poor dismal Nay Race. The waves cast up a boat with six American whalefishers, who had been shipwrecked off the coast of Sahalin; they are living now at the station and solemnly walk about the streets. They are waiting for the *Petersburg* and will sail with me.

I am not bringing you furs, there are none in Sahalin. Keep well and Heaven guard you all.

I am bringing you all presents. The cholera in Vladivostok and Japan is over.

TO A. S. SUVORIN.

MALAYA DMITROVKA, MOSCOW, December 9.

... Hurrah! Here at last I am sitting at my table at home! I pray to my faded penates and write to you. I have now a happy feeling as though I had not been away from home at all. I am well and thriving to the marrow of my bones. Here's a very brief report for you. I was in Sahalin not two months, as you have printed, but three months plus two days. I worked at high pressure. I made a full and minute census of the whole of Sahalin's population, and saw *everything* except the death penalty. When we see each other I will show you a whole trunkful of stuff about the convicts which is very valuable as raw material. I know a very great deal now, but I have brought away a horrid feeling. While I was staying in Sahalin, I only had a bitter feeling in my inside as though from rancid butter; and now, as I remember it, Sahalin seems to me a perfect hell. For two months I worked intensely, putting my back into it; in the third month I began to feel ill from the bitterness I have spoken of, from boredom, and the thought that the cholera would come from Vladivostok to Sahalin, and that so I was in danger of having to winter in the convict settlement. But, thank God! the cholera ceased, and on the 13th of October the steamer bore me away from Sahalin. I have been in Vladivostok. About the Primorsky Region and our Eastern sea-coast with its fleets, its problems, and its Pacific dreams altogether, I have only one thing to tell of: its crying poverty! Poverty, ignorance, and worthlessness, that might drive one to despair. One honest man for ninety-nine thieves, that are blackening the name of Russia.... We passed Japan because the cholera was there, and so I have not bought you anything Japanese, and the five hundred you gave me for your purchases I have spent on my own needs, for which you have, by law, the right to send me to a settlement in Siberia. The first foreign port we reached was Hong Kong. It is an exquisite bay. The traffic on the sea was such as I had never seen before even in pictures; excellent roads, trams, a railway to the mountains, a museum, botanical gardens; wherever you look you see the tenderest solicitude on the part of the English for the men in their service; there is even a club for the sailors. I went about in a jinrickshaw—that is, carried by men—bought all sorts of rubbish of the Chinese, and was moved to indignation at hearing my Russian fellow-travellers abuse the English for exploiting the natives. I thought: Yes, the English exploit the Chinese, the Sepoys, the Hindoos, but they do give them roads, aqueducts, museums, Christianity, and what do you give them?

When we left Hong Kong the boat began to rock. The steamer was empty and lurched through an angle of thirty-eight degrees, so that we were afraid it would upset. I am not subject to sea-sickness: that discovery was very agreeable to me. On the way to Singapore we threw two corpses into the sea. When one sees a dead man, wrapped in sailcloth, fly, turning somersaults in the water, and remembers that it is several miles to the bottom, one feels frightened, and for some reason begins to fancy that one will die oneself and will be thrown into the sea. Our horned cattle have fallen sick. Through the united verdict of Dr. Stcherbak and your humble servant, the cattle have been killed and thrown into the sea.

I have no clear memory of Singapore as, for some reason, I felt very sad while I was driving about it, and was almost weeping. Next after it comes Ceylon—an earthly Paradise. There in that Paradise I went more than a hundred versts on the railway and gazed at palm forests and bronze women to my heart's content.... After Ceylon we sailed for thirteen days and nights without stopping and were all stupid from boredom. I bear the heat well. The Red Sea is depressing; I felt touched as I gazed at Sinai.

God's world is a good place. The one thing not good in it is we. How little justice and humility there is in us. How little we understand true patriotism! A drunken, broken-down debauchee of a husband loves his wife and children, but of what use is that love? We, so we are told in our own newspapers, love our great motherland, but how does that love express itself? Instead of knowledge—insolence and immeasurable conceit; instead of work—sloth and swinishness; there is no justice, the conception of honour does not go beyond "the honour of the uniform"—the uniform which is so commonly seen adorning the prisoner's dock in our courts.

Work is what is wanted, and the rest can go to the devil. First of all we must be just, and all the rest will be added unto us,

I have a passionate desire to talk to you. My soul is in a ferment. I want no one else but you, for it is only with you I can talk.

How glad I am that everything was managed without Galkin-Vrasskoy's help. He didn't write one line about me, and I turned up in Sahalin utterly unknown.

MOSCOW,

December 24, 1890.

I believe in Koch and in spermine and praise God for it. All that—that is the kochines, spermines, and so on—seem to the public a kind of miracle that leaped forth from some brain, after the fashion of Pallas Athene; but people who have a closer acquaintance with the facts know that they are only the natural sequel of what has been done during the last twenty years. A great deal has been done, my dear fellow! Surgery alone has done so much that one is fairly dumbfounded at it. To one who is studying medicine now, the time before twenty years ago seems simply pitiable. My dear friend, if I were offered the choice between the "ideals" of the renowned "sixties," or the very poorest Zemstvo hospital of to-day, I should, without a moment's hesitation, choose the second.

Will kochine cure syphilis? It's possible. But as for cancer, you must allow me to have my doubts. Cancer is not a microbe; it's a tissue, growing in the wrong place, and like a noxious weed smothering all the neighbouring tissues. If N.'s uncle feels better, that is, because the microbes of erysipelas—that is, the elements that produce the disease of erysipelas—form a component part of kochine. It was observed long ago that with the development of erysipelas, the growth of malignant tumours is temporarily checked.

It's a strange business—while I was travelling to Sahalin and back I felt perfectly well, but now, at home, the devil knows what is happening to me. My head is continually aching, I have a feeling of languor all over, I am

- 139 -

quickly exhausted, apathetic, and worst of all, my heart is not beating regularly. My heart is continually stopping for a few seconds....

MOSCOW,

January, 1891.

I shall probably come to Petersburg on the 8th of January.... Since by February I shall not have a farthing, I must make haste and finish the novel [Footnote: "The Duel."] I've begun. There is something in the novel about which I must talk to you and ask your advice.

I spent Christmas in a horrible way. To begin with, I had palpitations of the heart; secondly, my brother Ivan came to stay and was ill with typhoid, poor fellow; thirdly, after my Sahalin labours and the tropics, my Moscow life seems to me now so petty, so bourgeois, and so dull, that I feel ready to bite; fourthly, working for my daily bread prevents my giving up my time to Sahalin; fifthly, my acquaintances bother me, and so on.

The poet Merezhkovsky has been to see me twice; he is a very intelligent man.

How sorry I am you did not see my mongoose. It is a wonderful creature.

TO HIS SISTER.

ST. PETERSBURG, January 14, 1891.

Unforeseen circumstances have kept me a few days longer. I am alive and well. There is no news. I saw Tolstoy's "The Power of Darkness" the other day, though. I have been to Ryepin's studio. What else? Nothing else. It's dull, in fact.

I went to-day to a dog-show; I went there with Suvorin, who at the moment I am writing these lines is standing by the table and asking me to write and tell you that I have been to the dog-show with the famous dog Suvorin....

January, later.

I am alive and well, I have no palpitations, I've no money either, and everything is going well.

I am paying visits and seeing acquaintances. I have to talk about Sahalin and India. It's horribly boring.

... Anna Ivanovna is as nice as ever, Suvorin talks as incessantly as ever.

I receive the most boring invitations to the most boring dinners. It seems I must make haste and get back to Moscow, as they won't let me work here.

Hurrah, we are avenged! To make up for our being so bored, the cotton ball has yielded 1,500 roubles clear profit, in confirmation of which I enclose a cutting from a newspaper.

If anything is collected for the benefit of the Sahalin schools, let me know at once.

How is my mongoose? Don't forget to give him food and drink, and beat him without mercy when he jumps on the table. Does he eat people? [Footnote: A naive question asked by a lady of Chekhov's acquaintance.]

Write how Ivan is....

January, later.

I am tired as a ballet dancer after five acts and eight tableaux. Dinners, letters which I am too lazy to answer, conversations and imbecilities of all sorts. I have to go immediately to dine in Vassilyevsky Ostrov, and I am bored and ought to work.

I'll stay another three days and see whether the ballet will go on the same, then I shall go home, or to see Ivan.

I am surrounded by a thick atmosphere of ill-feeling, extremely vague and to me incomprehensible. They feed me with dinners and pay me the vulgarest compliments, and at the same time they are ready to devour me.

What for? The devil only knows. If I were to shoot myself I should thereby provide the greatest gratification to nine-tenths of my friends and admirers. And how pettily they express their petty feelings!

... My greetings to Lydia Yegorovna Mizinov. I expect a programme from her. Tell her not to eat farinaceous food and to avoid Levitan. A better admirer than me she will not find in her Town Council nor in higher society.

January 16, 1891.

I have the honour to congratulate you and the hero of the name-day; [Footnote: It was the name-day of Chekhov himself.] I wish you and him health and prosperity, and above all that the mongoose should not break the crockery or tear the wall-paper. I shall celebrate my name-day at the Maly Yaroslavets restaurant, from the restaurant to the benefit performance, from the benefit performance to the restaurant again.

I am working, but with very great difficulty. No sooner have I written a line than the bell rings and someone comes in to talk to me about Sahalin. It's simply awful! ...

I have found Drishka. It appears that she is living in the same house as I am. She ran away from Moscow to Petersburg under romantic circumstances: she meant to marry a lawyer, plighted her troth to him, but an army captain turned up, and so on; she had to run away or the lawyer would have shot both Drishka and the captain with a pistol loaded with cranberries. She is prospering and is the same lively rogue as ever. I went to Svobodin's name-day party with her yesterday. She sang gipsy songs, and created such a sensation that all the great men kissed her hand.

Rumours have reached me that Lidia Stahievna is going to be married *par depit*. Is it true? Tell her that I shall carry her off from her husband *par depit*. I am a violent man.

Has not anything been collected for the benefit of the Sahalin schools? Let me know....

TO A. F. KONI.

PETERSBURG, January 16, 1891.

DEAR SIR, ANATOLY FYODOROVITCH,

I did not hasten to answer your letter because I am not leaving Petersburg before next Saturday. I am sorry I have not been to see Madame Naryshkin, but I think I had better defer my visit till my book has come out, when I shall be able to turn more freely to the material I have. My brief Sahalin past looms so immense in my imagination that when I want to speak about it I don't know where to begin, and it always seems to me that I have not said what was wanted.

I will try and describe minutely the position of the children and young people in Sahalin. It is exceptional. I saw starving children, I saw girls of thirteen prostitutes, girls of fifteen with child. Girls begin to live by prostitution from twelve years old, sometimes before menstruation has begun. Church and school exist only on paper, the children are educated by their environment and the convict surroundings. Among other things I have noted down a conversation with a boy of ten years old. I was making the census of the settlement of Upper Armudano; all the inhabitants are poverty-stricken, every one of them, and have the reputation of being desperate gamblers at the game of shtoss. I go into a hut; the people are not at home; on a bench sits a white-haired, round-shouldered, bare-footed boy; he seems lost in thought. We begin to talk.

I. "What is your father's second name?"

He. "I don't know."

I. "How is that? You live with your father and don't know what his name is? Shame!"

He. "He is not my real father."

I. "How is that?"

He. "He is living with mother."

I. "Is your mother married or a widow?"

He. "A widow. She followed her husband here."

I. "What has become of her husband, then?"

He. "She killed him."

I. "Do you remember your father?"

He. "No, I don't, I am illegitimate. I was born when mother was at Kara."

On the Amur steamer going to Sahalin, there was a convict with fetters on his legs who had murdered his wife. His daughter, a little girl of six, was with him. I noticed wherever the convict moved the little girl scrambled after him, holding on to his fetters. At night the child slept with the convicts and soldiers all in a heap together. I remember I was at a funeral in Sahalin. Beside the newly dug grave stood four convict bearers ex officio; the treasury clerk and I, in the capacity of Hamlet and Horatio, wandering about the cemetery; the dead woman's lodger, a Circassian, who had come because he had nothing better to do; and a convict woman who had come out of pity and had brought the dead woman's two children, one a baby, and the other, Alyoshka, a boy of four, wearing a woman's jacket and blue breeches with bright-coloured patches on the knees. It was cold and damp, there was water in the grave, the convicts were laughing. The sea was in sight. Alyoshka looked into the grave with curiosity; he tried to wipe his chilly nose, but the long sleeve of his jacket got into his way. When they began to fill in the grave I asked him: "Alyoshka, where is your mother?" He waved his hand with the air of a gentleman who has lost at cards, laughed, and said: "They have buried her!"

The convicts laughed, the Circassian turned and asked what he was to do with the children, saying it was not his duty to feed them.

Infectious diseases I did not meet with in Sahalin. There is very little congenital syphilis, but I saw blind children, filthy, covered with eruptions—all diseases that are evidence of neglect. Of course I am not going to settle the problem of the children. I don't know what ought to be done. But it seems to me that one will do nothing by means of philanthropy and what little is left of prison and other funds. To my thinking, to make something of great importance dependent upon charity, which in Russia always has a casual character, and on funds which do not exist, is pernicious. I should prefer it to be financed out of the government treasury.

TO A. S. SUVORIN.

MOSCOW, January 31, 1891.

At home I found depression. My nicest and most intelligent mongoose had fallen ill and was lying very quietly under a quilt. The little beast eats and drinks nothing. The climate has already laid its cold claw on it and means to kill it. What for?

We have received a dismal letter. In Taganrog we were on friendly terms with a well-to-do Polish family. The cakes and jam I ate in their house when I was a boy at school arouse in me now the most touching reminiscences; there used to be music, young ladies, home-made liqueurs, and catching goldfinches in the immense courtyard. The father had a post in the Taganrog customs and got into trouble. The investigation and trial ruined the family. There were two daughters and a son. When the elder daughter married a rascal of a Greek, the family took an orphan girl into the house to bring up. This little girl was attacked by disease of the knee and they amputated the leg. Then the son died of consumption, a medical student in his fourth year, an excellent fellow, a perfect Hercules, the hope of the family.... Then came terrible poverty.... The father took to wandering about the cemetery, longed to take to drink but could not: vodka simply made his head ache cruelly while his thoughts remained the same, just as sober and revolting. Now they write that the younger daughter, a beautiful, plump young girl, is consumptive.... The father writes to me of that and writes to me for a loan of *ten roubles*.... Ach!

I felt awfully unwilling to leave you, but still I am glad I did not remain another day—I went away and showed that I had strength of will. I am writing already. By the time you come to Moscow my novel [Footnote: "The Duel."] will be finished, and I will go back with you to Petersburg.

Tell Borya, Mitya, and Andrushka that I vituperate them. In the pocket of my greatcoat I found some notes on which was scrawled: "Anton Pavlovitch, for shame, for shame, for shame!" O pessimi discipuli! Utinam vos lupus devoret!

Last night I did not sleep, and I read through my "Motley Tales" for the second edition. I threw out about twenty stories.

MOSCOW,

February 5, 1891.

My mongoose has recovered and breaks crockery again with unfailing regularity.

I am writing and writing! I must own I was afraid that my Sahalin expedition would have put me out of the way of writing, but now I see that it is all right. I have written a great deal. I am writing diffusely a la Yasinsky. I want to get hold of a thousand roubles.

I shall soon begin to expect you. Are we going to Italy or not? We ought to.

In Petersburg I don't sleep at night, I drink and loaf about, but I feel immeasurably better than in Moscow. The devil only knows why it is so.

I am not depressed, because in the first place I am writing, and in the second, one feels that summer, which I love more than anything, is close at hand. I long to prepare my fishing tackle....

February 23.

Greetings, my dear friend.

Your telegram about the Tormidor upset me. I felt dreadfully attracted to Petersburg: now for the sake of Sardou and the Parisian visitors. But practical considerations pulled me up. I reflected that I must hurry on with my novel; that I don't know French, and so should only be taking up someone else's place in the box; that I have very little money, and so on. In short, as it seems to me now, I am a poor comrade, though apparently I acted sensibly.

My novel is progressing. It's all smooth, even, there is scarcely anything that is too long. But do you know what is very bad? There is no movement in my novel, and that frightens me. I am afraid it will be difficult to read to the middle, to say nothing of reading to the end. Anyway, I shall finish it. I shall bring Anna Pavlovna a copy on vellum paper to read in the bathroom. I should like something to sting her in the water, so that she would run out of the bathroom sobbing.

I was melancholy when you went away....

Send me some money. I have none and seem to have nowhere to borrow. By my reckoning I cannot under favourable circumstances get more than a thousand roubles from you before September. But don't send the money by post, as I can't bear going to post offices....

March 5.

We are going!!! I agree to go, where you like and when you like. My soul is leaping with delight. It would be stupid on my part not to go, for when would an opportunity come again? But, my dear friend, I leave you to weigh the following circumstances.

(1) My work is still far from being finished; if I put it by till May, I shall not be able to begin my Sahalin work before July, and that is risky. For my Sahalin impressions are already evaporating, and I run the risk of forgetting a great deal.

(2) I have absolutely no money. If without finishing my novel I take another thousand roubles for the tour abroad, and then for living after the tour, I shall get into such a tangle that the devil himself could not pull me out by the ears. I am not in a tangle yet because I am up to all sorts of dodges, and live more frugally than a mouse; but if I go abroad everything will go to the devil. My accounts will be in a mess and I shall get myself hopelessly in debt. The very thought of a debt of two thousand makes my heart sink.

There are other considerations, but they are all of small account beside that of money and work. And so, thoroughly digest my objections, put yourself into my skin for a moment, and decide, wouldn't it be better for me to stay at home? You will say all this is unimportant. But lay aside your point of view? and look at it from mine.

I await a speedy answer.

My novel [Footnote: "The Duel."] is progressing, but I have not got far.

I have been to the Kiselyovs'. The rooks are already arriving.

TO MADAME KISELYOV.

MOSCOW, March 11, 1891.

As I depart for France, Spain, and Italy, I beseech you, oh, Heavens, keep Babkino in good health and prosperity!

Yes, Marya Vladimirovna! As it is written in the scripture: he had not time to cry out, before a bear devoured him. So I had not time to cry out before an unseen power has drawn me again to the mysterious distance. To-day I am going to Petersburg, from there to Berlin, and so further.

Whether I climb Vesuvius or watch a bull-fight in Spain, I shall remember you in my holiest prayers. Good-bye.

I have been to a seminary and picked out a seminarist for Vassilisa. There were plenty with delicate feelings and responsive natures, but not one would consent. At first, especially when I told them that you sometimes had peas and radishes on your table, they consented; but when I accidentally let out that in the district captain's room there was a bedstead on which people were flogged, they scratched their heads and muttered that they must think it over. One, however, a pockmarked fellow called Gerasim Ivanovitch, with very delicate feelings and a responsive nature, is coming to see you in a day or two. I hope that Vassilisa and you will make him welcome. Snatch the chance: it's a brilliant match. You can flog Gerasim Ivanovitch, for he told me: "I am immensely fond of violent sensations;" when he is with you you had better lock the cupboard where the vodka is kept and keep the windows open, as the seminary inspiration and responsiveness is perceptible at every minute.

"What a happy girl is Vassilisa!"

Idiotik has not been to see me yet.

The hens peck the cock. They must be keeping Lent, or perhaps the virtuous widows don't care for their new suitor.

They have brought me a new overcoat with check lining.

Well, be in Heaven's keeping, happy, healthy and peaceful. God give you all everything good. I shall come back in Holy Week. Don't forget your truly devoted,

ANTON CHEKHOV.

TO HIS SISTER.

PETERSBURG, March 16. Midnight.

I have just seen the Italian actress Duse in Shakespeare's *Cleopatra*. I don't know Italian, but she acted so well that it seemed to me I understood every word. A remarkable actress! I have never seen anything like it before. I gazed at that Duse and felt overcome with misery at the thought that we have to educate our temperaments and tastes on such wooden actresses as N. and her like, whom we call great because we have seen nothing better. Looking at Duse I understood why it is that the Russian theatre is so dull.

I sent three hundred roubles to-day, did you get them?

After Duse it was amusing to read the address I enclose. [Footnote: A newspaper cutting containing an address: From the Students of the Technological Institute of Harkov to M. M. Solovtsov, was enclosed.] My God, how low taste and a sense of justice have sunk! And these are the students—the devil take them! Whether it is Solovtsov or whether it is Salvini, it's all the same to them, both equally "stir a warm response in the hearts of the young." They are worth a farthing, all those hearts.

We set off for Warsaw at half-past one to-morrow. My greetings to all, even the mongooses, though they don't deserve it. I will write.

VIENNA,

March 20, 1891.

MY DEAR CZECHS,

I write to you from Vienna, which I reached yesterday at four o'clock in the afternoon. Everything went well on the journey. From Warsaw to Vienna I travelled like a railway Nana in a luxurious compartment of the "Societe Internationale des Wagons-Lits." Beds, looking-glasses, huge windows, rugs, and so on.

Ah, my dears, if you only knew how nice Vienna is! It can't be compared with any of the towns I have seen in my life. The streets are broad and elegantly paved, there are numbers of boulevards and squares, the houses have always six or seven storeys, and shops—they are not shops, but a perfect delirium, a dream! There are myriads of neckties alone in the windows! Such amazing things made of bronze, china, and leather! The churches are huge, but they do not oppress one by their hugeness; they caress the eye, for it seems as though they are woven of lace. St. Stephen and the Votiv-Kirche are particularly fine. They are not like buildings, but like cakes for tea. The parliament, the town hall, and the university are magnificent. It is all magnificent, and I have for the first time realized, yesterday and to-day, that architecture is really an art. And here the art is not seen in little bits, as with us, but stretches over several versts. There are numbers of monuments. In every side street there is sure to be a bookshop. In the windows of the bookshops there are Russian books to be seen—not, alas, the works of Albov, of Barantsevitch, and of Chekhov, but of all sorts of anonymous authors who write and publish abroad. I saw "Renan," "The

Mysteries of the Winter Palace," and so on. It is strange that here one is free to read anything and to say what one likes. Understand, O ye peoples, what the cabs are like here! The devil take them! There are no droshkys, but they are all new, pretty carriages with one and often two horses. The horses are splendid. On the box sit dandies in top-hats and reefer jackets, reading the newspaper, all politeness and readiness to oblige.

The dinners are good. There is no vodka; they drink beer and fairly good wine. There is one thing that is nasty: they make you pay for bread. When they bring the bill they ask, *Wie viel brodchen?*—that is, how many rolls have you devoured? And you have to pay for every little roll.

The women are beautiful and elegant. Indeed, everything is diabolically elegant.

I have not quite forgotten German. I understand, and am understood.

When we crossed the frontier it was snowing. In Vienna there is no snow, but it is cold all the same.

I am homesick and miss you all, and indeed I am conscience-stricken, too, at deserting you all again. But there, never mind! I shall come back and stay at home for a whole year. I send my greetings to everyone, everyone.

I wish you all things good; don't forget me with my many transgressions. I embrace you, I bless you, send my greetings and remain,

Your loving

A. CHEKHOV.

Everyone who meets us recognises that we are Russians, and stares not at my face, but at my grizzled cap. Looking at my cap they probably think I am a very rich Russian Count.

TO HIS BROTHER IVAN.

VENICE, March 24, 1891.

I am now in Venice. I arrived here two days ago from Vienna. One thing I can say: I have never in my life seen a town more marvellous than Venice. It is perfectly enchanting, brilliance, joy, life. Instead of streets and roads there are canals; instead of cabs, gondolas. The architecture is amazing, and there is not a single spot that does not excite some historical or artistic interest. You float in a gondola and see the palace of the Doges, the house where Desdemona lived, homes of various painters, churches. And in the churches there are sculptures and paintings such as we have never dreamed of. In fact it is enchantment.

All day from morning till night I sit in a gondola and glide along the streets, or I saunter about the famous St. Mark's Square. The square is as level and clean as a parquet floor. Here there is St. Mark's—something impossible to describe—the Palace of the Doges, and other buildings which make me feel as I do listening to part singing—I feel the amazing beauty and revel in it.

And the evenings! My God! One might almost die of the strangeness of it. One goes in a gondola ... warmth, stillness, stars.... There are no horses in Venice, and so there is a silence here as in the open country. Gondolas flit to and fro, ... then a gondola glides by, hung with lanterns. In it are a double-bass, violins, a guitar, a mandolin and cornet, two or three ladies, several men, and one hears singing and music. They sing from operas. What voices! One goes on a little further and again meets a boat with singers, and then again, and the air is full, till midnight, of the mingled strains of violins and tenor voices, and all sorts of heart-stirring sounds.

Merezhkovsky, whom I have met here, is off his head with ecstasy. For us poor and oppressed Russians it is easy to go out of our minds here in a world of beauty, wealth, and freedom. One longs to remain here for ever, and when one stands in the churches and listens to the organ one longs to become a Catholic.

The tombs of Canova and Titian are magnificent. Here they bury great artists like kings in churches; here they do not despise art as with us; the churches provide a shelter for pictures and statues however naked they may be.

In the Palace of the Doges there is a picture in which there are about ten thousand human figures.

To-day is Sunday. There will be a band playing in St. Mark's Square....

If you ever happen to come to Venice it will be the best thing in your life. You ought to see the glass here! Your bottles [Footnote: His brother Ivan was teaching in a school attached to a glass factory.] are so hideous compared with the things here, that it makes one sick to think of them.

I will write again; meanwhile, good-bye.

TO MADAME KISELYOV.

VENICE, March 25.

I am in Venice. You may put me in a madhouse. Gondolas, St. Mark's Square, water, stars, Italian women, serenades, mandolins, Falernian wine— in fact all is lost!

Don't remember evil against me.

The shade of the lovely Desdemona sends a smile to the District Captain.

Greetings to all. ANTONIO.

The Jesuits send their love to you.

TO HIS SISTER,

VENICE, March 25, 1891.

Bewitching blue-eyed Venice sends her greetings to all of you. Oh, signori and signorine, what an exquisite town this Venice is! Imagine a town consisting of houses and churches such as you have never seen; an intoxicating architecture, everything as graceful and light as the birdlike gondola. Such houses and churches can only be built by people possessed of immense artistic and musical taste and endowed with a lion-like temperament. Now imagine in the streets and alleys, instead of pavement, water; imagine that there is not one horse in the town; that instead of cabmen you see gondoliers on their wonderful boats, light, delicate long-beaked birds which scarcely seem to touch the water and tremble at the tiniest wave. And all from earth to sky bathed in sunshine.

There are streets as broad as the Nevsky, and others in which you can bar the way by stretching out your arms. The centre of the town is St. Mark's Square with the celebrated cathedral of the same name. The cathedral is magnificent, especially on the outside. Beside it is the Palace of the Doges where Othello made his confession before the senators.

In short, there is not a spot that does not call up memories and touch the heart. For instance, the little house where Desdemona lived makes an impression that is difficult to shake off. The very best time in Venice is the evening. First the stars; secondly, the long canals in which the lights and stars are reflected; thirdly, gondolas, gondolas, and gondolas; when it is dark they seem to be alive. Fourthly, one wants to cry because on all sides one hears music and superb singing. A gondola glides up hung with many-coloured lanterns; there is light enough for one to distinguish a double-bass, a guitar, a mandolin, a violin.... Then another gondola like it.... Men and women sing, and how they sing! It's quite an opera.

Fifthly, it's warm.

In short, the man's a fool who does not go to Venice. Living is cheap here. Board and lodging costs eighteen francs a week—that is, six roubles each or twenty-five roubles a month. A gondolier asks a franc for an hour—that is, thirty kopecks. Admission to the academies, museums, and so on, is free. The Crimea is ten times as expensive, and the Crimea beside Venice is a cuttle-fish beside a whale.

I am afraid Father is angry with me for not having said good-bye to him. I ask his forgiveness.

What glass there is here! what mirrors! Why am I not a millionaire! ... Next year let us all take a summer cottage in Venice.

The air is full of the vibration of church bells: my dear Tunguses, let us all embrace Catholicism. If only you knew how lovely the organs are in the churches, what sculptures there are here, what Italian women on their knees with prayer-books!

Keep well and don't forget me, a sinner.

A picturesque railway line, of which I have been told a great deal, runs from Vienna to Venice. But I was disappointed in the journey. The mountains, the precipices, and the snowy crests I have seen in the Caucasus and Ceylon are far more impressive than here. *Addio.*

VENICE,

March 26, 1891.

It is pelting cats and dogs. *Venetia bella* has ceased to be *bella*. The water excites a feeling of dejected dreariness, and one longs to hasten somewhere where there is sun.

The rain has reminded me of my raincoat (the leather one); I believe the rats have gnawed it a little. If they have, send it to be mended as soon as you can....

How is Signor Mongoose? I am afraid every day of hearing that he is dead.

In describing the cheapness of Venetian life yesterday, I overdid it a bit. It is Madame Merezhkovsky's fault; she told me that she and her husband paid only six francs per week each. But instead of per week, read per day. Anyway, it is cheap. The franc here goes as far as a rouble.

We are going to Florence.

May the Holy Mother bless you.

I have seen Titian's Madonna. It's very fine. But it is a pity that here fine works are mixed up side by side with worthless things, that have been preserved and not flung away simply from the spirit of conservatism all-present in such creatures of habit as *messieurs les hommes*. There are many pictures the long life of which is quite incomprehensible.

The house where Desdemona used to live is to let.

BOLOGNA,

March 28, 1891.

I am in Bologna, a town remarkable for its arcades, slanting towers, and Raphael's pictures of "Cecilia." We are going on to-day to Florence.

FLORENCE,

March 29, 1891.

I am in Florence. I am worn out with racing about to museums and churches. I have seen the Venus of Medici, and I think that if she were dressed in modern clothes she would be hideous, especially about the waist.

The sky is overcast, and Italy without sun is like a face in a mask.

P. S.—Dante's monument is fine.

FLORENCE,

March 30, 1891.

I am in Florence. To-morrow we are going to Rome. It's cold. We have the spleen. You can't take a step in Florence without coming to a picture-shop or a statue-shop.

P. S.—Send my watch to be mended.

TO MADAME KISELYOV.

ROME, April 1, 1891.

The Pope of Rome charges me to congratulate you on your name-day and wish you as much money as he has rooms. He has eleven thousand! Strolling about the Vatican I was nearly dead with exhaustion, and when I got home I felt that my legs were made of cotton-wool.

I am dining at the table d'hote. Can you imagine just opposite me are sitting two Dutch girls: one of them is like Pushkin's Tatyana, and the other like her sister Olga. I watch them all through dinner, and imagine a neat, clean little house with a turret, excellent butter, superb Dutch cheese, Dutch herrings, a benevolent-looking pastor, a sedate teacher, ... and I feel I should like to marry a Dutch girl and be depicted with her on a tea-tray beside the little white house.

I have seen everything and dragged myself everywhere I was told to go. What was offered me to sniff at, I sniffed at. But meanwhile I feel nothing but exhaustion and a craving for cabbage-soup and buckwheat porridge. I was enchanted by Venice, beside myself; but since I have left it, it has been nothing but Baedeker and bad weather.

Good-bye for now, Marya Vladimirovna, and the Lord God keep you. Humble respects from me and the other Pope to his Honour, Vassilisa and Elizaveta Alexandrovna.

Neckties are marvellously cheap here. I think I may take to eating them. They are a franc a pair.

To-morrow I am going to Naples. Pray that I may meet there a beautiful Russian lady, if possible a widow or a divorced wife.

In the guide-books it says that a love affair is an essential condition for a tour in Italy. Well, hang them all! I am ready for anything. If there must be a love affair, so be it.

Don't forget your sinful, but sincerely devoted,

ANTON CHEKHOV,

My respects to the starlings.

TO HIS SISTER.

ROME, April 1, 1891.

When I got to Rome I went to the post-office and did not find a single letter. Suvorin has got several letters. I made up my mind to pay you out, not to write to you at all—but there, God bless you! I am not so very fond of letters, but when one is travelling nothing is so bad as uncertainty. How have you settled the summer villa question? Is the mongoose alive? And so on and so on.

I have been in St. Peter's, in the Capitol, in the Coliseum, in the Forum—I have even been in a *cafe'-chantant*, but did not derive from it the gratification I had expected. The weather is a drawback, it is raining. I am hot in my autumn overcoat, and cold in my summer one.

Travelling is very cheap. One may pay a visit to Italy with only four hundred roubles and go back with purchases. If I were travelling alone or with Ivan, I should have brought away the conviction that travelling in Italy was much cheaper than travelling in the Caucasus. But alas! I am with the Suvorins.... In Venice we lived in the best of hotels like Doges; here in Rome we live like Cardinals, for we have taken a salon of what was once the palace of Cardinal Conti, now the Hotel Minerva; two huge drawing-rooms, chandeliers, carpets, open fireplaces, and all sorts of useless rubbish, costing us forty francs a day.

My back aches, and the soles of my feet burn from tramping about. It's awful how we walk!

It seems odd to me that Levitan did not like Italy. It's a fascinating country. If I were a solitary person, an artist, and had money, I should live here in the winter. You see, Italy, apart from its natural scenery and warmth, is the one country in which you feel convinced that art is really supreme over everything, and that conviction gives one courage.

NAPLES,

April 4, 1891.

I arrived in Naples, went to the post-office and found there five letters from home, for which I am very grateful to you all. Well done, relations! Even Vesuvius is so touched it has gone out.

Vesuvius hides its top in clouds and can only be seen well in the evening. By day the sky is overcast. We are staying on the sea-front and have a view of everything: the sea, Vesuvius, Capri, Sorrento.... We drove in the daytime up to the monastery of St. Martini: the view from here is such as I have never seen before, a marvellous panorama. I saw something like it at Hong Kong when I went up the mountain in the railway.

In Naples there is a magnificent arcade. And the shops!! The shops make me quite giddy. What brilliance! You, Masha, and you, Lika, would be rabid with delight.

There is a wonderful aquarium in Naples. There are even sharks and squids. When a squid (an octopus) devours some animals it's a revolting sight.

I have been to a barber's and watched a young man having his beard clipped for a whole hour. He was probably engaged to be married or else a cardsharper. At the barber's the ceiling and all the four walls were made of looking-glass, so that you feel that you are not at a hairdresser's but at the Vatican where there are eleven thousand rooms. They cut your hair wonderfully.

I shan't bring you any presents, as you don't write to me about the summer villa and the mongoose. I bought you a watch, Masha, but I have cast it to the swine. But there, God forgive you!

P.S.—I shall be back by Easter, come and meet me at the station.

NAPLES,

April 7, 1891.

Yesterday I went to Pompeii and went over it. As you know, it is a Roman town buried under the lava and ashes of Vesuvius in 79 A.D. I walked about the streets of the town and saw the houses, the temples, the theatre, the squares.... I saw and marvelled at the faculty of the Romans for combining simplicity with convenience and beauty. After viewing Pompeii, I lunched at a restaurant and then decided to go to Vesuvius. The excellent red wine I had drunk had a great deal to do with this decision. I had to ride on horseback to the foot of Vesuvius. I have in consequence to-day a sensation in some parts of my mortal frame as though I had been in the Third Division, and had there been flogged. What an agonising business it is climbing up Vesuvius! Ashes, mountains of lava, solid waves of molten minerals, mounds of earth, and every sort of abomination. You take one step forward and fall half a step back, the soles of your feet hurt you, your breathing is oppressed.... You go on and on and on, and it is still a long way to the top. You wonder whether to turn back, but you are ashamed to turn back, you would be laughed at. The ascent began at half-past two, and ended at six. The crater of Vesuvius is a great many yards in diameter. I stood on its edge and looked down as into a cup. The soil around, covered by a layer of sulphur, was smoking vigorously. From the crater rose white stinking smoke; spurts of hot water and red-hot stones fly out while Satan lies snoring under cover of the smoke. The noise is rather mixed, you hear in it the beating of breakers and the roar of thunder, and the rumble of the railway line and the falling of planks. It is very terrible, and at the same time one has an impulse to jump right into the crater. I believe in hell now. The lava has such a high temperature that copper coins melt in it.

Coming down was as horrid as going up. You sink up to your knees in ashes. I was fearfully tired. I went back on horseback through a little village and by houses; there was a glorious fragrance and the moon was shining. I sniffed, gazed at the moon, and thought of *her*—that is, of Lika L.

All the summer, noble gentlemen, we shall have no money, and the thought of that spoils my appetite. I have got into debt for a thousand for a tour, which I could have made *solo* for three hundred roubles. All my hopes now are in the fools of amateurs who are going to act my "Bear."

Have you taken a house for the holidays, signori? You treat me piggishly, you write nothing to me, and I don't know what's going on, and how things are at home.

Humble respects to you all. Take care of yourselves, and don't completely forget me.

MONTE CARLO,

April 13, 1891.

I am writing to you from Monte Carlo, from the very place where they play roulette. I can't tell you how thrilling the game is. First of all I won eighty francs, then I lost, then I won again, and in the end was left with a loss of forty francs. I have twenty francs left, I shall go and try my luck again. I have been here since the morning, and it is twelve o'clock at night. If I had money to spare I believe I should spend the whole year gambling and walking about the magnificent halls of the casino. It is interesting to watch the ladies who lose thousands. This morning a young lady lost 5000 francs. The tables with piles of gold are interesting too. In fact it is beyond all words. This charming Monte Carlo is extremely like a fine ... den of thieves. The suicide of losers is quite a regular thing.

Suvorin *fils* lost 300 francs.

We shall soon see each other. I am weary of wandering over the face of the earth. One must draw the line. My heels are sore as it is.

TO HIS BROTHER MIHAIL.

NICE, Monday in Holy Week, April, 1891.

We are staying in Nice, on the sea-front. The sun is shining, it is warm, green and fragrant, but windy. An hour's journey from Nice is the famous Monaco. There is Monte Carlo, where roulette is played. Imagine the rooms of the Hall of Nobility but handsomer, loftier and larger. There are big tables, and on the tables roulette—which I will describe to you when I get home. The day before yesterday I went over there, played and lost. The game is fearfully fascinating. After losing, Suvorin *fils* and I fell to thinking it over, and thought out a system which would ensure one's winning. We went yesterday, taking five hundred francs each; at the first staking I won two gold pieces, then again and again; my waistcoat pockets bulged with gold. I had in hand French money even of the year 1808, as well as Belgian, Italian, Greek, and Austrian coins.... I have never before seen so much gold and silver. I began playing at five o'clock and by ten I had not a single franc in my pocket, and the only thing left me was the satisfaction of knowing that I had my return ticket to Nice. So there it is, my friends! You will say, of course: "What a mean thing to do! We are so poor, while he out there plays roulette." Perfectly just, and I give you permission to slay me. But I personally am much pleased with myself. Anyway, now I can tell my grandchildren that I have played roulette, and know the feeling which is excited by gambling.

Beside the Casino where roulette is played there is another swindle—the restaurants. They fleece one frightfully and feed one magnificently. Every dish is a regular work of art, before which one is expected to bow one's knee in homage and to be too awe-stricken to eat it. Every morsel is rigged out with lots of artichokes, truffles, and nightingales' tongues of all sorts. And, good Lord! how contemptible and loathsome this life is with its artichokes, its palms, and its smell of orange blossoms! I love wealth and luxury, but the luxury here, the luxury of the gambling saloon, reminds one of a luxurious water-closet. There is something in the atmosphere that offends one's sense of decency and vulgarizes the scenery, the sound of the sea, the moon.

Yesterday—Sunday—I went to the Russian church here. What was peculiar was the use of palm-branches instead of willows; and instead of boy choristers a choir of ladies, which gives the singing an operatic effect. They put foreign money in the plate; the verger and beadle speak French, and so on....

Of all the places I have been in hitherto Venice has left me the loveliest memories. Rome on the whole is rather like Harkov, and Naples is filthy. And the sea does not attract me, as I got tired of it last November and December.

I feel as though I have been travelling for a whole year. I had scarcely got back from Sahalin when I went to Petersburg, and then to Petersburg again, and to Italy....

If I don't manage to get home by Easter, when you break the fast, remember me in your prayers, and receive my congratulations from a distance, and my assurance that I shall miss you all horribly on Easter night.

TO HIS SISTER.

PARIS, April 21, 1891.

To-day is Easter. So Christ is risen! It's my first Easter away from home.

I arrived in Paris on Friday morning and at once went to the Exhibition. Yes, the Eiffel Tower is very very high. The other exhibition buildings I saw only from the outside, as they were occupied by cavalry brought there in anticipation of disorders. On Friday they expected riots. The people flocked in crowds about the streets, shouting and whistling, greatly excited, while the police kept dispersing them. To disperse a big crowd a dozen policemen are sufficient here. The police make a combined attack, and the crowd runs like mad. In one of these attacks the honour was vouchsafed to me—a policeman caught hold of me under my shoulder, and pushed me in front of him.

There was a great deal of movement, the streets were swarming and surging. Noise, hubbub. The pavements are filled with little tables, and at the tables sit Frenchmen who feel as though they were at home in the street. A magnificent people. There is no describing Paris, though; I will put off the description of it till I get home.

I heard the midnight service in the Church of the Embassy....

I am afraid you have no money.

Misha, get my pince-nez mended, for the salvation of your soul! I am simply a martyr without spectacles. I went to the Salon and couldn't see half the pictures, thanks to my short sight. By the way, the Russian artists are far more serious than the French.... In comparison with the landscape painters I saw here yesterday Levitan is a king....

PARIS,

April 24.

A change again. One of the Russian sculptors living in Paris has undertaken to do a bust of Suvorin, and this will keep us till Saturday.

... How are you managing without money? Bear it till Thursday.

Imagine my delight. I was in the Chamber of Deputies just at the time of the sitting when the Minister for Internal Affairs was called to account for the irregularities which the government had ventured upon in putting down the riots in Fourmis (there were many killed and wounded). It was a stormy and extremely interesting sitting.

Men who tie boa-constrictors round their bodies, ladies who kick up to the ceiling, flying people, lions, *cafe'-chantants*, dinners and lunches begin to sicken me. It is time I was home. I am longing to work.

TO A. S. SUVORIN.

ALEXIN, May 7, 1891.

The summer villa is all right. There are woods and the Oka: it is far away in the wilds, it is warm, nightingales sing, and so on. It is quiet and peaceful, and in bad weather it will be dull and depressing here. After travelling abroad, life at a summer villa seems a little mawkish. I feel as though I had been taken prisoner and put into a fortress. But I am contented all the same. In Moscow I received from the Society of Dramatic Authors not two hundred roubles, as I expected, but three hundred. It's very kind on the part of fortune.

Well, my dear sir, I owe you, even if we adopt your reckoning, not less than eight hundred roubles. In June or July, when my money will be at the shop, I will write to Zandrok to send all that comes to me to you in Feodosia, and do not try and prevent me. I give you my word of honour that when I have paid my debts and settled with you, I'll accept a loan of 2,000 from you. Do not imagine that it is disagreeable to me to be in your debt. I lend other people money, and so I feel I have the right to borrow money, but I am afraid of getting into difficulties and the habit of being in debt. You know I owe your firm a devilish lot.

There is a fine view from my window. Trains are continually passing. There is a bridge across the Oka.

ALEXIN,

May 10, 1891.

Yes, you are right, my soul needs balsam. I should read now with pleasure, even with joy, something serious, not merely about myself but things in general. I pine for serious reading, and recent Russian criticism does not nourish but simply irritates me. I could read with enthusiasm something new about Pushkin or Tolstoy. That would be balsam for my idle mind.

I am homesick for Venice and Florence too, and am ready to climb Vesuvius again; Bologna has been effaced from my memory and grown dim. As for Nice and Paris, when I recall them "I look on my life with loathing."

In the last number of *The Messenger of Foreign Literature* there is a story by Ouida, translated from the English by our Mihail. Why don't I know foreign languages? It seems to me I could translate magnificently. When I read anyone else's translation I keep altering and transposing the words in my brain, and the result is something light, ethereal, like lacework.

On Mondays, Tuesdays, and Wednesdays I write my Sahalin book, on the other days, except Sunday, my novel, and on Sundays, short stories. I work with zest. The weather has been superb every day; the site of our summer villa is dry and healthy. There is a lot of woodland. There are a lot of fish and crayfish in the Oka. I see the trains and the steamers. Altogether if it were not for being somewhat cramped I should be very very much pleased with it.

I don't intend to get married. I should like to be a little bald old man sitting at a big table in a fine study....

ALEXIN,

May 13, 1891.

I am going to write you a Christmas story—that's certain. Two, indeed, if you like. I sit and write and write ...; at last I have set to work. I am only sorry that my cursed teeth are aching and my stomach is out of order.

I am a dilatory but productive author. By the time I am forty I shall have hundreds of volumes, so that I can open a bookshop with nothing but my own works. To have a lot of books and to have nothing else is a horrible disgrace.

My dear friend, haven't you in your library Tagantsev's "Criminal Law"? If you have, couldn't you send it me? I would buy it, but I am now "a poor relation"—a beggar and as poor as Sidor's goat. Would you telephone to your shop, too, to send me, on account of favours to come, two books: "The Laws relating to Exiles," and "The Laws relating to Persons under Police Control." Don't imagine that I want to become a procurator; I want these works for my Sahalin book. I am going to direct my attack chiefly against life sentences, in which I see the root of all the evils; and against the laws dealing with exiles, which are fearfully out of date and contradictory.

TO L. S. MIZINOV.

ALEXIN, May 17, 1891.

Golden, mother-of-pearl, and *fil d'Ecosse* Lika! The mongoose ran away the day before yesterday, and will never come back again. It is dead. That is the first thing.

The second thing is, that we are moving our residence to the upper storey of the house of B.K.—the man who gave you milk to drink and forgot to give you strawberries. We will let you know the day we move in due time. Come to smell the flowers, to walk, to fish, and to blubber. Ah, lovely Lika! When you bedewed my right shoulder with your tears (I have taken out the spots with benzine), and when slice after slice you ate our bread and meat, we greedily devoured your face and head with our eyes. Ah, Lika, Lika, diabolical beauty! ...

When you are at the Alhambra with Trofimov I hope you may accidentally jab out his eye with your fork.

TO A. S. SUVORIN.

ALEXIN, May 18, 1891.

... I get up at five o'clock in the morning; evidently when I am old I shall get up at four. My forefathers all got up very early, before the cock. And I notice people who get up very early are horribly fussy. So I suppose I shall be a fussy, restless old man....

BOGIMOVO,

May 20.

... The carp bite capitally. I forgot all my sorrows yesterday; first I sat by the pond and caught carp, and then by the old mill and caught perch.

... The last two proclamations—about the Siberian railway and the exiles—pleased me very much. The Siberian railway is called a national concern, and the tone of the proclamation guarantees its speedy completion; and convicts who have completed such and such terms as settlers are allowed to return to Russia without the right to live in the provinces of Petersburg and Moscow. The newspapers have let this pass unnoticed, and yet it is something which has never been in Russia before— it is the first step towards abolishing the life sentence which has so long weighed on the public conscience as unjust and cruel in the extreme....

BOGIMOVO,

May 27, 4 o'clock in the Morning.

The mongoose has run away into the woods and has not come back. It is cold. I have no money. But nevertheless, I don't envy you. One cannot live in town now, it is both dreary and unwholesome. I should like you to be sitting from morning till dinner-time in this verandah, drinking tea and writing something artistic, a play or something; and after dinner till evening, fishing and thinking peaceful thoughts. You have long ago earned the right which is denied you now by all sorts of chance circumstances, and it seems to me shameful and unjust that I should live more peacefully than you. Is it possible that you will stay all June in town? It's really terrible....

... By the way, read Grigorovitch's letter to my enemy Anna Ivanovna. Let her soul rejoice. "Chekhov belongs to the generation which has perceptibly begun to turn away from the West and concentrate more closely on their own world...." "Venice and Florence are nothing else than dull towns for a man of any intelligence...." *Merci*, but I don't understand persons of such intelligence. One would have to be a bull to "turn away from the West" on arriving for the first time in Venice or Florence. There is very little intelligence in doing so. But I should like to know who is taking the trouble to announce to the whole universe that I did not like foreign parts. Good Lord! I never let drop one word about it. I liked even Bologna. Whatever ought I to have done? Howled with rapture? Broken the windows? Embraced Frenchmen? Do they say I gained no ideas? But I fancy I did....

We must see each other—or more correctly, I must see you. I am missing you already, although to-day I caught two hundred and fifty-two carp and one crayfish.

BOGIMOVO,

June 4, 1891.

Why did you go away so soon? I was very dull, and could not get back into my usual petty routine very quickly afterwards. As luck would have it, after you went away the weather became warm and magnificent, and the fish began to bite.

... The mongoose has been found. A sportsman with dogs found him on this side of the Oka in a quarry; if there had not been a crevice in the quarry the dogs would have torn the mongoose to pieces. It had been astray in the woods for eighteen days. In spite of the climatic conditions, which are awful for it, it had grown fat—such is the effect of freedom. Yes, my dear sir, freedom is a grand thing.

I advise you again to go to Feodosia by the Volga. Anna Ivanovna and you will enjoy it, and it will be new and interesting for the children. If I were free I would come with you. It's snug now on those Volga steamers, they feed you well and the passengers are interesting.

Forgive me for your having been so uncomfortable with us. When I am grown up and order furniture from Venice, as I certainly shall do, you won't have such a cold and rough time with me.

TO L. S. MIZINOV.

BOGIMOVO, June 12, 1891.

Enchanting, amazing Lika!

Captivated by the Circassian Levitan, you have completely forgotten that you promised my brother Ivan you would come on the 1st of June, and you do not answer my sister's letter at all. I wrote to you from Moscow to invite you, but my letter, too, remained a voice crying in the wilderness. Though you are received in aristocratic society, you have been badly brought up all the same, and I don't regret having once chastised you with a switch. You must understand that expecting your arrival from day to day not only wearies us, but puts us to expense. In an ordinary way we only have for dinner what is left of yesterday's soup, but when we expect visitors we have also a dish of boiled beef, which we buy from the neighbouring cooks.

We have a magnificent garden, dark avenues, snug corners, a river, a mill, a boat, moonlight, nightingales, turkeys. In the pond and river there are very intelligent frogs. We often go for walks, during which I usually close my eyes and crook my right arm in the shape of a bread-ring, imagining that you are walking by my side.

... Give my greetings to Levitan. Please ask him not to write about you in every letter. In the first place it is not magnanimous on his part, and in the second, I have no interest whatever in his happiness.

Be well and happy and don't forget us. I have just received your letter, it is filled from top to bottom with such charming expressions as: "The devil choke you!" "The devil flay you!" "Anathema!" "A good smack," "rabble," "overeaten myself." Your friends—such as Trophim—with their cabmen's talk certainly have an improving influence on you.

You may bathe and go for evening walks. That's all nonsense. All my inside is full of coughs, wet and dry, but I bathe and walk about, and yet I am alive....

TO L. S. MIZINOV.

(Enclosing a photograph of a young man inscribed "To Lida from Petya.")

PRECIOUS LIDA!

Why these reproaches! I send you my portrait. To-morrow we shall meet. Do not forget your Petya. A thousand kisses!!!

I have bought Chekhov's stories. How delightful! Mind you buy them. Remember me to Masha Chekhov. What a darling you are!

TO THE SAME.

I love you passionately like a tiger, and I offer you my hand.

Marshal of Nobility,

GOLOVIN RTISHTCHEV.

P.S.—Answer me by signs. You do squint.

TO HIS SISTER.

BOGIMOVO, June, 1891.

Masha! Make haste and come home, as without you our intensive culture is going to complete ruin. There is nothing to eat, the flies are sickening. The mongoose has broken a jar of jam, and so on, and so on.

All the summer visitors sigh and lament over your absence. There is no news.... The spiderman is busy from morning to night with his spiders. He has already described five of the spider's legs, and has only three left to do. When he has finished with spiders he will begin upon fleas, which he will catch on his aunt. The K's sit every evening at the club, and no hints from me will prevail on them to move from the spot.

It is hot, there are no mushrooms. Suvorin has not come yet....

Come soon for it is devilishly dull. We have just caught a frog and given it to the mongoose. It has eaten it.

TO MADAME KISELYOV.

ALEXIN, July 20, 1891.

Greetings, honoured Marya Vladimirovna.

For God's sake write what you are doing, whether you are all well and how things are in regard to mushrooms and gudgeon.

We are living at Bogimovo in the province of Kaluga.... It's a huge house, a fine park, the inevitable views, at the sight of which I am for some reason expected to say "Ach!" A river, a pond with hungry carp who love to get on to the hook, a mass of sick people, a smell of iodoform, and walks in the evenings. I am busy with my Sahalin; and in the intervals, that I may not let my family starve, I cherish the muse and write stories. Everything goes on in the old way, there is nothing new. I get up every day at five o'clock, and prepare my coffee with my own hands—a sign that I have already got into old bachelor habits and am resigned to them. Masha is painting, Misha wears his cockade creditably, father talks about bishops, mother bustles about the house, Ivan fishes. On the same estate with us there is living a zoologist called Wagner and his family, and some Kisilyovs—not the Kisilyovs, but others, not the real ones.

Wagner catches ladybirds and spiders, and Kisilyov the father sketches, as he is an artist. We get up performances, *tableaux-vivants*, and picnics. It is very gay and amusing, but I have only to catch a perch or find a mushroom for my head to droop, and my thoughts to be carried back to the past, and my brain and soul begin in a funereal voice to sing the duet "We are parted." The "deposed idol and the deserted temple" rise up before my imagination, and I think devoutly: "I would exchange all the zoologists and great artists in the world for one little Idiotik." [Footnote: Madame Kisilyov's son.] The weather has all the while been hot and dry, and only to-day there has been a crash of thunder and the gates of heaven are open. One longs to get away somewhere—for instance, to America, or Norway.... Be well and happy, and may the good spirits, of whom there are so many at Babkino, have you in their keeping.

TO HIS BROTHER ALEXANDR.

ALEXIN, July, 1891.

MY PHOTOGRAPHIC AND PROLIFIC BROTHER!

I got a letter from you a long time ago with the photographs of Semashko, but I haven't answered till now, because I have been all the time trying to formulate the great thoughts befitting my answer. All our people are alive and well, we often talk of you, and regret that your prolificness prevents you from coming to us here where you would be very welcome. Father, as I have written to you already, has thrown up Ivanygortch, and is living with us. Suvorin has been here twice; he talked about you, and caught fish. I am up to my neck in work with Sahalin, and other things no less wearisome and hard labour. I dream of winning forty thousand, so as to cut myself off completely from writing, which I am sick of, to buy a little bit of land and live like a hermit in idle seclusion, with you and Ivan in the neighbourhood—I dream of presenting you with fifteen acres each as poor relations. Altogether I have a dreary existence, I am sick of toiling over lines and halfpence, and old age is creeping nearer and nearer.

Your last story, in my opinion, shared by Suvorin, is good. Why do you write so little?

The zoologist V. A. Wagner, who took his degree with you, is staying in the same courtyard. He is writing a very solid dissertation. Kisilyov, the artist, is living in the same yard too. We go walks together in the evenings and discuss philosophy....

TO A. S. SUVORIN.

BOGIMOVO, July 24, 1891.

... Thanks for the five kopecks addition. Alas, it will not settle my difficulties! To save up a reserve, as you write, and extricate myself from the abyss of halfpenny anxieties and petty terrors, there is only one resource left me—an immoral one. To marry a rich woman or give out Anna Karenin as my work. And as that is impossible I dismiss my difficulties in despair and let things go as they please.

You once praised Rod, a French writer, and told me Tolstoy liked him. The other day I happened to read a novel of his and flung up my hands in amazement. He is equivalent to our Matchtet, only a little more intelligent. There is a terrible deal of affectation, dreariness, straining after originality, and as little of anything artistic as there was salt in that porridge we cooked in the evening at Bogimovo. In the preface this Rod regrets that he was in the past a "naturalist," and rejoices that the spiritualism of the latest recruits of literature has replaced materialism. Boyish boastfulness which is at the same time coarse and clumsy.... "If we are not as talented as you, Monsieur Zola, to make up for it we believe in God." ...

July 29.

Well, thank God! To-day I have received from the bookshop notice that there is 690 roubles 6 kopecks coming to me. I have written in answer that they are to send five hundred roubles to Feodosia and the other one hundred and ninety to me. And so I am left owing you only one hundred and seventy. That is comforting, it's an advance anyway. To meet the debt to the newspaper I am arming myself with an immense story which I shall finish in a day or two and send. I ought to knock three hundred roubles off the debt, and get as much for myself. Ough! ...

August 6.

... The death of a servant in the house makes a strange impression, doesn't it? The man while he was alive attracted attention only so far as he was one's "man"; but when he is dead he suddenly engrosses the attention of all, lies like a weight on the whole house, and becomes the despotic master who is talked of to the exclusion of everything.

... I shall finish my story to-morrow or the day after, but not to-day, for it has exhausted me fiendishly towards the end. Thanks to the haste with which I have worked at it, I have wasted a pound of nerves over it. The composition of it is a little complicated. I got into difficulties and often tore up what I had written, and for days at a time was dissatisfied with my work—that is why I have not finished it till now. How awful it is! I must rewrite it! It's impossible to leave it, for it is in a devil of a mess. My God! if the public likes my works as little as I do those of other people which I am reading, what an ass I am! There is something asinine about our writing....

To my great pleasure the amazing astronomer has arrived. She is angry with you, and calls you for some reason an "eloquent gossip." To begin with, she is free and independent; and then she has a poor opinion of men; and further, according to her, everyone is a savage or a ninny—and you dared to give her my address with the words "the being you adore lives at ...," and so on. Upon my word, as though one could suspect earthly feelings in astronomers who soar among the clouds! She talks and laughs all day, is a capital mushroom-gatherer, and dreams of the Caucasus to which she is departing today.

August 18.

At last I have finished my long, wearisome story [Footnote: "The Duel."] and am sending it to you in Feodosia. Please read it. It is too long for the paper, and not suitable for dividing into parts. Do as you think best, however....

There are more than four signatures of print in the story. It's awful. I am exhausted, and dragged the end, like a train of waggons on a muddy night in autumn, at a walking pace with halts—that is why I am late with it....

August 18.

Speaking of Nikolay and the doctor who attends him, you emphasize that "all that is done without love, without self-sacrifice, even in regard to trifling conveniences." You are right, speaking of people generally, but what would you have the doctors do? If, as your old nurse says, "The bowel has burst," what's one to do, even if one is ready to give one's life to the sufferer? As a rule, while the family, the relations, and the servants are doing "everything they can" and are straining every nerve, the doctor sits and looks like a fool, with his hands folded, disconsolately ashamed of himself and his science, and trying to preserve external tranquillity....

Doctors have loathsome days and hours, such as I would not wish my worst enemy. It is true that ignoramuses and coarse louts are no rarity among doctors, nor are they among writers, engineers, people in general; but those loathsome days and hours of which I speak fall to the lot of doctors only, and for that, truly, much may be forgiven them....

The amazing astronomer is at Batum now. As I told her I should go to Batum too, she will send her address to Feodosia. She has grown cleverer than ever of late. One day I overheard a learned discussion between her and the zoologist Wagner, whom you know. It seemed to me that in comparison with her the learned professor was simply a schoolboy. She has excellent logic and plenty of good common sense, but no rudder, ... so that she drifts and drifts, and doesn't know where she is going....

A woman was carting rye, and she fell off the waggon head downwards. She was terribly injured: concussion of the brain, straining of the vertebrae of the neck, sickness, fearful pains, and so on. She was brought to me. She was moaning and groaning and praying for death, and yet she looked at the man who brought her and muttered: "Let the lentils go, Kirila, you can thresh them later, but thresh the oats now." I told her that she could talk about oats afterwards, that there was something more serious to talk about, but she said to me: "His oats are ever so good!" A managing, vigilant woman. Death comes easy to such people....

August 28.

I send you Mihailovsky's article on Tolstoy. Read it and grow perfect. It's a good article, but it's strange; one might write a thousand such articles and things would not be one step forwarder, and it would still remain unintelligible why such articles are written....

I am writing my Sahalin, and I am bored, I am bored.... I am utterly sick of life.

Judging from your telegram I have not satisfied you with my story. You should not have hesitated to send it back to me.

Oh, how weary I am of sick people! A neighbouring landowner had a nervous stroke and they trundled me off to him in a scurvy jolting britchka. Most of all I am sick of peasant women with babies, and of powders which it is so tedious to weigh out.

There is a famine year coming. I suppose there will be epidemics of all sorts and risings on a small scale....

August 28.

So you like my story? [Footnote: "The Duel."] Well, thank God! Of late I have become devilishly suspicious and uneasy. I am constantly fancying that my trousers are horrid, and that I am writing not as I want to, and that I am giving my patients the wrong powders. It must be a special neurosis.

If Ladzievsky's surname is really horrible, you can call him something else. Let him be Lagievsky, let von Koren remain von Koren. The multitude of Wagners, Brandts, and so on, in all the scientific world, make a Russian name out of the question for a zoologist—though there is Kovalevsky. And by the way, Russian life is so mixed up nowadays that any surnames will do.

Sahalin is progressing. There are times when I long to sit over it from three to five years, and work at it furiously; but at times, in moments of doubt, I could spit on it. It would be a good thing, by God! to devote three years to it. I shall write a great deal of rubbish, because I am not a specialist, but really I shall write something sensible too. It is such a good subject, because it would live for a hundred years after me, as it would be the literary source and aid for all who are studying prison organization, or are interested in it.

You are right, your Excellency, I have done a great deal this summer. Another such summer and I may perhaps have written a novel and bought an estate. I have not only paid my way, but even paid off a thousand roubles of debt.

... Tell your son that I envy him. And I envy you too, and not because your wives have gone away, but because you are bathing in the sea and living in a warm house. I am cold in my barn. I should like new carpets, an open fireplace, bronzes, and learned conversations. Alas! I shall never be a Tolstoyan. In women I love beauty above all things; and in the history of mankind, culture, expressed in carpets, carriages with springs, and keenness of wit. Ach! To make haste and become an old man and sit at a big table! ...

P.S.—If we were to cut the zoological conversations out of "The Duel" wouldn't it make it more living? ...

MOSCOW,

September 8.

I have returned to Moscow and am keeping indoors. My family is busy trying to find a new flat but I say nothing because I am too lazy to turn round. They want to move to Devitchye Polye for the sake of cheapness.

The title you recommend for my novel—"Deception"—will not do: it would only be appropriate if it were a question of conscious lying. Unconscious lying is not deception but a mistake. Tolstoy calls our having money and eating meat lying—that's too much....

Death gathers men little by little, he knows what he is about. One might write a play: an old chemist invents the elixir of life—take fifteen drops and you live for ever; but he breaks the phial from terror, lest such carrion as himself and his wife might live for ever. Tolstoy denies mankind immortality, but my God! how much that is personal there is in it! The day before yesterday I read his "Afterword." Strike me dead! but it is stupider and stuffier than "Letters to a Governor's Wife," which I despise. The devil take the philosophy of the great ones of this world! All the great sages are as despotic as generals, and as ignorant and as indelicate as generals, because they feel secure of impunity. Diogenes spat in people's faces, knowing that he would not suffer for it. Tolstoy abuses doctors as scoundrels, and displays his ignorance in great questions because he's just such a Diogenes who won't be locked up or abused in the newspapers. And so to the devil with the philosophy of all the great ones of this world! The whole of it with its fanatical "Afterwords" and "Letters to a Governor's Wife" is not worth one little mare in his "Story of a Horse...."

TO E. M. S.

MOSCOW, September 16.

So we old bachelors smell of dogs? So be it. But as for specialists in feminine diseases being at heart rakes and cynics, allow me to differ. Gynaecologists have to do with deadly prose such as you have never dreamed of, and to which perhaps, if you knew it, you would, with the ferocity characteristic of your imagination, attribute a worse smell than that of dogs. One who is always swimming in the sea loves dry land; one who for ever is plunged in prose passionately longs for poetry. All gynaecologists are idealists. Your doctor reads poems, your instinct prompted you right; I would add that he is a great liberal, a bit of a mystic, and that he dreams of a wife in the style of the Nekrassov Russian woman. The famous Snyegirev cannot speak of the "Russian woman" without a quiver in his voice. Another gynaecologist whom I know is in love with a mysterious lady in a veil whom he has only seen from a distance. Another one goes to all the first performances at the theatre and then is loud in his abuse, declaring that authors ought to represent only ideal women, and so on. You have omitted to consider also that a good gynaecologist cannot be a stupid man or a mediocrity. Intellect has a brighter lustre than baldness, but you have noticed the baldness and emphasized it—and have flung the intellect overboard. You have noticed, too, and emphasized that a fat man—brrr!—exudes a sort of greasiness, but you completely lose sight of the fact that he is a professor—that is, that he has spent several years in thinking and doing something which sets him high above millions of men, high above all the Verotchkas and Taganrog Greek girls, high above dinners and wines of all sorts. Noah had three sons, Shem, Ham, and Japheth. Ham only noticed that his father was a drunkard, and completely lost sight of the fact that he was a genius, that he had built an ark and saved the world.

Writers must not imitate Ham, bear that in mind.

I do not venture to ask you to love the gynaecologist and the professor, but I venture to remind you of the justice which for an objective writer is more precious than the air he breathes.

The girl of the merchant class is admirably drawn. That is a good passage in the doctor's speech in which he speaks of his lack of faith in medicine, but there is no need to make him drink after every sentence....

Then from the particular to the general! Let me warn you. This is not a story and not a novel and not a work of art, but a long row of heavy, gloomy barrack buildings. Where is your construction which at first so enchanted your humble servant? Where is the lightness, the freshness, the grace? Read your story through: a description of a dinner, then a description of passing ladies and girls, then a description of a company, then a description of a dinner, ... and so on endlessly. Descriptions and descriptions and no action at all. You ought to begin straight away with the merchant's daughter, and keep to her, and chuck out Verotchka and the Greek girls and all the rest, except the doctor and the merchant family.

Excuse this long letter.

TO A. S. SUVORIN.

MOSCOW, October 16, 1891.

I congratulate you on your new cook, and wish you an excellent appetite. Wish me the same, for I am coming to see you soon—sooner than I had intended—and shall eat for three. I simply must get away from home, if only for a fortnight. From morning till night I am unpleasantly irritable, I feel as though someone were drawing a blunt knife over my soul, and this irritability finds external expression in my hurrying off to bed early and avoiding conversation. Nothing I do succeeds. I began a story for the *Sbornik*; I wrote half and threw it up, and then began another; I have been struggling for more than a week with this story, and the time when I shall finish it and when I shall set to work and finish the first story, for which I am to be paid, seems to me far away. I have not been to the province of Nizhni Novgorod yet, for reasons not under my control, and I don't know when I shall go. In fact it's a hopeless mess—a silly muddle and not life. And I desire nothing now so much as to win two hundred thousand....

Ah, I have such a subject for a novel! If I were in a tolerable humour I could begin it on the first of November and finish it on the first of December. I would make five signatures of print. And I long to write as I did at Bogimovo—i.e., from morning till night and in my sleep.

Don't tell anyone I am coming to Petersburg. I shall live incognito. In my letters I write vaguely that I am coming in November....

Shall I remind you of Kashtanka, or forget about her? Won't she lose her childhood and youth if we don't print her? However, you know best....

P. S.—If you see my brother Alexandr, tell him that our aunt is dying of consumption. Her days are numbered. She was a splendid woman, a saint.

If you want to visit the famine-stricken provinces, let us go together in January, it will be more conspicuous then....

MOSCOW,

October 19, 1891.

What a splendid little letter has come from you! It is warmly and eloquently written, and every thought in it is true. To talk now of laziness and drunkenness, and so on, is as strange and tactless as to lecture a man on the conduct of life at a moment when he is being sick or lying ill of typhus. There is always a certain element of insolence in being well-fed, as in every kind of force, and that element finds expression chiefly in the well-fed man preaching to the hungry. If consolation is revolting at a time of real sorrow, what must be the effect of preaching morality; and how stupid and insulting that preaching must seem. These moral people imagine that if a man is fifteen roubles in arrears with his taxes he must be a wastrel, and ought not to drink; but they ought to reckon up how much states are in debt, and prime ministers, and what the debts of all the marshals of nobility and all the bishops taken together come to. What do the Guards owe! Only their tailors could tell us that....

You have told them to send me four hundred? Vivat dominus Suvorin! So I have already received from your firm 400 + 100 + 400. Altogether I shall get for "The Duel" as I calculated, about fourteen hundred, so five hundred will go towards my debt. Well, and for that thank God! By the spring I must pay off all my debt or I shall go into a decline, for in the spring I want another advance from all my editors. I shall take it and escape to Java....

Ah, my friends, how bored I am! If I am a doctor I ought to have patients and a hospital; if I am a literary man I ought to live among people instead of in a flat with a mongoose, I ought to have at least a scrap of social and political life—but this life between four walls, without nature, without people, without a country, without health and appetite, is not life, but some sort of ... and nothing more.

For the sake of all the perch and pike you are going to catch on your Zaraish estate, I entreat you to publish the English humorist Bernard. [Translator's Note: ? Bernard Shaw.] ...

TO MADAME LINTVARYOV.

MOSCOW, October 25, 1891.

HONOURED NATALYA MIHAILOVNA,

I have not gone to Nizhni as I meant to, but am sitting at home, writing and sneezing. Madame Morozov has seen the Minister, he has absolutely prohibited private initiative in the work of famine relief, and actually waved her out of his presence. This has reduced me to apathy at once. Add to that, complete lack of money, sneezing, a mass of work, the illness of my

aunt who died to-day, the indefiniteness, the uncertainty in fact—
everything has come together to hinder a lazy person like me. I have put off
my going away till the first of December.

We felt dull without you for a long time, and when the Shah of Persia
[Footnote: A. I. Smagin.] went away it was duller still. I have given orders
that no one is to be admitted, and sit in my room like a heron in the reeds; I
see no one, and no one sees me. And it is better so, or the public would
pull the bell off, and my study would be turned into a smoking and talking
room. It's dull to live like this, but what am I to do? I shall wait till the
summer and then let myself go.

I shall sell the mongoose by auction. I should be glad to sell N. and his
poems too, but no one would buy him. He dashes in to see me almost
every evening as he used to do, and bores me with his doubts, his struggles,
his volcanoes, slit nostrils, atamans, the life of the free, and such tosh, for
which God forgive him.

Russkiya Vyedomosti is printing a *Sbornik* for the famine fund. With
your permission, I shall send you a copy.

Well, good health and happiness to you; respects and greetings to all
yours from

> *the Geographer,*
>
> *A. CHEKHOV.*

P. S.—All my family send their regards.

We are all well but sorrowful. Our aunt was a general favourite, and was
considered among us the incarnation of goodness, kindness, and justice, if
only all that can be incarnated. Of course we shall all die, but still it is sad.

In April I shall be in your parts. By the spring I hope I shall have heaps
of money. I judge by the omen: no money is a sign of money coming.

TO A. S. SUVORIN.

MOSCOW, October 25, 1891.

Print "The Duel" not twice a week but only once. To print it twice is
breaking a long-established custom of the paper, and it would seem as
though I were robbing the other contributors of one day a week; and
meanwhile it makes no difference to me or my novel whether it is printed

once a week or twice. The literary brotherhood in Petersburg seems to talk of nothing but the uncleanness of my motives. I have just received the good news that I am to be married to the rich Madame Sibiryakov. I get a lot of agreeable news altogether.

I wake up every night and read "War and Peace." One reads it with the same interest and naive wonder as though one had never read it before. It's amazingly good. Only I don't like the passages in which Napoleon appears. As soon as Napoleon comes on the scene there are forced explanations and tricks of all sorts to prove that he was stupider than he really was. Everything that is said and done by Pierre, Prince Andrey, or the absolutely insignificant Nikolay Rostov—all that is good, clever, natural, and touching; everything that is thought and done by Napoleon is not natural, not clever, inflated and worthless.

When I live in the provinces (of which I dream now day and night), I shall practice as a doctor and read novels.

I am not coming to Petersburg.

If I had been by Prince Andrey I should have saved him. It is strange to read that the wound of a prince, a rich man spending his days and nights with a doctor and being nursed by Natasha and Sonya, should have smelt like a corpse. What a scurvy affair medicine was in those days! Tolstoy could not help getting soaked through with hatred for medicine while he was writing his thick novel....

MOSCOW,

November 18, 1891.

... I have read your letter about the influenza and Solovyov. I was unexpectedly aware of a dash of cruelty in it. The phrase "I hate" does not suit you at all; and a public confession "I am a sinner, a sinner, a sinner," is such pride that it made me feel uncomfortable. When the pope took the title "holiness," the head of the Eastern church, in pique, called himself "The servant of God's servants." So you publicly expatiate on your sinfulness from pique of Solovyov, who has the impudence to call himself orthodox. But does a word like orthodoxy, Judaism, or Catholicism contain any implication of exceptional personal merit or virtue? To my thinking everybody is bound to call himself orthodox if he has that word inscribed on his passport. Whether you believe or not, whether you are a prince of this world or an exile in penal servitude, you are, for practical purposes, orthodox. And Solovyov made no sort of pretension when he said he was no Jew or Chaldean but orthodox....

I still feel dull, blighted, foolish, and indifferent, and I am still sneezing and coughing, and I am beginning to think I shall not get back to my former health. But that's all in God's hands. Medical treatment and anxiety about one's physical existence arouse in me a feeling not far from loathing. I am not going to be doctored. I will take water and quinine, but I am not going to let myself be sounded....

I had only just finished this letter when I received yours. You say that if I go into the wilds I shall be quite cut off from you. But I am going to live in the country in order to be nearer Petersburg. If I have no flat in Moscow you must understand, my dear sir, I shall spend November, December, and January in Petersburg: that will be possible then. I shall be able to be idle all the summer too; I shall look out for a house in the country for you, but you are wrong in disliking Little Russians, they are not children or actors in the province of Poltava, but genuine people, and cheerful and well-fed into the bargain.

Do you know what relieves my cough? When I am working I sprinkle the edge of the table with turpentine with a sprayer and inhale its vapour. When I go to bed I spray my little table and other objects near me. The fine drops evaporate sooner than the liquid itself. And the smell of turpentine is pleasant. I drink Obersalzbrunnen, avoid hot things, talk little, and blame myself for smoking so much. I repeat, dress as warmly as possible, even at home. Avoid draughts at the theatre. Treat yourself like a hothouse plant or you will not soon be rid of your cough. If you want to try turpentine, buy the French kind. Take quinine once a day, and be careful to avoid constipation. Influenza has completely taken away from me any desire to drink spirituous liquors. They are disgusting to my taste. I don't drink my two glasses at night, and so it is a long time before I can get to sleep. I want to take ether.

I await your story. In the summer let us each write a play. Yes, by God! why the devil should we waste our time....

TO E. M. S.

MOSCOW, November 19, 1891.

HONOURED ELENA MIHAILOVNA,

I am at home to all commencing, continuing, and concluding authors—that is my rule, and apart from your authorship and mine, I regard a visit from you as a great honour to me. Even if it were not so, even if for some reason I did not desire your visit, even then I should have received you, as I have enjoyed the greatest hospitality from your family. I did not receive you, and at once asked my brother to go to you and explain the cause. At the moment your card was handed me I was ill and undressed—forgive these homely details—I was in my bedroom, while there were persons in my study whose presence would not have been welcome to you. And so—to see you was physically impossible, and this my brother was to have explained to you, and you, a decent and good-hearted person, ought to have understood it; but you were offended. Well, I can't help it....

But can you really have written only fifteen stories?—at this rate you won't learn to write till you are fifty.

I am in bad health; for over a month I have had to keep indoors—influenza and cough.

All good wishes.

Write another twenty stories and send them. I shall always read them with pleasure, and practice is essential for you.

TO A. S. SUVORIN.

MOSCOW, November 22, 1891.

My health is on the road to improvement. My cough is less, my strength is greater. My mood is livelier, and there is sunrise in my head. I wake up in the morning in good spirits, go to bed without gloomy thoughts, and at dinner I am not ill-humoured and don't say nasty things to my mother.

I don't know when I shall come to you. I have heaps of work *pour manger.* Till the spring I must work—that is, at senseless grind. A ray of liberty has beamed upon my horizon. There has come a whiff of freedom. Yesterday I got a letter from the province of Poltava. They write they have found me a suitable place. A brick house of seven rooms with an iron roof, lately built and needing no repairs, a stable, a cellar, an icehouse, eighteen acres of land, an excellent meadow for hay, an old shady garden on the bank of the river Psyol. The river bank is mine; on that side there is a marvellous view over a wide expanse. The price is merciful. Three thousand, and two thousand deferred payment over several years. Five in all. If heaven has mercy upon me, and the purchase comes off, I shall move there in March *for good*, to live quietly in the lap of nature for nine months and the rest of the year in Petersburg. I am sending my sister to look at the place.

Ach! liberty, liberty! If I can live on not more than two thousand a year, which is only possible in the country, I shall be absolutely free from all anxieties over money coming in and going out. Then I shall work and read, read ... in a word it will be marmelad. [Translator's Note: A kind of sweetmeat made by boiling down fruit to the consistency of damson cheese.] ...

MOSCOW,

November 30, 1891.

I return you the two manuscripts you sent me. One story is an Indian Legend—The Lotus Flower, Wreaths of Laurel, A Summer Night, The Humming Bird—that in India! He begins with Faust thirsting for youth and ends with "the bliss of the true life," in the style of Tolstoy. I have cut out parts, polished it up, and the result is a legend of no great value, indeed, but light, and it may be read with interest. The other story is illiterate, clumsy, and womanish in structure, but there is a story and a certain raciness. I have cut it down to half as you see. Both stories could be printed....

I keep dreaming and dreaming. I dream of moving from Moscow into the country in March, and in the autumn coming to Petersburg to stay till the spring. I long to spend at least one winter in Petersburg, and that's only possible on condition I have no perch in Moscow. And I dream of how I shall spend five months talking to you about literature, and do as I think best in the *Novoye Vremya*, while in the country I shall go in for medicine heart and soul.

Boborykin has been to see me. He is dreaming too. He told me that he wants to write something in the way of the physiology of the Russian novel, its origin among us, and the natural course of its development. While he was talking I could not get rid of the feeling that I had a maniac before me, but a literary maniac who put literature far above everything in life. I so rarely see genuine literary people at home in Moscow that a conversation with Boborykin seemed like heavenly manna, though I don't believe in the physiology of the novel and the natural course of its development—that is, there may exist such a physiology in nature, but I don't believe with existing methods it can be detected. Boborykin dismisses Gogol absolutely and refuses to recognize him as a forerunner of Turgenev, Gontcharov, and Tolstoy.... He puts him apart, outside the current in which the Russian novel has flowed. Well, I don't understand that. If one takes the standpoint of natural development, it's impossible to put not only Gogol, but even a dog barking, outside the current, for all things in nature influence one another, and even the fact that I have just sneezed is not without its influence on surrounding nature....

Good health to you! I am reading Shtchedrin's "Diary of a Provincial." How long and boring it is! And at the same time how like real life!

TO N. A. LEIKIN.

MOSCOW, December 2, 1891.

I am writing to ask you a great favour, dear Nikolay Alexandrovitch. This is what it is. Until last year I have always lived with my university diploma, which by land and by sea has served me for a passport; but every time it has been *vise* the police have warned me that one cannot live with a diploma, and that I ought to get a passport from "the proper department." I have asked everyone what this "proper department" means, and no one has given me an answer. A year ago the Moscow head police officer gave me a passport on the condition that within a year I should get a passport from "the proper department." I can't make head or tail of it! The other day I learned that as I have never been in the government service and by education am a doctor, I ought to be registered in the class of professional citizens, and that a certain department, I believe the heraldic, will furnish me with a certificate which will serve me as a passport for all the days of my life. I remembered that you had lately received the grade of professional citizen, and with it a certificate, and that therefore you must have applied somewhere and to someone and so, in a sense, are an old campaigner. For God's sake advise me to what department I ought to apply. What petition ought I to write, and how many stamps ought I to put on it? What documents must be enclosed with the petition? and so on, and so on. In the town hall there is a "passport bureau." Could not that bureau reveal the mystery if it is not sufficiently clear to you?

Forgive me for troubling you, but I really don't know to whom to apply, and I am a very poor lawyer myself....

Your "Medal" is often given at Korsh's Theatre, and with success. It is played together with Myasnitsky's "Hare." I haven't seen them, but friends tell me that a great difference is felt between the two plays: that "The Medal" in comparison with "The Hare" seems something clean, artistic, and having form and semblance. There you have it! Literary men are swept out of the theatre, and plays are written by nondescript people, old and young, while the journals and newspapers are edited by tradesmen, government clerks, and young ladies. But there, the devil take them! ...

TO E. P. YEGOROV.

MOSCOW, December 11, 1891.

HONOURED EVGRAF PETROVITCH,

I write to explain why my journey to you did not come off. I was intending to come to you not as a special correspondent, but on a commission from, or more correctly by agreement with, a small circle of people who want to do something for the famine-stricken peasants. The point is that the public does not trust the administration and so is deterred from subscribing. There are a thousand legends and fables about the waste, the shameless theft, and so on. People hold aloof from the Episcopal department and are indignant with the Red Cross. The owner of our beloved Babkino, the Zemsky Natchalnik, rapped out to me, bluntly and definitely: "The Red Cross in Moscow are thieves." Such being the state of feeling, the government can scarcely expect serious help from the public. And yet the public wants to help and its conscience is uneasy. In September the educated and wealthy classes of Moscow formed themselves into circles, thought, talked, and applied for advice to leading persons; everyone was talking of how to get round the government and organize independently. They decided to send to the famine-stricken provinces their own agents, who should make acquaintance with the position on the spot, open feeding centres, and so on. Some of the leaders of these circles, persons of weight, went to Durnovo to ask permission, and Durnovo refused it, declaring that the organization of relief must be left to the Episcopal department and the Red Cross. In short, private initiative was suppressed at its first efforts. Everyone was cast down and dispirited; some were furious, some simply washed their hands of the whole business. One must have the courage and authority of Tolstoy to act in opposition to all prohibitions and prevailing sentiments, and to follow the dictates of duty.

Well, now about myself. I am in complete sympathy with individual initiative, for every man has the right to do good in the way he thinks best; but all the discussion concerning the government, the Red Cross, and so on, seemed to me inopportune and impractical. I imagined that with coolness and good humour, one might get round all the terrors and delicacy of the position, and that there was no need to go to the Minister about it. I went to Sahalin without a single letter of recommendation, and yet I did everything I wanted to. Why cannot I go to the famine-stricken provinces? I remembered, too, such representatives of the government as you, Kiselyov, and all the Zemsky Natchalniks and tax inspectors of my acquaintance—all extremely decent people, worthy of complete confidence. And I resolved—if only for a small region—to combine the two elements of officialdom and private initiative. I want to come and consult you as soon as I can. The public trusts me; it would trust you, too, and I might reckon on succeeding. Do you remember I wrote to you? Suvorin came to Moscow at the time; I complained to him that I did not know your address. He telegraphed to Baranov, and Baranov was so kind as to send it to me. Suvorin was ill with influenza; as a rule when he comes to Moscow we spend whole days together discussing literature, of which he has a wide knowledge; we did the same on this occasion, and in consequence I caught his influenza, was laid up, and had a raging cough. Korolenko was in Moscow, and he found me ill. Lung complications kept me ill for a whole month, confined to the house and unable to do anything. Now I am on the way to recovery, though I still cough and am thin. There is the whole story for you. If it had not been for the influenza we might together perhaps have succeeded in extracting two or three thousand or more from the public.

Your exasperation with the press I can quite understand. The lucubrations of the journalists annoy you who know the true position of affairs, in the same way as the lucubrations of the profane about diphtheria annoy me as a doctor. But what would you have? Russia is not England and is not France. Our newspapers are not rich and they have very few men at their disposal. To send to the Volga a professor of the Petrovsky Academy or an Engelhardt is expensive: to send a talented and business-like member of the staff is impossible too—he is wanted at home. The *Times* could organize a census in the famine-stricken provinces at its own expense, could settle a Kennan in every district, paying him forty roubles a day, and then something sensible could be done; but what can the *Russkiya Vyedomosti* or the *Novoye Vremya* do, who consider an income of a hundred thousand as the wealth of Croesus? As for the correspondents themselves, they are townsmen who know the country only from Glyeb Uspensky. Their position is an utterly false one, they must fly into a district, sniff about, write, and dash on further. The Russian correspondent has neither material resources, nor freedom, nor authority. For two hundred roubles a month he gallops on and on, and only prays they may not be angry with him for his involuntary and inevitable misrepresentations. He feels guilty—though it is not he that is to blame but Russian darkness. The newspaper correspondents of the west have excellent maps, encyclopaedias, and statistics; in the west they could write their reports, sitting at home, but among us a correspondent can extract information only from talk and rumour. Among us in Russia only three districts have been investigated: the Tcherepov district, the Tambov district, and one other. That is all in the whole of Russia. The newspapers tell lies, the correspondents are duffers, but what's to be done? If our press said nothing the position would be still more awful, you'll admit that.

Your letter and your scheme for buying the cattle from the peasants has stirred me up. I am ready with all my heart and all my strength to follow your lead and do whatever you think best. I have thought it over for a long time, and this is my opinion: it is no use to reckon upon the rich. It is too late. Every wealthy man has by now forked out as many thousands as he is destined to. Our one resource now is the middle-class man who subscribes by the rouble and the half-rouble. Those who in September were talking about private initiative will by now have found themselves a niche in various boards and committees and are already at work. So only the middle-class man is left. Let us open a subscription list. You shall write a letter to the editors, and I will get it printed in *Russkiya Vyedomosti* and *Novoye Vremya*. To combine the two elements above mentioned, we might both sign the letter. If that is inconvenient to you from an official point of view, one might write in the third person as a communication that in the fifth section of the Nizhni Novgorod district this and that had been organized, that things were, thank God! going successfully and that subscriptions could be sent to the Zemsky Natchalnik, E. P. Yegorov, or to A. P. Chekhov, or to the editor of such and such papers. We need only to write at some length. Write in full detail, I will add something, and the thing will be done. We must ask for subscriptions and not for loans. No one will come forward with a loan; it is uncomfortable. It is hard to give, but it is harder still to take back.

I have only one rich acquaintance in Moscow, V. A. Morozov, a lady well-known for her philanthropy. I went to see her yesterday with your letter. I talked with her and dined with her. She is absorbed now in the committee of education, which is organizing relief centres for the school-children, and is giving everything to that. As education and horses are incommensurables, V. A. promised me the co-operation of the committee if we would start centres for feeding the school-children and send detailed information about it. I felt it awkward to ask her for money on the spot, for people beg and beg of her and fleece her like a fox. I only asked her when she had any committees and board meetings not to forget us, and she promised she would not....

If any roubles or half-roubles come in I will send them on to you without delay. Dispose of me and believe me that it would be a real happiness to me to do at least something, for so far I have done absolutely nothing for the famine-stricken peasants and for those who are helping them.

TO A. I. SMAGIN.

MOSCOW, December 11, 1891.

... Well, now I have something to tell you, my good sir. I am sitting at home in Moscow, but meantime my enterprise in the Nizhni Novgorod province is in full swing already! Together with my friend the Zemsky Natchalnik, an excellent man, we are hatching a little scheme, on which we expect to spend a hundred thousand or so, in the most remote section of the province, where there are no landowners nor doctors, nor even well-educated young ladies who are now to be found in numbers even in hell. Apart from famine relief of all sorts, we are making it our chief object to save the crops of next year. Owing to the fact that the peasants are selling their horses for next to nothing, there is a grave danger that the fields will not be ploughed for the spring corn, so that the famine will be repeated next year. So we are going to buy up the horses and feed them, and in spring give them back to their owners; our work is already firmly established, and in January I am going there to behold its fruits. Here is my object in writing to you. If in the course of some noisy banquet you or anyone else should chance to collect, if only half a rouble, for the famine fund, or if some Korobotchka bequeaths a rouble for that object, or if you yourself should win a hundred roubles, remember us sinners in your prayers, and spare us a part of your wealth! Not at once but when you like, only not later than in the spring....

TO A. S. SUVORIN.

MOSCOW, December 11, 1891.

... I am coming to you. My lying is unintentional. I have no money at all. I shall come when I get the various sums owing to me. Yesterday I got one hundred and fifty roubles, I shall soon get more, then I shall fly to you.

In January I am going to Nizhni Novgorod province: there my scheme is working already. I am very, very glad. I am going to write to Anna Pavlovna.

Ah, if you knew how agonizingly my head aches to-day! I want to come to Petersburg if only to lie motionless indoors for two days and only go out to dinner. For some reason I feel utterly exhausted. It's all this cursed influenza.

How many persons could you and would you undertake to feed? Tolstoy! ah, Tolstoy! In these days he is not a man but a super-man, a Jupiter. In the *Sbornik* he has published an article about the relief centres, and the article consists of advice and practical instructions. So business-like, simple, and sensible that, as the editor of *Russkiya Vyedomosti* said, it ought to be printed in the *Government Gazette*, instead of in the *Sbornik*....

December 13, 1891.

Now I understand why you don't sleep well at night. If I had written a story like that I should not have slept for ten nights in succession. The most terrible passage is where Varya strangles the hero and initiates him into the mysteries of the life beyond the grave. It's terrifying and consistent with spiritualism. You mustn't cut out a single word from Varya's speeches, especially where they are both riding on horseback. Don't touch it. The idea of the story is good, and the incidents are fantastic and interesting....

But why do you talk of our "nervous age"? There really is no nervous age. As people lived in the past so they live now, and the nerves of to-day are no worse than the nerves of Abraham, Isaac, and Jacob. Since you have already written the ending I shall not put you out by sending you mine. I was inspired and could not resist writing it. You can read it if you like. Stories are good in this way, that one can sit over them, pen in hand, for days together, and not notice how time passes, and at the same time be conscious of life of a sort. That's from the hygienic point of view. And from the point of view of usefulness and so on, to write a fairly good story and give the reader ten to twenty interesting minutes—that, as Gilyarovsky says, is not a sheep sneezing....

I have a horrible headache again to-day. I don't know what to do. Yes, I suppose it's old age, or if it's not that it's something worse.

A little old gentleman brought me one hundred roubles to-day for the famine.

TO A. I. SMAGIN.

MOSCOW, December 16, 1891.

... Alas! if I don't move into the country this year, and if the purchase of the house and land for some reason does not come off, I shall be playing the part of a great villain in regard to my health. It seems to me that I am dried and warped like an old cupboard, and that if I go on living in Moscow next season, and give myself up to scribbling excesses, Gilyarovsky will read an excellent poem to welcome my entrance into that country place where there is neither sitting nor standing nor sneezing, but only lying down and nothing more. Do you know why you have no success with women? Because you have the most hideous, heathenish, desperate, tragic handwriting....

TO A. N. PLESHTCHEYEV.

MOSCOW, December 25, 1891.

DEAR ALEXEY NIKOLAEVITCH,

Yesterday I chanced to learn your address, and I write to you. If you have a free minute please write to me how you are in health, and how you are getting on altogether. Write, if only a couple of lines.

I have had influenza for the last six weeks. There has been a complication of the lungs and I have a cruel cough. In March I am going south to the province of Poltava, and shall stay there till my cough is gone. My sister has gone down there to buy a house and garden.

Literary doings here are quiet but life is bustling. There is a great deal of talk about the famine, and a great deal of work resulting from the said talk. The theatres are empty, the weather is wretched, there are no frosts at all. Jean Shteheglov is captivated by the Tolstoyans. Merezhkovsky sits at home as of old, lost in a labyrinth of deep researches, and as of old is very nice; of Chekhov they say he has married the heiress Sibiryakov and got five millions dowry—all Petersburg is talking of it. For whose benefit and for what object this slander, I am utterly unable to imagine. It's positively sickening to read letters from Petersburg.

I have not seen Ostrovsky this year....

We shall probably not meet very soon, as I am going away in March and shall not return to the North before November. I shall not keep a flat in Moscow, as that pleasure is beyond my means. I shall stay in Petersburg.

I embrace you warmly. By the way, a little explanation in private. One day at dinner in Paris, persuading me to remain there, you offered to lend me money. I refused, and it seemed to me my refusal hurt and vexed you, and I fancied that when we parted there was a touch of coldness on your side. Possibly I am mistaken, but if I am right I assure you, my dear friend, on my word of honour, that I refused not because I did not care to be under an obligation to you, but simply from a feeling of self-preservation; I was behaving stupidly in Paris, and an extra thousand francs would only have been bad for my health. Believe me that if I had needed it, I would have asked you for a loan as readily as Suvorin.

God keep you.

TO V. A. TIHONOV.

MOSCOW, February 22, 1892.

... You are mistaken in thinking you were drunk at Shtcheglov's name-day party. You had had a drop, that was all. You danced when they all danced, and your jigitivka on the cabman's box excited nothing but general delight. As for your criticism, it was most likely far from severe, as I don't remember it. I only remember that Vvedensky and I for some reason roared with laughter as we listened to you.

Do you want my biography? Here it is. I was born in Taganrog in 1860. I finished the course at Taganrog high school in 1879. In 1884 I took my degree in medicine at the University of Moscow. In 1888 I gained the

Pushkin prize. In 1890 I made a journey to Sahalin across Siberia and back by sea. In 1891 I made a tour in Europe, where I drank excellent wine and ate oysters. In 1892 I took part in an orgy in the company of V. A. Tihonov at a name-day party. I began writing in 1879. The published collections of my works are: "Motley Tales," "In the Twilight," "Stories," "Surly People," and a novel, "The Duel." I have sinned in the dramatic line too, though with moderation. I have been translated into all the languages with the exception of the foreign ones, though I have indeed long ago been translated by the Germans. The Czechs and the Serbs approve of me also, and the French are not indifferent. The mysteries of love I fathomed at the age of thirteen. With my colleagues, doctors, and literary men alike, I am on the best of terms. I am a bachelor. I should like to receive a pension. I practice medicine, and so much so that sometimes in the summer I perform post-mortems, though I have not done so for two or three years. Of authors my favourite is Tolstoy, of doctors Zaharin.

All that is nonsense though. Write what you like. If you haven't facts make up with lyricism.

TO A. S. KISELYOV.

MELIHOVO, STATION LOPASNYA, MOSCOW-KURSK LINE. March 7, 1892.

This is our new address. And here are the details for you. If a peasant woman has no troubles she buys a pig. We have bought a pig, too, a big cumbersome estate, the owner of which would in Germany infallibly be made a *herzog*. Six hundred and thirty-nine acres in two parts with land not ours in between. Three hundred acres of young copse, which in twenty years will look like a wood, at present is a thicket of bushes. They call it "shaft wood," but to my mind the name of "switch wood" would be more appropriate, since one could make nothing of it at present but switches. There is a fruit-garden, a park, big trees, long avenues of limes. The barns and sheds have been recently built, and have a fairly presentable appearance. The poultry house is made in accordance with the latest deductions of science, the well has an iron pump. The whole place is shut off from the world by a fence in the style of a palisade. The yard, the garden, the park, and the threshing-floor are shut off from each other in the same way. The house is good and bad. It's more roomy than our Moscow flat, it's light and warm, roofed with iron, and stands in a fine position, has a verandah into the garden, French windows, and so on, but it is bad in not being lofty, not sufficiently new, having outside a very stupid and naive appearance, and inside swarms with bugs and beetles which could only be got rid of by one means—a fire: nothing else would do for them.

There are flower-beds. In the garden fifteen paces from the house is a pond (thirty-five yards long, and thirty-five feet wide), with carp and tench in it, so that you can catch fish from the window. Beyond the yard there is another pond, which I have not yet seen. In the other part of the estate there is a river, probably a nasty one. Two miles away there is a broad river full of fish. We shall sow oats and clover. We have bought clover seed at ten roubles a pood, but we have no money left for oats. The estate has been bought for thirteen thousand. The legal formalities cost about seven hundred and fifty roubles, total fourteen thousand. The artist who sold it was paid four thousand down, and received a mortgage for five thousand at five per cent, for five years. The remaining four thousand the artist will receive from the Land Bank when in the spring I mortgage the estate to a bank. You see what a good arrangement. In two or three years I shall have five thousand, and shall pay off the mortgage, and shall be left with only the four thousand debt to the bank; but I have got to live those two of three years, hang it all! What matters is not the interest—that is small, not more than five hundred roubles a year—but that I shall be obliged all the time to think about quarter-days and all sorts of horrors attendant on being in debt. Moreover, your honour, as long as I am alive and earning four or five thousand a year, the debts will seem a trifle, and even a convenience, for to pay four hundred and seventy interest is much easier than to pay a thousand for a flat in Moscow; that is all true. But what if I depart from you sinners to another world—that is, give up the ghost? Then the ducal estate with the debts would seem to my parents in their green old age and to my sister such a burden that they would raise a wail to heaven.

I was completely cleaned out over the move.

Ah, if you could come and see us! In the first place it would be very delightful and interesting to see you; and in the second, your advice would save us from a thousand idiocies. You know we don't understand a thing about it. Like Raspluev, all I know about agriculture is that the earth is black, and nothing more. Write. How is it best to sow clover?—among the rye, or among the spring wheat? ...

TO I. L. SHTCHEGLOV.

MELIHOVO, March 9, 1892.

... Yes, such men as Ratchinsky are very rare in this world. I understand your enthusiasm, my dear fellow. After the suffocation one feels in the proximity of A. and B.—and the world is full of them—Ratchinsky with his ideas, his humanity, and his purity, seems like a breath of spring. I am ready to lay down my life for Ratchinsky; but, dear friend,—allow me that "but" and don't be vexed—I would not send my children to his school. Why? I received a religious education in my childhood—with church singing, with reading of the "apostles" and the psalms in church, with regular attendance at matins, with obligation to assist at the altar and ring the bells. And, do you know, when I think now of my childhood, it seems to me rather gloomy. I have no religion now. Do you know, when my brothers and I used to stand in the middle of the church and sing the trio "May my prayer be exalted," or "The Archangel's Voice," everyone looked at us with emotion and envied our parents, but we at that moment felt like little convicts. Yes, dear boy! Ratchinsky I understand, but the children who are trained by him I don't know. Their souls are dark for me. If there is joy in their souls, then they are happier than I and my brothers, whose childhood was suffering.

It is nice to be a lord. There is plenty of room, it's warm, people are not continually pulling at the bell; and it is easy to descend from one's lordship and serve as concierge or porter. My estate, sir, cost thirteen thousand, and I have only paid a third, the rest is a debt which will keep me long years on the chain.

Come and see me, Jean, together with Suvorin. Make a plan with him. I have such a garden! Such a naive courtyard, such geese! Write a little oftener.

TO A. S. SUVORIN.

MELIHOVO, March 17, 1892.

... Ah, my dear fellow, if only you could take a holiday! Living in the country is inconvenient. The insufferable time of thaw and mud is beginning, but something marvellous and moving is taking place in nature, the poetry and novelty of which makes up for all the discomforts of life. Every day there are surprises, one better than another. The starlings have returned, everywhere there is the gurgling of water, in places where the snow has thawed the grass is already green. The day drags on like eternity.

One lives as though in Australia, somewhere at the ends of the earth; one's mood is calm, contemplative, and animal, in the sense that one does not regret yesterday or look forward to tomorrow. From here, far away, people seem very good, and that is natural, for in going away into the country we are not hiding from people but from our vanity, which in town among people is unjust and active beyond measure. Looking at the spring, I have a dreadful longing that there should be paradise in the other world. In fact, at moments I am so happy that I superstitiously pull myself up and remind myself of my creditors, who will one day drive me out of the Australia I have so happily won....

TO MADAME AVILOV.

MELIHOVO, March 19, 1892.

HONOURED LIDYA ALEXYEVNA,

I have read your story "On the Road." If I were the editor of an illustrated magazine, I should publish the story with great pleasure; but here is my advice as a reader: when you depict sad or unlucky people, and want to touch the reader's heart, try to be colder—it gives their grief as it were a background, against which it stands out in greater relief. As it is, your heroes weep and you sigh. Yes, you must be cold.

But don't listen to me, I am a bad critic. I have not the faculty of forming my critical ideas clearly. Sometimes I make a regular hash of it....

TO A. S. SUVORIN.

MELIHOVO, March, 1892.

The cost of labour is almost nil, and so I am very well off. I begin to see the charms of capitalism. To pull down the stove in the servants' quarters and build up there a kitchen stove with all its accessories, then to pull down the kitchen stove in the house arid put up a Dutch stove instead, costs twenty roubles altogether. The price of two men to dig, twenty-five kopecks. To fill the ice cellar it costs thirty kopecks a day to the workmen. A young labourer who does not drink or smoke, and can read and write, whose duties are to work the land and clean the boots and look after the flower-garden, costs five roubles a month. Floors, partitions, papering walls—all that is cheaper than mushrooms. And I am at ease. But if I were to pay for labour a quarter of what I get for my leisure I should be ruined in a month, as the number of stove-builders, carpenters, joiners, and so on, threatens to go for ever after the fashion of a recurring decimal. A spacious life not cramped within four walls requires a spacious pocket too. I have bored you already, but I must tell you one thing more: the clover seed costs one hundred roubles a *pood*, and the oats needed for seed cost more than a hundred. Think of that! They prophesy a harvest and wealth for me, but what is that to me! Better five kopecks in the present than a rouble in the future. I must sit and work. I must earn at least five hundred roubles for all these trifles. I have earned half already. And the snow is melting, it is warm, the birds are singing, the sky is bright and spring-like.

I am reading a mass of things. I have read Lyeskov's "Legendary Characters," religious and piquant—a combination of virtue, piety, and lewdness, but very interesting. Read it if you haven't read it. I have read again Pisarev's "Criticism of Pushkin." Awfully naive. The man pulls Onyegin and Tatyana down from their pedestals, but Pushkin remains unhurt. Pisarev is the grandfather and father of all the critics of to-day, including Burenin—the same pettiness in disparagement, the same cold and conceited wit, and the same coarseness and indelicacy in their attitude to people. It is not Pisarev's ideas that are brutalizing, for he has none, but his coarse tone. His attitude to Tatyana, especially to her charming letter, which I love tenderly, seems to me simply abominable. The critic has the foul aroma of an insolent captious procurator.

We have almost finished furnishing; only the shelves for my books are not done yet. When we take out the double windows we shall begin painting everything afresh, and then the house will have a very presentable appearance.

There are avenues of lime-trees, apple-trees, cherries, plums, and raspberries in the garden....

MELIHOVO,

April 6, 1892.

It is Easter. There is a church here, but no clergy. We collected eleven roubles from the whole parish and got a priest from the Davydov

Monastery, who began celebrating the service on Friday. The church is very old and chilly, with lattice windows. We sang the Easter service—that is, my family and my visitors, young people. The effect was very good and harmonious, particularly the mass. The peasants were very much pleased, and they say they have never had such a grand service. Yesterday the sun shone all day, it was warm. In the morning I went into the fields, from which the snow has gone already, and spent half an hour in the happiest frame of mind: it was amazingly nice! The winter corn is green already, and there is grass in the copse.

You will not like Melihovo, at least at first. Here everything is in miniature; a little avenue of lime-trees, a pond the size of an aquarium, a little garden and park, little trees; but when you have walked about it once or twice the impression of littleness goes off. There is great feeling of space in spite of the village being so near. There is a great deal of forest around. There are numbers of starlings, and the starling has the right to say of itself: "I sing to my God all the days of my life." It sings all day long without stopping....

MELIHOVO,

April 8, 1892.

If Shapiro were to present me with the gigantic photograph of which you write, I should not know what to do with it. A cumbersome present. You say that I used to be younger. Yes, imagine! Strange as it may seem, I have passed thirty some time ago, and I already feel forty close at hand. I have grown old not in body only, but in spirit. I have become stupidly indifferent to everything in the world, and for some reason or other the beginning of this indifference coincided with my tour abroad. I get up and go to bed feeling as though interest in life had dried up in me. This is either the illness called in the newspapers nervous exhaustion, or some working of the spirit not clear to the consciousness, which is called in novels a spiritual revulsion. If it is the latter it is all for the best, I suppose.

The artist Levitan is staying with me. Yesterday evening I went out with him shooting. He shot at a snipe; the bird, shot in the wing, fell into a pool. I picked it up: a long beak, big black eyes, and beautiful plumage. It looked at me with surprise. What was I to do with it? Levitan scowled, shut his eyes, and begged me, with a quiver in his voice: "My dear fellow, hit him on the head with the butt-end of your gun." I said: "I can't." He went on nervously, shrugging his shoulders, twitching his head and begging me to; and the snipe went on looking at me in wonder. I had to obey Levitan and kill it. One beautiful creature in love the less, while two fools went home and sat down to supper.

Jean Shtcheglov, in whose company you were so bored for a whole evening, is a great opponent of every sort of heresy, and amongst others of feminine intellect; and yet if one compares him with K., for instance, beside her he seems like a foolish little monk. By the way, if you see K., give her my greetings, and tell her that we are expecting her here. She is very interesting in the open air and far more intelligent than in town....

TO MADAME AVILOV.

MELIHOVO, April 29, 1892.

... Yes, it is nice now in the country, not only nice but positively amazing. It's real spring, the trees are coming out, it is hot. The nightingales are singing, and the frogs are croaking in all sorts of tones. I haven't a halfpenny, but the way I look at it is this: the rich man is not he who has plenty of money, but he who has the means to live now in the luxurious surroundings given us by early spring. Yesterday I was in Moscow, but I almost expired there of boredom and all manner of disasters. Would you believe it, a lady of my acquaintance, aged forty-two, recognized herself in the twenty-year-old heroine of my story, "The Grasshopper" and all Moscow is accusing me of libelling her. The chief proof is the external likeness. The lady paints, her husband is a doctor, and she is living with an artist.

I am finishing a story ("Ward No. 6"), a very dull one, owing to a complete absence of woman and the element of love. I can't endure such stories. I write it as it were by accident, thoughtlessly.

Yes, I wrote to you once that you must be unconcerned when you write pathetic stories. And you did not understand me. You may weep and moan over your stories, you may suffer together with your heroes, but I consider one must do this so that the reader does not notice it. The more objective, the stronger will be the effect.

TO A. S. SUVORIN.

MELIHOVO, May 15, 1892.

... I have got hold of the peasants and the shopkeepers here. One had a haemorrhage from the throat, another had his arm crushed by a tree, a third had his little daughter sick.... It seems they would be in a desperate case without me. They bow respectfully to me as Germans do to their pastor, I am friends with them, and all goes well....

May 28, 1892.

Life is short, and Chekhov, from whom you are expecting an answer, would like it to flash by brilliantly and with dash. He would go to Prince's Island, to Constantinople, and again to India and Sahalin.... But in the first place he is not free, he has a respectable family who need his protection. In the second, he has a large dose of cowardice. Looking towards the future I call nothing but cowardice. I am afraid of getting into a muddle, and every journey complicates my financial position. No, don't tempt me without need. Don't write to me of the sea.

It is hot here. There are warm rains, the evenings are enchanting. Three-quarters of a mile from here there is a good bathing place and good sport for picnics, but no time to bathe or go to picnics. Either I am writing and gnashing my teeth, or settling questions of halfpence with carpenters and labourers. Misha was cruelly reprimanded by his superiors for coming to me every week instead of staying at home, and now there is no one but me to look after the farming, in which I have no faith, as it is on a petty scale, and more like a gentlemanly hobby than real work. I have bought three mousetraps, and catch twenty-five mice a day and carry them away to the copse. It is lovely in the copse....

Our starlings, old and young, suddenly flew away. This puzzled us, for it won't be time for their migration for ever so long; but suddenly we learn that the other day clouds of grasshoppers from the south, which were taken for locusts, flew over Moscow. One wonders how did our starlings find out that on precisely such a day and so many miles from Melihovo these insects would fly past? Who told them about it? Truly this is a great mystery....

June 16.

... You want me to write my impressions to you.

My soul longs for breadth and altitude, but I am forced to lead a narrow life spent over trashy roubles and kopecks. There is nothing more vulgar than a petty bourgeois life with its halfpence, its victuals, its futile talk, and its useless conventional virtue; my heart aches from the consciousness that I am working for money, and money is the centre of all I do. This aching feeling, together with a sense of justice, makes my writing a contemptible pursuit in my eyes: I don't respect what I write, I am apathetic and bored with myself, and glad that I have medicine which, anyway, I practise not for the sake of money. I ought to have a bath in sulphuric acid and flay off my skin, and then grow a new hide....

MELIHOVO,

August 1.

My letters chase you, but do not catch you. I have written to you often, and among other places to St. Moritz. Judging from your letters you have had nothing from me. In the first place, there is cholera in Moscow and about Moscow, and it will be in our parts some day soon. In the second place, I have been appointed cholera doctor, and my section includes twenty-five villages, four factories, and one monastery. I am organizing the building of barracks, and so on, and I feel lonely, for all the cholera business is alien to my heart, and the work, which involves continual driving about, talking, and attention to petty details, is exhausting for me. I have no time to write. Literature has been thrown aside for a long time now, and I am poverty-stricken, as I thought it convenient for myself and my independence to refuse the remuneration received by the section doctors. I am bored, but there is a great deal that is interesting in cholera if you look at it from a detached point of view. I am sorry you are not in Russia. Material for short letters is being wasted. There is more good than bad, and in that cholera is a great contrast to the famine which we watched in the winter. Now all are working—they are working furiously. At the fair at Nizhni they are doing marvels which might force even Tolstoy to take a respectful attitude to medicine and the intervention of cultured people generally in life. It seems as though they had got a hold on the cholera. They have not only decreased the number of cases, but also the percentage of deaths. In immense Moscow the cholera does not exceed fifty cases a week, while on the Don it is a thousand a day—an impressive difference. We district doctors are getting ready; our plan of action is definite, and there are grounds for supposing that in our parts we too shall decrease the percentage of mortality from cholera. We have no assistants, one has to be doctor and sanitary attendant at one and the same time. The peasants are rude, dirty in their habits, and mistrustful; but the thought that our labours are not thrown away makes all that scarcely noticeable. Of all the Serpuhovo doctors I am the most pitiable; I have a scurvy carriage and horses, I don't know the roads, I see nothing by evening light, I have no money, I am very quickly exhausted, and worst of all, I can never forget that I ought to be writing, and I long to spit on the cholera and sit down and write to you, and I long to talk to you. I am in absolute loneliness.

Our farming labours have been crowned with complete success. The harvest is considerable, and when we sell the corn Melihovo will bring us more than a thousand roubles. The kitchen garden is magnificent. There are perfect mountains of cucumbers and the cabbage is wonderful. If it were not for the accursed cholera I might say that I have never spent a summer so happily as this one.

Nothing has been heard of cholera riots yet. There is talk of some arrests, some manifestoes, and so on. They say that A., the writer, has been condemned to fifteen years' penal servitude. If the socialists are really going to exploit the cholera for their own ends I shall despise them. Revolting means for good ends make the ends themselves revolting. Let them get a lift on the backs of the doctors and feldshers, but why lie to the peasants? Why persuade them that they are right in their ignorance and that their coarse prejudices are the holy truth? If I were a politician I could never bring myself to disgrace my present for the sake of the future, even though I were promised tons of felicity for an ounce of mean lying. Write to me as often as possible in consideration of my exceptional position. I cannot be in a good mood now, and your letters snatch me away from cholera concerns, and carry me for a brief space to another world....

August 16.

I'll be damned if I write to you again. I have written to Abbazzio, to St. Moritz. I have written a dozen times at least, so far you have not sent me one correct address, and so not one of my letters has reached and my long description and lectures about the cholera have been wasted. It's mortifying. But what is most mortifying is that after a whole series of letters from me about our exertions against the cholera, you all at once write me from gay Biarritz that you envy my leisure! Well, Allah forgive you!

Well, I am alive and in good health. The summer was a splendid one, dry, warm, abounding in the fruits of the earth, but its whole charm was from July onwards, spoilt by news of the cholera. While you were inviting me in your letters first to Vienna, and then to Abbazzio I was already one of the doctors of the Serpuhovo Zemstvo, was trying to catch the cholera by its tail and organizing a new section full steam. In the morning I have to see patients, and in the afternoon drive about. I drive, I give lectures to the natives, treat them, get angry with them, and as the Zemstvo has not granted me a single kopeck for organizing the medical centres I cadge from the wealthy, first from one and then from another. I turn out to be an excellent beggar; thanks to my beggarly eloquence, my section has two excellent barracks with all the necessaries, and five barracks that are not excellent, but horrid. I have saved the Zemstvo from expenditure even on disinfectants. Lime, vitriol, and all sorts of stinking stuff I have begged from the manufacturers for all my twenty-five villages. In fact Kolomin ought to be proud of having been at the same high school with me. My soul is exhausted. I am bored. Not to belong to oneself, to think about nothing but diarrhoea, to start up in the night at a dog's barking and a knock at the gate ("Haven't they come for me?"), to drive with disgusting horses along unknown roads; to read about nothing but cholera, and to expect nothing but cholera, and at the same time to be utterly uninterested in that disease, and in the people whom one is serving—that, my good sir, is a hash which wouldn't agree with anyone. The cholera is already in Moscow and in the Moscow district. One must expect it from hour to hour. Judging from its course in Moscow one must suppose that it is already declining and that the bacillus is losing its strength. One is bound to think, too, that it is powerfully affected by the measures that have been taken in Moscow and among us. The educated classes are working vigorously, sparing neither themselves nor their purses; I see them every day, and am touched, and when I remember how Zhitel and Burenin used to vent their acrid spleen on these same educated people I feel almost suffocated. In Nizhni the doctors and the cultured people generally have done marvels. I was overwhelmed with enthusiasm when I read about the cholera. In the good old times, when people were infected and died by thousands, the amazing conquests that are being made before our eyes could not even be dreamed of. It's a pity you are not a doctor and cannot share my delight—that is, fully feel and recognize and appreciate all that is being done. But one cannot tell about it briefly.

The treatment of cholera requires of the doctor deliberation before all things—that is, one has to devote to each patient from five to ten hours or even longer. As I mean to employ Kantani's treatment—that is clysters of tannin and sub-cutaneous injection of a solution of common salt—my position will be worse than foolish; while I am busying myself over one patient, a dozen can fall ill and die. You see I am the only man for twenty-five villages, apart from a feldsher who calls me "your honour," does not venture to smoke in my presence, and cannot take a step without me. If there are isolated cases I shall be capital; but if there is an epidemic of only five cases a day, then I shall do nothing but be irritable and exhausted and feel myself guilty.

Of course there is no time even to think of literature. I am writing nothing. I refused remuneration so as to preserve some little freedom of action for myself, and so I have not a halfpenny. I am waiting till they have threshed and sold the rye. Until then I shall be living on "The Bear" and mushrooms, of which there are endless masses here. By the way, I have never lived so cheaply as now. We have everything of our own, even our own bread. I believe in a couple of years all my household expenses will not exceed a thousand roubles a year.

When you learn from the newspapers that the cholera is over, you will know that I have gone back to writing again. Don't think of me as a literary man while I am in the service of the Zemstvo. One can't do two things at once.

You write that I have given up Sahalin. I cannot abandon that child of mine. When I am oppressed by the boredom of belles-lettres I am glad to turn to something else. The question when I shall finish Sahalin and when I shall print does not strike me as being important. While Galkin-Vrasskoy reigns over the prison system I feel very much disinclined to bring out my book. Of course if I am driven to it by need, that is a different matter.

In all my letters I have pertinaciously asked you one question, which of course you are not obliged to answer: "Where are you going to be in the autumn, and wouldn't you like to spend part of September and October with me in Feodosia or the Crimea?" I have an impatient desire to eat, drink, and sleep, and talk about literature—that is, do nothing, and at the same time feel like a decent person. However, if my idleness annoys you, I can promise to write with or beside you, a play or a story.... Eh? Won't you? Well, God be with you, then.

The astronomer has been here twice. I felt bored with her on both occasions. Svobodin has been here too. He grows better and better. His serious illness has made him pass through a spiritual metamorphosis.

See what a long letter I have written, even though I don't feel sure that the letter will reach you. Imagine my cholera-boredom, my cholera-loneliness, and compulsory literary inactivity, and write to me more, and oftener. Your contemptuous feeling for France I share. The Germans are far above them, though for some reason they are called stupid. And the Franco-Russian Entente Cordiale I am as fond of as Tolstoy is. There's something nastily suggestive about these cordialities. On the other hand I was awfully pleased at Virchow's visit to us.

We have raised a very nice potato and a divine cabbage. How do you manage to get on without cabbage-soup? I don't envy you your sea, nor your freedom, nor the happy frame of mind you are in abroad. The Russian summer is better than anything. And by the way, I don't feel any great longing to be abroad. After Singapore, Ceylon, and perhaps even our Amur, Italy and even the crater of Vesuvius do not seem fascinating. After being in India and China I did not see a great difference between other European countries and Russia.

A neighbour of ours, the owner of the renowned Otrad, Count X, is staying now at Biarritz, having run away from the cholera; he gave his doctor only five hundred roubles for the campaign against the cholera. His sister, the countess, who is living in my section, when I went to discuss the provision of barracks for her workmen, treated me as though I had come to apply for a situation. It mortified me, and I told her a lie, pretending to be a rich man. I told the same lie to the Archimandrite, who refuses to provide quarters for the cases which may occur in the monastery. To my question what would he do with the cases that might be taken ill in his hostel, he answered me: "They are persons of means and will pay you themselves...." Do you understand? And I flared up, and said I did not care about payment, as I was well off, and that all I wanted was the security of the monastery.... There are sometimes very stupid and humiliating positions.... Before the count went away I met his wife. Huge diamonds in her ears, wearing a bustle, and not knowing how to hold herself. A millionaire. In the company of such persons one has a stupid schoolboy feeling of wanting to be rude.

The village priest often comes and pays me long visits; he is a very good fellow, a widower, and has some illegitimate children.

Write or there will be trouble....

MELIHOVO,

October 10, 1892.

Your telegram telling me of Svobodin's death caught me just as I was going out of the yard to see patients. You can imagine my feelings. Svobodin stayed with me this summer; he was very sweet and gentle, in a serene and affectionate mood, and became very much attached to me. It was evident to me that he had not very long to live, it was evident to him too. He had the thirst of the aged for everyday peace and quiet, and had grown to detest the stage and everything to do with the stage and dreaded returning to Petersburg. Of course I ought to go to the funeral, but to begin with, your telegram came towards evening, and the funeral is most likely tomorrow, and secondly the cholera is twenty miles away, and I cannot leave my centre. There are seven cases in one village, and two have died already. The cholera may break out in my section. It is strange that with winter coming on the cholera is spreading over a wider and wider region.

I have undertaken to be the section doctor till the fifteenth of October—my section will be officially closed on that day. I shall dismiss my feldsher, close the barracks, and if the cholera comes, I shall cut rather a comic figure. Add to that the doctor of the next section is ill with pleurisy and so, if the cholera appears in his section, I shall be bound, from a feeling of comradeship, to undertake his section.

So far I have not had a single case of cholera, but I have had epidemics of typhus, diphtheria, scarlatina, and so on. At the beginning of summer I had a great deal of work, then towards the autumn less and less.

The sum of my literary achievement this summer, thanks to the cholera, has been almost nil. I have written little, and have thought about literature even less. However, I have written two small stories—one tolerable, one bad.

Life has been hard work this summer, but it seems, to me now that I have never spent a summer so well as this one. In spite of the turmoil of the cholera, and the poverty which has kept tight hold of me all the summer, I have liked the life and wanted to live. How many trees I have planted! Thanks to our system of cultivation, Melihovo has become unrecognizable, and seems now extraordinarily snug and beautiful, though very likely it is good for nothing. Great is the power of habit and the sense of property. And it's marvellous how pleasant it is not to have to pay rent. We have made new acquaintances and formed new relations. Our old terrors in facing the peasants now seem ludicrous. I have served in the Zemstvo, have presided at the Sanitary Council and visited the factories, and I liked all that. They think of me now as one of themselves, and stay the night with me when they pass through Melihovo. Add to that, that we have bought ourselves a new comfortable covered carriage, have made a new road, so that now we don't drive through the village. We are digging a pond.... Anything else? In fact hitherto everything has been new and interesting, but how it will be later on, I don't know. There is snow already, it is cold, but I don't feel drawn to Moscow. So far I have not had any feeling of dulness.

The educated people here are very charming and interesting. What matters most, they are honest. Only the police are unattractive.

We have seven horses, a broad-faced calf, and puppies, called Muir and Merrilees....

November 22, 1892.

Snow is falling by day, while at night the moon is shining its utmost, a gorgeous amazing moon. It is magnificent. But nevertheless, I marvel at the fortitude of landowners who spend the winter in the country; there's so little to do that if anyone is not in one way or another engaged in intellectual work, he is inevitably bound to become a glutton or a drunkard, or a man like Turgenev's Pigasov. The monotony of the snowdrifts and the bare trees, the long nights, the moonlight, the deathlike stillness day and night, the peasant women and the old ladies—all that disposes one to indolence, indifference, and an enlarged liver....

November 25, 1892.

It is easy to understand you, and there is no need for you to abuse yourself for obscurity of expression. You are a hard drinker, and I have regaled you with sweet lemonade, and you, after giving the lemonade its due, justly observe that there is no spirit in it. That is just what is lacking in our productions—the alcohol which could intoxicate and subjugate, and you state that very well. Why not? Putting aside "Ward No. 6" and myself, let us discuss the matter in general, for that is more interesting. Let me discuss the general causes, if that won't bore you, and let us include the whole age. Tell me honestly, who of my contemporaries—that is, men between thirty and forty-five—have given the world one single drop of alcohol? Are not Korolenko, Nadson, and all the playwrights of to-day, lemonade? Have Ryepin's or Shishkin's pictures turned your head? Charming, talented, you are enthusiastic; but at the same time you can't forget that you want to smoke. Science and technical knowledge are passing through a great period now, but for our sort it is a flabby, stale, and dull time. We are stale and dull ourselves, we can only beget gutta-percha boys, [Footnote: An allusion to Grigorovitch's well-known story.] and the only person who does not see that is Stassov, to whom nature has given a rare faculty for getting drunk on slops. The causes of this are not to be found in our stupidity, our lack of talent, or our insolence, as Burenin imagines, but in a disease which for the artist is worse than syphilis or sexual exhaustion. We lack "something," that is true, and that means that, lift the robe of our muse, and you will find within an empty void. Let me remind you that the writers, who we say are for all time or are simply good, and who intoxicate us, have one common and very important characteristic; they are going towards something and are summoning you towards it, too, and you feel not with your mind, but with your whole being, that they have some object, just like the ghost of Hamlet's father, who did not come and disturb the imagination for nothing. Some have more immediate objects—the abolition of serfdom, the liberation of their country, politics, beauty, or simply vodka, like Denis Davydov; others have remote objects—God, life beyond the grave, the happiness of humanity, and so on. The best of them are realists and paint life as it is, but, through every line's being soaked in the consciousness of an object, you feel, besides life as it is, the life which ought to be, and that captivates you. And we? We! We paint life as it is, but beyond that—nothing at all.... Flog us and we can do no more! We have neither immediate nor remote aims, and in our soul there is a great empty space. We have no politics, we do not believe in revolution, we have no God, we are not afraid of ghosts, and I personally am not afraid even of death and blindness. One who wants nothing, hopes for nothing, and fears nothing, cannot be an artist. Whether it is a disease or not—what it is does not matter; but we ought to recognize that our position is worse than a governor's. I don't know how it will be with us in ten or twenty years— then circumstances may be different, but meanwhile it would be rash to expect of us anything of real value, apart from the question whether we have talent or not. We write mechanically, merely obeying the long-established arrangement in accordance with which some men go into the government service, others into trade, others write.... Grigorovitch and you think I am clever. Yes, I am at least so far clever as not to conceal from myself my disease, and not to deceive myself, and not to cover up my own emptiness with other people's rags, such as the ideas of the sixties, and so on. I am not going to throw myself like Garshin over the banisters, but I am not going to flatter myself with hopes of a better future either. I am not to blame for my disease, and it's not for me to cure myself, for this disease, it must be supposed, has some good purpose hidden from us, and is not sent in vain....

February, 1893.

My God! What a glorious thing "Fathers and Children" is! It is positively terrifying. Bazarov's illness is so powerfully done that I felt ill and had a sensation as though I had caught the infection from him. And the end of Bazarov? And the old men? And Kukshina? It's beyond words. It's simply a work of genius. I don't like the whole of "On the Eve," only Elena's father and the end. The end is full of tragedy. "The Dog" is very good, the language is wonderful in it. Please read it if you have forgotten it. "Acia" is charming, "A Quiet Backwater" is too compressed and not satisfactory. I don't like "Smoke" at all. "The House of Gentlefolk" is weaker than "Fathers and Children," but the end is like a miracle, too. Except for the old woman in "Fathers and Children"—that is, Bazarov's mother—and the mothers as a rule, especially the society ladies, who are, however, all alike (Liza's mother, Elena's mother), and Lavretsky's mother, who had been a serf, and the humble peasant woman, all Turgenev's girls and women are insufferable in their artificiality, and—forgive my saying it—falsity. Liza and Elena are not Russian girls, but some sort of Pythian prophetesses, full of extravagant pretensions. Irina in "Smoke," Madame Odintsov in "Fathers and Children," all the lionesses, in fact, fiery, alluring, insatiable creatures for ever craving for something, are all nonsensical. When one thinks of Tolstoy's "Anna Karenin," all these young ladies of Turgenev's, with their seductive shoulders, fade away into nothing. The negative types of women where Turgenev is slightly caricaturing (Kukshina) or jesting (the descriptions of balls) are wonderfully drawn, and so successful, that, as the saying is, you can't pick a hole in it.

The descriptions of nature are fine, but ... I feel that we have already got out of the way of such descriptions and that we need something different....

April 26, 1893.

... I am reading Pisemsky. His is a great, very great talent! The best of his works is "The Carpenters' Guild." His novels are exhausting in their minute detail. Everything in him that has a temporary character, all his digs at the critics and liberals of the period, all his critical observations with their assumption of smartness and modernity, and all the so-called profound reflections scattered here and there—how petty and naive it all is to our modern ideas! The fact of the matter is this: a novelist, an artist, ought to pass by everything that has only a temporary value. Pisemsky's people are living, his temperament is vigorous. Skabitchevsky in his history attacks him for obscurantism and treachery, but, my God! of all contemporary writers I don't know a single one so passionately and earnestly liberal as Pisemsky. All his priests, officials, and generals are regular blackguards. No one was so down on the old legal and military set as he.

By the way, I have read also Bourget's "Cosmopolis." Rome and the Pope and Correggio and Michael Angelo and Titian and doges and a fifty-year-old beauty and Russians and Poles are all in Bourget, but how thin and strained and mawkish and false it is in comparison even with our coarse and simple Pisemsky! ...

What a good thing I gave up the town! Tell all the Fofanovs, Tchermnys, *et tutti quanti* who live by literature, that living in the country is immensely cheaper than living in the town. I experience this now every day. My family costs me nothing now, for lodging, bread, vegetables, milk, butter, horses, are all our own. And there is so much to do, there is not time to get through it all. Of the whole family of Chekhovs, I am the only one to lie down, or sit at the table: all the rest are working from morning till night. Drive the poets and literary men into the country. Why should they live in starvation and beggary? Town life cannot give a poor man rich material in the sense of poetry and art. He lives within four walls and sees people only at the editors' offices and in eating-shops....

MELIHOVO,

January 25, 1894.

I believe I am mentally sound. It is true I have no special desire to live, but that is not, so far, disease, but something probably passing and natural. It does not follow every time that an author describes someone mentally deranged, that he is himself deranged. I wrote "The Black Monk" without any melancholy ideas, through cool reflection. I simply had a desire to describe megalomania. The monk floating across the country was a dream, and when I woke I told Misha about it. So you can tell Anna Ivanovna that poor Anton Pavlovitch, thank God! has not gone out of his mind yet, but that he eats a great deal at supper and so he dreams of monks.

I keep forgetting to write to you: read Ertel's story "The Seers" in "Russkaya Mysl." There is poetry and something terrible in the old-fashioned fairy-tale style about it. It is one of the best new things that has come out in Moscow....

YALTA,

March 27, 1894.

I am in good health generally, ill in certain parts. For instance, a cough, palpitations of the heart, haemorrhoids. I had palpitations of the heart incessantly for six days, and the sensation all the time was loathsome. Since I have quite given up smoking I have been free from gloomy and anxious moods. Perhaps because I am not smoking, Tolstoy's morality has ceased to touch me; at the bottom of my heart I take up a hostile attitude towards it, and that of course is not just. I have peasant blood in my veins, and you won't astonish me with peasant virtues. From my childhood I have believed in progress, and I could not help believing in it since the difference between the time when I used to be thrashed and when they gave up thrashing me was tremendous.... But Tolstoy's philosophy touched me profoundly and took possession of me for six or seven years, and what affected me was not its general propositions, with which I was familiar beforehand, but Tolstoy's manner of expressing it, his reasonableness, and probably a sort of hypnotism. Now something in me protests, reason and justice tell me that in the electricity and heat of love for man there is something greater than chastity and abstinence from meat. War is an evil and legal justice is an evil; but it does not follow from that that I ought to wear bark shoes and sleep on the stove with the labourer, and so on, and so on. But that is not the point, it is not a matter of *pro and con*; the thing is that in one way or another Tolstoy has passed for me, he is not in my soul, and he has departed from me, saying: "I leave this your house empty." I am untenanted. I am sick of theorizing of all sorts, and such bounders as Max Nordau I read with positive disgust. Patients in a fever do not want food, but they do want something, and that vague craving they express as "longing for something sour." I, too, want something sour, and that's not a mere chance feeling, for I notice the same mood in others around me. It is just as if they had all been in love, had fallen out of love, and now were looking for some new distraction. It is very possible and very likely that the Russians will pass through another period of enthusiasm for the natural sciences, and that the materialistic movement will be fashionable. Natural science is performing miracles now. And it may act upon people like Mamay, and dominate them by its mass and grandeur. All that is in the hands of God, however. And theorizing about it makes one's head go round.

TO L. S. MIZINOV.

YALTA, March 27, 1894.

DEAR LIKA,

Thanks for your letter. Though you do scare me in your letter saying you are soon going to die, though you do taunt me with having rejected you, yet thank you all the same; I know perfectly well you are not going to die, and that no one has rejected you.

I am in Yalta and I am dreary, very dreary indeed. The aristocracy, so to call it, are performing "Faust," and I go to the rehearsals and there I enjoy the spectacle of a perfect flower-bed of black, red, flaxen, and brown heads; I listen to the singing and I eat. At the house of the principal of the high school I eat tchibureks, and saddle of lamb with boiled grain; in various estimable families I eat green soup; at the confectioner's I eat—in my hotel also. I go to bed at ten and I get up at ten, and after dinner I lie down and rest, and yet I am bored, dear Lika. I am not bored because "my ladies" are not with me, but because the northern spring is better than the spring here, and because the thought that I must, that I ought to write never leaves me for an instant. To write and write and write! It is my opinion that true happiness is impossible without idleness. My ideal is to be idle and to love a plump girl. My loftiest happiness is to walk or to sit doing nothing; my favourite occupation is to gather up what is not wanted (leaves, straws, and so on) and to do what is useless. Meanwhile, I am a literary man, and have to write here in Yalta. Dear Lika, when you become a great singer and are paid a handsome salary, then be charitable to me, marry me, and keep me at your expense, that I may be free to do nothing. If you really are going to die, it might be undertaken by Varya Eberly, whom, as you know, I love. I am so all to pieces with the perpetual thought of work I ought to do and can't avoid that for the last week I have been continually tormented with palpitations of the heart. It's a loathsome sensation.

I have sold my fox-skin greatcoat for twenty roubles! It cost sixty, but as forty roubles' worth of fur has peeled off it, twenty roubles was not too low a price. The gooseberries are not ripe here yet, but it is warm and bright, the trees are coming out, the sea looks like summer, the young ladies are yearning for sensations: but yet the north is better than the south of Russia, in spring at any rate. In our part nature is more melancholy, more lyrical, more Levitanesque; here it is neither one thing nor the other, like good, sonorous, but frigid verse. Thanks to my palpitations I haven't drunk wine for a week, and that makes the surroundings seem even poorer....

M. gave a concert here, and made one hundred and fifty roubles clear profit. He roared like a grampus but had an immense success. I am awfully sorry I did not study singing; I could have roared too, as my throat is rich in husky elements, and they say I have a real octave. I should have earned money, and been a favourite with the ladies....

TO HIS BROTHER ALEXANDR.

MELIHOVO, April 15, 1894.

... I have come back from the flaming Tavrida and am already sitting on the cool banks of my pond. It's very warm, however: the thermometer runs up to twenty-six....

I am busy looking after the land: I am making new avenues, planting flowers, chopping down dead trees, and chasing the hens and the dogs out of the garden. Literature plays the part of Erakit, who was always in the background. I don't want to write, and indeed, it's hard to combine a desire to live and a desire to write....

TO A. S. SUVORIN.

Of course it is very nice in the country; in fine weather Russia is an extraordinarily beautiful and enchanting country, especially for those who have been born and spent their childhood in the country. But you will never buy yourself an estate, as you don't know what you want. To like an estate you must make up your mind to buy it; so long as it is not yours it will seem comfortless and full of defects. My cough is considerably better, I am sunburnt, and they tell me I am fatter, but the other day I almost fell down and I fancied for a minute that I was dying. I was walking along the avenue with the prince, our neighbour, and was talking when all at once something seemed to break in my chest, I had a feeling of warmth and suffocation, there was a singing in my ears, I remembered that I had been having palpitations for a long time and thought—"they must have meant something then." I went rapidly towards the verandah on which visitors were sitting, and had one thought—that it would be awkward to fall down and die before strangers; but I went into my bedroom, drank some water, and recovered.

So you are not the only one who suffers from staggering!

I am beginning to build a pretty lodge....

May 9.

I have no news. The weather is most exquisite, and in the foliage near the house a nightingale is building and shouting incessantly. About twelve miles from me there is the village of Pokrovskoe-Meshtcherskoe; the old manor house there is now the lunatic asylum of the province. The Zemsky doctors from the whole Moscow province met there on the fourth of May, to the number of about seventy-five; I was there too. There are a great many patients but all that is interesting material for alienists and not for psychologists. One patient, a mystic, preaches that the Holy Trinity has come upon earth in the form of the metropolitan of Kiev, Ioannikiy. "A limit of ten years has been given us; eight have passed, only two years are left. If we do not want Russia to fall into ruins like Sodom, all Russia must go in a procession with the Cross to Kiev, as Moscow went to Troitsa, and pray there to the divine martyr in the noble form of the metropolitan Ioannikiy." This queer fellow is convinced that the doctors in the asylum are poisoning him, and that he is being saved by the miraculous intervention of Christ in the form of the metropolitan. He is continually praying to the East and singing, and, addressing himself to God, invariably adds the words, "in the noble form of the metropolitan Ioannikiy." He has a lovely expression of face....

From the madhouse I returned late at night in my troika. Two-thirds of the way I had to drive through the forest in the moonlight, and I had a wonderful feeling such as I have not had for a long time, as though I had come back from a tryst. I think that nearness to nature and idleness are essential elements of happiness; without them it is impossible....

TO MADAME AVILOV.

MELIHOVO, July, 1894.

I have so many visitors that I cannot answer your last letter. I want to write at length but am pulled up at the thought that any minute they may come in and hinder me. And in fact while I write the word "hinder," a girl has come in and announced that a patient has arrived; I must go.... I have grown to detest writing, and I don't know what to do. I would gladly take up medicine and would accept any sort of post, but I no longer have the physical elasticity for it. When I write now or think I ought to write I feel as much disgust as though I were eating soup from which I had just removed a beetle—forgive the comparison. What I hate is not the writing itself, but the literary entourage from which one cannot escape, and which one takes everywhere as the earth takes its atmosphere....

TO A. S. SUVORIN.

MELIHOVO, August 15, 1894.

Our trip on the Volga turned out rather a queer one in the end. Potapenko and I went to Yaroslav to take a steamer from there to

Tsaritsyn, then to Kalatch, from there by the Don to Taganrog. The journey from Yaroslav to Nizhni is beautiful, but I had seen it before. Moreover, it was very hot in the cabin and the wind lashed in our faces on deck. The passengers were an uneducated set, whose presence was irritating. At Nizhni we were met by N., Tolstoy's friend. The heat, the dry wind, the noise of the fair and the conversation of N. suddenly made me feel so suffocated, so ill at ease, and so sick, that I took my portmanteau and ignominiously fled to the railway station.... Potapenko followed me. We took the train for Moscow, but we were ashamed to go home without having done anything, and we decided to go somewhere if it had to be to Lapland. If it had not been for his wife our choice would have fallen on Feodosia, but ... alas! we have a wife living at Feodosia. We thought it over, we talked it over, we counted over our money, and came to the Psyol to Suma, which you know.... Well, the Psyol is magnificent. There is warmth, there is space, an immensity of water and of greenery and delightful people. We spent six days on the Psyol, ate and drank, walked and did nothing: my ideal of happiness, as you know, is idleness. Now I am at Melihovo again. There is a cold rain, a leaden sky, mud.

It sometimes happens that one passes a third-class refreshment room and sees a cold fish, cooked long before, and wonders carelessly who wants that unappetising fish. And yet undoubtedly that fish is wanted, and will be eaten, and there are people who will think it nice. One may say the same of the works of N. He is a bourgeois writer, writing for the unsophisticated public who travel third class. For that public Tolstoy and Turgenev are too luxurious, too aristocratic, somewhat alien and not easily digested. There is a public which eats salt beef and horse-radish sauce with relish, and does not care for artichokes and asparagus. Put yourself at its point of view, imagine the grey, dreary courtyard, the educated ladies who look like cooks, the smell of paraffin, the scantiness of interests and tasks—and you will understand N. and his readers. He is colourless; that is partly because the life he describes lacks colour. He is false because bourgeois writers cannot help being false. They are vulgar writers perfected. The vulgarians sin together with their public, while the bourgeois are hypocritical with them and flatter their narrow virtue.

MELIHOVO,

February 25, 1895.

... I should like to meet a philosopher like Nietzsche somewhere in a train or a steamer, and to spend the whole night talking to him. I consider his philosophy won't last long, however. It's more showy than convincing....

MELIHOVO,

March 16, 1895.

Instead of you, heaven has sent me N., who has come to see me with E. and Z., two young duffers who never miss a single word but induce in the whole household a desperate boredom. N. looks flabby and physically slack; he has gone off, but has become warmer and more good-natured; he must be going to die. When my mother was ordering meat from the butcher, she said he must let us have better meat, as N. was staying with us from Petersburg.

"What N.?" asked the butcher in surprise—"the one who writes books?" and he sent us excellent meat. So the butcher does not know that I write books, for he never sends anything but gristle for my benefit....

Your little letter about physical games for students will do good if only you will go on insisting on the subject. Games are absolutely essential. Playing games is good for health and beauty and liberalism, since nothing is so conducive to the blending of classes, et cetera, as public games. Games would give our solitary young people acquaintances; young people would more frequently fall in love; but games should not be instituted before the Russian student ceases to be hungry. No skating, no croquet, can keep the student cheerful and confident on an empty stomach.

MELIHOVO,

March 23, 1895.

I told you that Potapenko was a man very full of life, but you did not believe me. In the entrails of every Little Russian lie hidden many treasures. I fancy when our generation grows old, Potapenko will be the gayest and jolliest old man of us all.

By all means I will be married if you wish it. But on these conditions: everything must be as it has been hitherto—that is, she must live in Moscow while I live in the country, and I will come and see her. Happiness continued from day to day, from morning to morning, I cannot stand. When every day I am told of the same thing, in the same tone of voice, I become furious. I am furious, for instance, in the society of S., because he is very much like a woman ("a clever and responsive woman") and because in his presence the idea occurs to me that my wife might be like him. I promise you to be a splendid husband, but give me a wife who, like the moon, won't appear in my sky every day; I shan't write any better for being married....

Mamin-Sibiryak is a very nice fellow and an excellent writer. His last novel "Bread" is praised; Lyeskov was particularly enthusiastic about it. There are undoubtedly fine things in his work, and in his more successful stories the peasants are depicted every bit as well as in "Master and Man."

This is the fourth year I have been living at Melihovo. My calves have turned into cows, my copse has grown at least a yard higher, my heirs will make a capital bargain over the timber and will call me an ass, for heirs are never satisfied.

MELIHOVO,

March 30, 1895.

... We have spring here but there are regular mountains of snow, and there is no knowing when it will thaw. As soon as the sun hides behind a cloud there begins to be a chill breath from the snow, and it is horrible. Masha is already busy in the flower-beds and borders. She tires herself out and is constantly cross, so there is no need for her to read Madame Smirnov's article. The advice given is excellent; the young ladies will read it, and it will be their salvation. Only one point is not clear: how are they going to get rid of the apples and cabbages if the estate is far from the town, and of what stuff are they going to make their own dresses if their rye does not sell at all, and they have not a halfpenny? To live on one's land by the labour of one's own hands and the sweat of one's brow is only possible on one condition; that is, if one works oneself like a peasant, without regard for class or sex. There is no making use of slaves nowadays, one must take the scythe and axe oneself, and if one can't do that, no gardens will help one. Even the smallest success in farming is only gained in Russia at the price of a cruel struggle with nature, and wishing is not enough for the struggle, you need bodily strength and grit, you want traditions—and have young ladies all that? To advise young ladies to take up farming is much the same as to advise them to be bears, and to bend yokes....

I have no money, but I live in the country: there are no restaurants and no cabmen, and money does not seem to be needed.

MELIHOVO,

April 13, 1895.

I am sick of Sienkiewicz's "The Family of the Polonetskys." It's the Polish Easter cake with saffron. Add Potapenko to Paul Bourget, sprinkle with Warsaw eau-de-Cologne, divide in two, and you get Sienkiewicz. "The Polonetskys" is unmistakably inspired by Bourget's "Cosmopolis," by Rome and by marriage (Sienkiewicz has lately got married). We have the catacombs and a queer old professor sighing after idealism, and Leo XIII, with the unearthly face among the saints, and the advice to return to the prayer-book, and the libel on the decadent who dies of morphinism after confessing and taking the sacrament—that is, after repenting of his errors in the name of the Church. There is a devilish lot of family happiness and talking about love, and the hero's wife is so faithful to her husband and so subtly comprehends "with her heart" the mysteries of God and life, that in the end one feels mawkish and uncomfortable as after a slobbering kiss. Sienkiewicz has evidently not read Tolstoy, and does not know Nietzsche, he talks about hypnotism like a shopman; on the other hand every page is positively sprinkled with Rubens, Borghesi, Correggio, Botticelli—and that is done to show off his culture to the bourgeois reader and make a long nose on the sly at materialism. The object of the novel is to lull the bourgeoisie to sleep in its golden dreams. Be faithful to your wife, pray with her over the prayer-book, save money, love sport, and all is well with you in this world and the next. The bourgeoisie is very fond of so-called practical types and novels with happy endings, since they soothe it with the idea that one can both accumulate capital and preserve innocence, be a beast and at the same time be happy....

I wish you every sort of blessing. I congratulate you on the peace between Japan and China, and hope we may quickly obtain a Feodosia free from ice on the East Coast, and may make a railway to it.

The peasant woman had not troubles enough so she bought a pig. And I fancy we are saving up a lot of trouble for ourselves with this ice-free port. [Footnote: Prophetic of Port Arthur and the Japanese War.] It will cost us dearer than if we were to take it into our heads to wage war on all Japan. However, *futura sunt in manibus deorum.*

MELIHOVO,

October 21, 1895.

Thanks for your letter, for your warm words and your invitation. I will come, but most likely not before the end of November, as I have a devilish lot to do. First in the spring I am going to build a new school in the village where I am school warden; before beginning I have to make a plan and calculations, and to drive off here and there, and so on. Secondly—can you imagine it—I am writing a play which I shall probably not finish before the end of November. I am writing it not without pleasure, though I swear fearfully at the conventions of the stage. It's a comedy, there are three women's parts, six men's, four acts, landscapes (view over a lake); a great deal of conversation about literature, little action, tons of love. [Footnote: "The Seagull."] I read of Ozerova's failure and was sorry, for nothing is more painful than failing.... I have read of the success of the "Powers of Darkness" in your theatre.... When I was at Tolstoy's in August, he told me, as he was wiping his hands after washing, that he wouldn't alter his play. And now, remembering that, I fancy that he knew even then that his play would be passed by the censor *in toto.* I spent two days and a night with him. He made a delightful impression, I felt as much at ease as though I were at home, and our talks were easy....

MOSCOW,

October 26, 1895.

Tolstoy's daughters are very nice. They adore their father and have a fanatical faith in him and that means that Tolstoy really is a great moral force, for if he were insincere and not irreproachable his daughters would be the first to take up a sceptical attitude to him, for daughters are like sparrows: you don't catch them with empty chaff.... A man can deceive his fiancee or his mistress as much as he likes, and, in the eyes of a woman he loves, an ass may pass for a philosopher; but a daughter is a different matter....

MELIHOVO,

November 21, 1895.

Well, I have finished with the play. I began it *forte* and ended it *pianissimo*—contrary to all the rules of dramatic art. It has turned into a novel. I am rather dissatisfied than satisfied with it, and reading over my new-born play, I am more convinced than ever that I am not a dramatist. The acts are very short. There are four of them. Though it is so far only the skeleton of a play, a plan which will be altered a million times before the coming season, I have ordered two copies to be typed and will send you one, only don't let anyone read it....

TO HIS BROTHER MIHAIL.

PETERSBURG, October 15, 1896.

... My "Seagull" comes on on the seventeenth of October. Madame Kommissarzhevsky acts amazingly. There is no news. I am alive and well. I shall be at Melihovo about the twenty-fifth or towards the end of October. On the twenty-ninth is the meeting of the Zemstvo, at which I must be present as there will be a discussion about roads....

TO A. S. SUVORIN.

PETERSBURG, October 18, 1896.

I am off to Melihovo. All good wishes.... Stop the printing of the plays. I shall never forget yesterday evening, but still I slept well, and am setting off in a very tolerable good humour.

Write to me.... I have received your letter. I am not going to produce the play in Moscow. I shall *never* either write plays or have them acted.

TO HIS SISTER.

PETERSBURG, October 18, 1896.

I am setting off to Melihovo. I shall be there tomorrow between one or two o'clock in the afternoon. Yesterday's adventure did not astonish or greatly disappoint me, for I was prepared for it by the rehearsals—and I don't feel particularly bad.

When you come to Melihovo bring Lika with you.

TO HIS BROTHER MIHAIL.

PETERSBURG, October 18, 1896.

The play has fallen flat, and come down with a crash. There was an oppressive strained feeling of disgrace and bewilderment in the theatre. The actors played abominably stupidly. The moral of it is, one ought not to write plays.

TO A. S. SUVORIN.

MELIHOVO, October 22, 1896.

In your last letter (of October 18) you three times call me womanish, and say that I was in a funk. Why this libel? After the performance I had supper at Romanov's. On my word of honour. Then I went to bed, slept soundly, and next day went home without uttering a sound of complaint. If I had been in a funk I should have run from editor to editor and actor to actor, should have nervously entreated them to be considerate, should nervously have inserted useless corrections and should have spent two or three weeks in Petersburg fussing over my "Seagull," in excitement, in a cold perspiration, in lamentation.... When you were with me the night after the performance you told me yourself that it would be the best thing for me to go away; and next morning I got a letter from you to say good-bye. How did I show funk? I acted as coldly and reasonably as a man who has made an offer, received a refusal, and has nothing left but to go. Yes, my vanity was stung, but you know it was not a bolt from the blue; I was expecting a failure, and was prepared for it, as I warned you with perfect sincerity beforehand.

When I got home I took a dose of castor oil, and had a cold bath, and now I am ready to write another play. I no longer feel exhausted and irritable, and am not afraid that Davydov and Jean will come to me and talk about the play. I agree with your corrections, and a thousand thanks for them. Only please don't regret that you were not at the rehearsals. You know there was in reality only one rehearsal, at which one could make out nothing. One could not see the play at all through the loathsome acting.

I have got a telegram from Potapenko—"A colossal success." I have had a letter from Mlle. Veselitsky (Mikulitch) whom I don't know. She expresses her sympathy in a tone as if one of my family were dead. It's really quite inappropriate; that's all nonsense, though.

My sister is delighted with you and Anna Ivanovna, and I am inexpressibly glad of it, for I love your family like my own. She hastened home from Petersburg, possibly imagining that I would hang myself....

TO E. M. S.

MELIHOVO, November, 1896.

If, O honoured "One of the Audience", you are writing of the first performance, then allow—oh, allow me to doubt your sincerity. You hasten to pour healing balsam on the author's wounds, supposing that, under the circumstances, that is more necessary and better than sincerity; you are kind, very kind, and it does credit to your heart. At the first performance I did not see all, but what I did see was dingy, grey, dismal and wooden. I did not distribute the parts and was not given new scenery. There were only two rehearsals, the actors did not know their parts—and the result was a general panic and utter depression; even Madame Kommissarzhevsky's acting was not up to much, though at one of the rehearsals she acted marvellously, so that people sitting in the stalls wept with bowed heads.

In any case I am grateful and very, very much touched. All my plays are being printed, and as soon as they are ready I shall send you a copy....

TO A. F. KONI.

MELIHOVO, November 11, 1896.

You cannot imagine how your letter rejoiced me. I saw from the front only the two first acts of my play. Afterwards I sat behind the scenes and felt the whole time that "The Seagull" was a failure. After the performance that night and next day, I was assured that I had hatched out nothing but idiots, that my play was clumsy from the stage point of view, that it was not clever, that it was unintelligible, even senseless, and so on and so on. You can imagine my position—it was a collapse such as I had never dreamed of! I felt ashamed and vexed, and I went away from Petersburg full of doubts of all sorts. I thought that if I had written and put on the stage a play so obviously brimming over with monstrous defects, I had lost all instinct and that, therefore, my machinery must have gone wrong for good. After I had reached home, they wrote to me from Petersburg that the second and third performances were a success; several letters, some signed, some anonymous, came praising the play and abusing the critics. I read them with pleasure, but still I felt vexed and ashamed, and the idea forced itself upon me that if kind-hearted people thought it was necessary to comfort me, it meant that I was in a bad way. But your letter has acted upon me in a most definite way. I have known you a long time, I have a deep respect for you, and I believe in you more than in all the critics taken together—you felt that when you wrote your letter, and that is why it is so excellent and convincing. My mind is at rest now, and I can think of the play and the performance without loathing. Kommissarzhevskaia is a wonderful actress. At one of the rehearsals many people were moved to tears as they looked at her, and said that she was the first actress in Russia to-day; but at the first performance she was affected by the general attitude of hostility to my "Seagull," and was, as it were, intimidated by it and lost her voice. Our press takes a cold tone to her that doesn't do justice to her merits, and I am sorry for her. Allow me to thank you with all my heart for your letter. Believe me, I value the feelings that prompted you to write it far more than I can express in words, and the sympathy you call "unnecessary" at the end of your letter I shall never never forget, whatever happens.

TO V. I. NEMIROVITCH-DANTCHENKO.

MELIHOVO, November 26, 1896.

DEAR FRIEND,

I am answering the chief substance of your letter—the question why we so rarely talk of serious subjects. When people are silent, it is because they have nothing to talk about or because they are ill at ease. What is there to talk about? We have no politics, we have neither public life nor club life, nor even a life of the streets; our civic existence is poor, monotonous, burdensome, and uninteresting—and to talk is as boring as corresponding with L. You say that we are literary men, and that of itself makes our life a rich one. Is that so? We are stuck in our profession up to our ears, it has gradually isolated us from the external world, and the upshot of it is that we have little free time, little money, few books, we read little and reluctantly, we hear little, we rarely go anywhere. Should we talk about literature? ... But we have talked about it already. Every year it's the same thing again and again, and all we usually say about literature may be reduced to discussing who write better, and who write worse. Conversations upon wider and more general topics never catch on, because when you have tundras and Esquimaux all round you, general ideas, being so inappropriate to the reality, quickly lose shape and slip away like thoughts of eternal bliss. Should we talk of personal life? Yes, that may sometimes be interesting and we might perhaps talk about it; but there again we are constrained, we are reserved and insincere: we are restrained by an instinct of self-preservation and we are afraid. We are afraid of being overheard by some uncultured Esquimaux who does not like us, and whom we don't like either. I personally am afraid that my acquaintance, N., whose cleverness attracts us, will hold forth with raised finger, in every railway carriage and every house about me, settling the question why I became so intimate with X. while I was beloved by Z. I am afraid of our morals, I am afraid of our ladies.... In short, for our silence, for the frivolity and dulness of our conversations, don't blame yourself or me, blame what the critics call "the age," blame the climate, the vast distances, what you will, and let circumstances go on their own fateful, relentless course, hoping for a better future.

TO A. S. SUVORIN.

MELIHOVO, January 11, 1897.

We are having a census. They have served out to the numerators detestable inkpots, detestable clumsy badges like the labels of a brewery, and portfolios into which the census forms will not fit—giving the effect of a sword that won't go into its sheath. It is a disgrace. From early morning I go from hut to hut, and knock my head in the low doorways which I can't get used to, and as ill-luck will have it my head aches hellishly; I have migraine and influenza. In one hut a little girl of nine years old, boarded out from the foundling hospital, wept bitterly because all the other little girls in the hut were Mihailovnas while she was called Lvovna after her godfather. I said call yourself Mihailovna. They were all highly delighted, and began thanking me. That's what's called making friends with the Mammon of Unrighteousness.

The "Journal of Surgery" has been sanctioned by the Censor. We are beginning to bring it out. Be so good as to do us a service—have the enclosed advertisement printed on your front page and charge it to my account. The journal will be a very good one, and this advertisement can lead to nothing but unmistakable and solid benefit. It's a great benefit, you know, to cut off people's legs.

While we are on medical topics—a remedy for cancer has been found. For almost a year past, thanks to a Russian doctor Denisenko, they have been trying the juice of the celandine, and one reads of astonishing results. Cancer is a terrible unbearable disease, the death from it is agonizing; you can imagine how pleasant it is for a man initiated into the secrets of Aesculapius to read of such results....

MOSCOW,

February 8, 1897.

The census is over. I was pretty sick of the business, as I had both to enumerate and to write till my fingers ached, and to give lectures to fifteen numerators. The numerators worked excellently, with a pedantic exactitude almost absurd. On the other hand the Zemsky Natchalniks, to whom the census was entrusted in the districts, behaved disgustingly. They did nothing, understood little, and at the most difficult moments used to report themselves sick. The best of them turned out to be a man who drinks and draws the long bow *a la* Hlestakov [Translator's Note: A character in Gogol's "Inspector General."]—but was all the same a character, if only from the point of view of comedy, while the others were colourless beyond words, and it was annoying beyond words to have anything to do with them.

I am in Moscow at the Great Moscow Hotel. I am staying a short time, ten days, and then going home. The whole of Lent and the whole of April after it, I shall have to be busy again with carpenters and so on. I am building a school again. A deputation came to me from the peasants begging me for it, and I had not the courage to refuse. The Zemstvo is giving a thousand roubles, the peasants have collected three hundred, and that is all, while the school will not cost less than three thousand. So again I shall have all the summer to be thinking about money, and scraping it together here and there. Altogether life in the country is full of work and care....

The police have made a raid upon Tchertkov, the well-known Tolstoyan, have carried off all that the Tolstoyans had collected relating to the Duhobors and sectarians—and so all at once as though by magic all evidence against Pobyedonostsev and his angels has vanished. Goremykin called upon Tchertkov's mother and said: "Your son must make the choice—either the Baltic Province where Prince Hilkov is already living in exile, or a foreign country." Tchertkov has chosen London.

He is setting off on the thirteenth of February. L. N. Tolstoy has gone to Petersburg to see him off; and yesterday they sent his winter overcoat after him. A great many are going to see him off, even Sytin, and I am sorry that I cannot do the same. I don't cherish tender sentiments for Tchertkov, but the way he has been treated fills me with intense, intense indignation....

MOSCOW,

April 1, 1897.

The doctors have diagnosed tuberculosis in the upper part of the lungs, and have ordered me to change my manner of life. I understand their diagnosis but I don't understand their prescription, because it is almost impossible. They tell me I must live in the country, but you know living permanently in the country involves continual worry with peasants, with animals, with elementary forces of all kinds, and to escape from worries and anxieties in the country is as difficult as to escape burns in hell. But still I will try to change my life as far as possible, and have already, through Masha, announced that I shall give up medical practice in the country. This will be at the same time a great relief and a great deprivation to me. I shall drop all public duties in the district, shall buy a dressing-gown, bask in the sun, and eat a great deal. They tell me to eat six times a day and are indignant with me for eating, as they think, very little. I am forbidden to talk much, to swim, and so on, and so on.

Except my lungs, all my organs were found to be healthy. Hitherto I fancied I drank just so much as not to do harm; now it turns out on investigation that I was drinking less than I was entitled to. What a pity!

The author of "Ward No. 6" has been moved from Ward No. 16 to Ward No. 14. There is plenty of room here, two windows, lighting a la Potapenko, three tables. There is very little haemorrhage. After the evening when Tolstoy was here (we talked for a long time) at four o'clock in the morning I had violent haemorrhage again.

Melihovo is a healthy place; it stands exactly on a watershed, on high ground, so that there is never fever or diphtheria in it. They have decided, after general consultation, that I am not to go away anywhere but to go on living at Melihovo. I must only arrange the house somewhat more comfortably....

MOSCOW,

April 7, 1897.

... You write that my ideal is laziness. No, it is not laziness. I despise laziness as I despise weakness and lack of mental and moral energy. I was not talking of laziness but of leisure, and I did not say leisure was an ideal but only one of the essential conditions of personal happiness.

If the experiments with Koch's new serum give favourable results, I shall go of course to Berlin. Feeding is absolutely no use to me. Here for the last fortnight they have been feeding me zealously, but it's no use, I have not gained weight.

I ought to get married. Perhaps a cross wife would cut down the number of my visitors by at least a half. Yesterday they were coming all day long, it was simply awful. They came two at a time—and each one begs me not to speak and at the same time asks me questions....

TO A. I. ERTEL.

MELIHOVO, April 17, 1897.

DEAR FRIEND ALEXANDR IVANOVITCH,

I am now at home. For a fortnight before Easter I was lying in Ostroumov's clinic and was spitting blood. The doctor diagnosed tuberculosis in the lungs. I feel splendid, nothing aches, nothing is uneasy inside, but the doctors have forbidden me *vinum*, movement, and conversation, they have ordered me to eat a great deal, and forbidden me to practise—and I feel as it were dreary.

I hear nothing about the People's Theatre. At the congress it was spoken of apathetically, without interest, and the circle that had undertaken to write its constitution and set to work have evidently cooled off a little. It is due to the spring, I suppose. The only one of the circle I saw was Goltsev, and I had not time to talk to him about the theatre.

There is nothing new. A dead calm in literature. In the editor's offices they are drinking tea and cheap wine, drinking it without relish as they walk about, evidently from having nothing to do. Tolstoy is writing a little book about Art. He came to see me in the clinic, and said that he had flung aside his novel "Resurrection" as he did not like it, and was writing only about Art, and had read sixty books about Art. His idea is not a new one; all intelligent old men in all the ages have sung the same tune in different keys. Old men have always been prone to see the end of the world, and have always declared that morality was degenerating to the uttermost point, that Art was growing shallow and wearing thin, that people were growing feebler, and so on, and so on.

Lyov Nikolaevitch wants to persuade us in his little book that at the present time Art has entered upon its final phase, that it is in a blind alley, from which it has no outlet (except retreat).

I am doing nothing, I feed the sparrows with hemp-seed and prune a rose-tree a day. After my pruning, the roses flower magnificently. I am not looking after the farming.

Keep well, dear Alexandr Ivanovitch, thank you for your letter and friendly sympathy. Write to me for the sake of my infirmity, and don't blame me too much for my carelessness in correspondence.

In future I am going to try and answer your letters as soon as I have read them. Warmest greetings.

TO SUVORIN.

MELIHOVO, July 12, 1897.

... I am reading Maeterlinck, I have read his "Les Aveugles," "L'Intrus," and am reading "Aglavaine et Selysette." They are all strange wonderful things, but they make an immense impression, and if I had a theatre I should certainly stage "Les Aveugles." There is, by the way, a magnificent scenic effect in it, with the sea and a lighthouse in the distance. The public is semi-idiotic, but one might avoid the play's failing by writing the contents of the play—in brief, of course—on the programme, saying the play is the work of Maeterlinck, a Belgian author and decadent, and that what happens in it is that an old man, who leads about some blind men, has died in silence and that the blind men, not knowing this, are sitting and waiting for his return....

TO MADAME AVILOV.

NICE, October 6, 1897.

... You complain that my heroes are gloomy—alas! that's not my fault. This happens apart from my will, and when I write it does not seem to me that I am writing gloomily; in any case, as I work I am always in excellent spirits. It has been observed that gloomy, melancholy people always write cheerfully, while those who enjoy life put their depression into their writings. And I am a man who enjoys life; the first thirty years of my life I have lived as they say in pleasure and content....

TO F. D. BATYUSHKOV.

NICE, December 15, 1897.

... In one of your letters you expressed a desire that I should send you an international story, taking for my subject something from the life here. Such a story I can write only in Russia from reminiscences. I can only write from reminiscences, and I have never written directly from Nature. I have let my memory sift the subject, so that only what is important or typical is left in it as in a filter....

TO A. S. SUVORIN.

NICE, January 4, 1898.

... Judging from the extract printed in *Novoye Vremya*, Tolstoy's article on Art does not seem interesting. All that is old. He says about Art that it is decrepit, that it has got into a blind alley, that it is not what it ought to be, and so on, and so on. That's just like saying the desire to eat and drink has grown old, has outlived its day, and is not what it ought to be. Of course hunger is an old story, in the desire to eat we have got into a blind alley, but still eating is necessary, and we shall go on eating however the philosophers and irate old men moralise....

TO F. D. BATYUSHKOV.

NICE, January 28, 1898.

... We talk of nothing here but Zola and Dreyfus. The immense majority of educated people are on Zola's side and believe that Dreyfus is innocent.

Zola has gained immensely in public esteem; his letters of protest are like a breath of fresh air, and every Frenchman has felt that, thank God! there is still justice in the world, and that if an innocent man is condemned there is still someone to champion him. The French papers are extremely interesting while the Russian are worthless. *Novoye Vremya* is simply loathsome....

TO A. S. SUVORIN.

NICE, February 6, 1898.

... You write that you are annoyed with Zola, and here everyone has a feeling as though a new, better Zola had arisen. In his trial he has been cleansed as though in turpentine from grease-spots, and now shines before the French in his true brilliance. There is a purity and moral elevation that was not suspected in him. You should follow the whole scandal from the very beginning. The degradation of Dreyfus, whether it was just or not, made on all (you were of the number I remember) a painful and depressing impression. It was noticed that at the time of the sentence Dreyfus behaved like a decent well-disciplined officer, while those present at the sentence, the journalists for instance, shouted at him, "Hold your tongue, Judas,"— that is, behaved badly and indecently. Everyone came back from the sentence dissatisfied and with a troubled conscience. Dreyfus' counsel Demange, an honest man, who even during the preliminary stages of the trial felt that something shifty was being done behind the scenes, was particularly dissatisfied—and then the experts who, to convince themselves that they had not made a mistake, kept talking of nothing but Dreyfus, of his being guilty, and kept wandering all over Paris! ...

Of the experts one turned out to be mad, the author of a monstrously absurd project; two were eccentric creatures.

People could not help talking of the Intelligence Department at the War Office, that military consistory which is employed in hunting for spies and reading other people's letters; it began to be said that the head of that Department, Sandhen, was suffering from progressive paralysis; Paty de Clam has shown himself to be something after the style of Tausch of Berlin; Picquart suddenly took his departure mysteriously, causing a lot of talk. All at once a series of gross judicial blunders came to light. By degrees people became convinced that Dreyfus had been condemned on the strength of a secret document, which had been shown neither to the accused man nor his defending counsel, and decent law-abiding people saw in this a fundamental breach of justice. If the latter were the work not simply of Wilhelm, but of the centre of the solar system, it ought to have been shown to Demange. All sorts of guesses were made as to the contents of this letter, the most impossible stories circulated. Dreyfus was an officer, the military were suspect; Dreyfus was a Jew, the Jews were suspect. People began talking about militarism, about the Jews. Such utterly disreputable people as Drumont held up their heads; little by little they stirred up a regular pother on a substratum of anti-semitism, on a substratum that smelt of the shambles. When something is wrong with us we look for the causes outside ourselves, and readily find them. "It's the Frenchman's nastiness, it's the Jews', it's Wilhelm's." Capital, brimstone, the freemasons, the Syndicate, the Jesuits—they are all bogeys, but how they relieve our uneasiness! They are of course a bad sign. Since the French have begun talking about the Jews, about the Syndicate, it shows they are feeling uncomfortable, that there is a worm gnawing at them, that they feel the need of these bogeys to soothe their over-excited conscience.

Then this Esterhazy, a duellist, in the style of Turgenev's duellists, an insolent ruffian, who had long been an object of suspicion, and was not respected by his comrades; the striking resemblance of his handwriting with that of the *bordereau*, the Uhlan's letters, his threats which for some reason he does not carry out; finally the judgment, utterly mysterious, strangely deciding that the *bordereau* was written in Esterhazy's handwriting but not by his hand! ... And the gas has been continually accumulating, there has come to be a feeling of acute tension, of overwhelming oppression. The fighting in the court was a purely nervous manifestation, simply the hysterical result of that tension, and Zola's letter and his trial are a manifestation of the same kind. What would you have? The best people, always in advance of the nation, were bound to be the first to raise an agitation—and so it has been. The first to speak was Scherer-Kestner, of whom Frenchmen who know him intimately (according to Kovalevsky) say that he is a "sword-blade," so spotless and without blemish is he. The second is Zola, and now he is being tried.

Yes, Zola is not Voltaire, and we are none of us Voltaires, but there are in life conjunctions of circumstances when the reproach that we are not Voltaires is least of all appropriate. Think of Korolenko, who defended the Multanovsky natives and saved them from penal servitude. Dr. Haas is not a Voltaire either, and yet his wonderful life has been well spent up to the end.

I am well acquainted with the case from the stenographers' report, which is utterly different from what is in the newspapers, and I have a clear view of Zola. The chief point is that he is sincere—that is, he bases his judgments simply on what he sees, and not on phantoms like the others. And sincere people can be mistaken, no doubt of it, but such mistakes do less harm than calculated insincerity, prejudgments, or political considerations. Let Dreyfus be guilty, and Zola is still right, since it is the duty of writers not to accuse, not to prosecute, but to champion even the guilty once they have been condemned and are enduring punishment. I shall be told: "What of the political position? The interests of the State?" But great writers and artists ought to take part in politics only so far as they have to protect themselves from politics. There are plenty of accusers, prosecutors, and gendarmes without them, and in any case, the role of Paul suits them better than that of Saul. Whatever the verdict may be, Zola will anyway experience a vivid delight after the trial, his old age will be a fine old age, and he will die with a conscience at peace, or at any rate greatly solaced. The French are very sick. They clutch at every word of comfort and at every genuine reproach coming to them from outside. That is why Bernstein's letter and our Zakrevsky's article (which was read here in the Novosti) have had such a great success here, and why they are so disgusted by abuse of Zola, such as the gutter press, which they despise, flings at him every day. However neurotic Zola may be, still he stands before the court of French common sense, and the French love him for it and are proud of him, even though they do applaud the Generals who, in the simplicity of their hearts, scare them first with the honour of the army, then with war....

TO HIS BROTHER ALEXANDR.

NICE, February 23, 1898.

... *Novoye Vremya* has behaved simply abominably about the Zola case. The old man and I have exchanged letters on the subject (in a tone of great moderation, however), and have both dropped the subject.

I don't want to write and I don't want his letters, in which he keeps justifying the tactlessness of his paper by saying he loves the military: I don't want them because I have been thoroughly sick of it all for a long time past. I love the military too, but I would not if I had a newspaper allow the *cactuses* to print Zola's novel *for nothing* in the Supplement, while they pour dirty water over this same Zola in the paper—and what for? For what not one of the cactuses has ever known—for a noble impulse and moral purity. And in any case to abuse Zola when he is on his trial—that is unworthy of literature....

TO HIS BROTHER MIHAIL.

YALTA, October 26, 1898.

... I am buying a piece of land in Yalta and am going to build so as to have a place in which to spend the winters. The prospect of continual wandering with hotel rooms, hotel porters, chance cooking, and so on, and so on, alarms my imagination. Mother will spend the winter with me. There is no winter here; it's the end of October, but the roses and other flowers are blooming freely, the trees are green and it is warm.

There is a great deal of water. Nothing will be needed apart from the house, no outbuildings of any sort; it will all be under one roof. The coal, wood and everything will be in the basement. The hens lay the whole year round, and no special house is needed for them, an enclosure is enough. Close by there is a baker's shop and the bazaar, so that it will be very cosy for Mother and very convenient. By the way, there are chanterelles and boletuses to be gathered all the autumn, and that will be an amusement for Mother. I am not doing the building myself, the architect is doing it all. The houses will be ready by April. The grounds, for a town house, are considerable. There will be a garden and flowerbeds, and a vegetable garden. The railway will come to Yalta next year....

As for getting married, upon which you are so urgent—what am I to say to you? To marry is interesting only for love; to marry a girl simply because she is nice is like buying something one does not want at the bazaar solely because it is of good quality.

The most important screw in family life is love, sexual attraction, one flesh, all the rest is dreary and cannot be reckoned upon, however cleverly we make our calculations. So the point is not in the girl's being nice but in her being loved; putting it off as you see counts for little....

My "Uncle Vanya" is being done all over the province, and everywhere with success. So one never knows where one will gain and where one will lose; I had not reckoned on that play at all....

TO GORKY.

Your last letter has given me great pleasure. I thank you with all my heart. "Uncle Vanya" was written long, long ago; I have never seen it on the stage. Of late years it has often been produced at provincial theatres. I feel cold about my plays as a rule; I gave up the theatre long ago, and feel no desire now to write for the stage.

You ask what is my opinion of your stories. My opinion? The talent is unmistakable and it is a real, great talent. For instance, in the story "In the Steppe" it is expressed with extraordinary vigour, and I actually felt a pang of envy that it was not I who had written it. You are an artist, a clever man, you feel superbly, you are plastic—that is, when you describe a thing you see it and you touch it with your hands. That is real art. There is my opinion for you, and I am very glad I can express it to you. I am, I repeat, very glad, and if we could meet and talk for an hour or two you would be convinced of my high appreciation of you and of the hopes I am building on your gifts.

Shall I speak now of defects? But that is not so easy. To speak of the defects of a talent is like speaking of the defects of a great tree growing in the garden; what is chiefly in question, you see, is not the tree itself but the tastes of the man who is looking at it. Is not that so?

I will begin by saying that to my mind you have not enough restraint. You are like a spectator at the theatre who expresses his transports with so little restraint that he prevents himself and other people from listening. This lack of restraint is particularly felt in the descriptions of nature with which you interrupt your dialogues; when one reads those descriptions one wishes they were more compact, shorter, put into two or three lines. The frequent mention of tenderness, whispering, velvetiness, and so on, give those descriptions a rhetorical and monotonous character—and they make one feel cold and almost exhaust one. The lack of restraint is felt also in the descriptions of women ("Malva," "On the Raft") and love scenes. It is not vigour, not breadth of touch, but just lack of restraint. Then there is the frequent use of words quite unsuitable in stories of your type. "Accompaniment," "disc," "harmony," such words spoil the effect. You often talk of waves. There is a strained feeling and a sort of circumspection in your descriptions of educated people; that is not because you have not observed educated people sufficiently, you know them, but you don't seem to know from what side to approach them.

How old are you? I don't know you, I don't know where you came from or who you are, but it seems to me that while you are still young you ought to leave Nizhni and spend two or three years rubbing shoulders with literature and literary people; not to learn to crow like the rest of us and to sharpen your wits, but to take the final plunge head first into literature and to grow to love it. Besides, the provinces age a man early. Korolenko, Potapenko, Mamin, Ertel, are first-rate men; you would perhaps at first feel their company rather boring, but in a year or two you would grow used to them and appreciate them as they deserve, and their society would more than repay you for the disagreeableness and inconvenience of life in the capital....

YALTA,

January 3, 1899.

... Apparently you have misunderstood me a little. I did not write to you of coarseness of style, but only of the incongruity of foreign, not genuinely Russian, or rarely used words. In other authors such words as, for instance, "fatalistically," pass unnoticed, but your things are musical, harmonious, and every crude touch jars fearfully. Of course it is a question of taste, and perhaps this is only a sign of excessive fastidiousness in me, or the conservatism of a man who has adopted definite habits for himself long ago. I am resigned to "a *collegiate assessor*," and "a *captain* of the second *rank*" in descriptions, but "*flirt*" and "*champion*" when they occur in descriptions excite repulsion in me.

Are you self-educated? In your stories you are completely an artist and at the same time an "educated" man in the truest sense.

Nothing is less characteristic of you than coarseness, you are clever and subtle and delicate in your feelings. Your best things are "In the Steppe," and "On the Raft,"—did I write to you about that? They are splendid things, masterpieces, they show the artist who has passed through a very good school. I don't think that I am mistaken. The only defect is the lack of restraint, the lack of grace. When a man spends the least possible number of movements over some definite action, that is grace. One is conscious of superfluity in your expenditure.

The descriptions of nature are the work of an artist; you are a real landscape painter. Only the frequent personification (anthropomorphism) when the sea breathes, the sky gazes, the steppe barks, nature whispers, speaks, mourns, and so on—such metaphors make your descriptions somewhat monotonous, sometimes sweetish, sometimes not clear; beauty and expressiveness in nature are attained only by simplicity, by such simple phrases as "The sun set," "It was dark," "It began to rain," and so on—and that simplicity is characteristic of you in the highest degree, more so perhaps than of any other writer....

TO A. S. SUVORIN.

YALTA, January 17, 1899.

... I have been reading Tolstoy's son's story: "The Folly of the Mir." The construction of the story is poor, indeed it would have been better to write it simply as an article, but the thought is treated with justice and passion. I am against the Commune myself. There is sense in the Commune when one has to deal with external enemies who make frequent invasions, and with wild animals; but now it is a crowd artificially held together, like a crowd of convicts. They will tell us Russia is an agricultural country. That is so, but the Commune has nothing to do with that, at any rate at the present time. The commune exists by husbandry, but once husbandry begins to pass into scientific agriculture the commune begins to crack at every seam, as the commune and culture are not compatible ideas. Our national drunkenness and profound ignorance are, by the way, sins of the commune system....

TO HIS BROTHER MIHAIL.

YALTA, February 6, 1899.

... Being bored, I am reading "The Book of my Life" by Bishop Porfiry. This passage about war occurs in it:

"Standing armies in time of peace are locusts devouring the people's bread and leaving a vile stench in society, while in time of war they are artificial fighting machines, and when they grow and develop, farewell to freedom, security, and national glory! ... They are the lawless defenders of unjust and partial laws, of privilege and of tyranny." ...

That was written in the forties....

TO I. I. ORLOV.

YALTA, February 22, 1899.

... In your letter there is a text from Scripture. To your complaint in regard to the tutor and failures of all sorts I will reply by another text: "Put not thy trust in princes nor in any sons of man" ... and I recall another expression in regard to the sons of man, those in particular who so annoy you: they are the sons of their age.

Not the tutor but the whole educated class—that is to blame, my dear sir. While the young men and women are students they are a good honest set, they are our hope, they are the future of Russia, but no sooner do those students enter upon independent life and become grown up than our hope and the future of Russia vanishes in smoke, and all that is left in the filter is doctors owning house property, hungry government clerks, and thieving engineers. Remember that Katkov, Pobyedonostsev, Vishnegradsky, were nurselings of the Universities, that they were our Professors—not military despots, but professors, luminaries.... I don't believe in our educated class, which is hypocritical, false, hysterical, badly educated and indolent. I don't believe in it even when it's suffering and complaining, for its oppressors come from its own entrails. I believe in individual people, I see salvation in individual personalities scattered here and there all over Russia—educated people or peasants—they have strength though they are few. No prophet is honoured in his own country, but the individual personalities of whom I am speaking play an unnoticed part in society, they are not domineering, but their work can be seen; anyway, science is advancing and advancing, social self-consciousness is growing, moral questions begin to take an uneasy character, and so on, and so on-and all this is being done in spite of the prosecutors, the engineers, and the tutors, in spite of the intellectual class en masse and in spite of everything....

TO MADAME AVILOV.

I shall not be at the writers' congress. In the autumn I shall be in the Crimea or abroad—that is, of course, if I am alive and free. I am going to spend the whole summer on my own place in the Serpuhov district. [Footnote: Melihovo.]

By the way, in what district of the Tula province have you bought your estate? For the first two years after buying an estate one has a hard time, at moments it is very bad indeed, but by degrees one is led to Nirvana, by sweet habit. I bought an estate and mortgaged it, I had a very hard time the first years (famine, cholera). Afterwards everything went well, and now it is pleasant to remember that I have somewhere near the Oka a nook of my own. I live in peace with the peasants, they never steal anything from me, and when I walk through the village the old women smile and cross themselves. I use the formal address to all except children, and never shout at them; but what has done most to build up our good relations is medicine. You will be happy on your estate, only please don't listen to anyone's advice and gloomy prognostications, and don't at first be disappointed, or form an opinion about the peasants. The peasants behave sullenly and not genuinely to all new-comers, and especially so in the Tula province. There is indeed a saying: "He's a good man though he is from Tula."

So here's something like a sermon for you, you see, madam. Are you satisfied?

Do you know L. N. Tolstoy? Will your estate be far from Tolstoy's? If it is near I shall envy you. I like Tolstoy very much.

Speaking of new writers, you throw Melshin in with a whole lot. That's not right. Melshin stands apart. He is a great and unappreciated writer, an intelligent, powerful writer, though perhaps he will not write more than he has written already. Kuprin I have not read at all. Gorky I like, but of late he has taken to writing rubbish, revolting rubbish, so that I shall soon give up reading him. "Humble People" is good, though one could have done without Buhvostov, whose presence brings into the story an element of strain, of tiresomeness and even falsity. Korolenko is a delightful writer. He is loved—and with good reason. Apart from all the rest there is sobriety and purity in him.

You ask whether I am sorry for Suvorin. Of course I am. He is paying heavily for his mistakes. But I'm not at all sorry for those who are surrounding him....

TO GORKY.

MOSCOW, April 25, 1899.

... The day before yesterday I was at L. N. Tolstoy's; he praised you very highly and said that you were "a remarkable writer." He likes your "The Fair" and "In the Steppe" and does not like "Malva." He said: "You can invent anything you like, but you can't invent psychology, and in Gorky one comes across just psychological inventions: he describes what he has never felt." So much for you! I said that when you were next in Moscow we would go together to see him.

When will you be in Moscow? On Thursday there will be a private performance—for me—of "The Seagull." If you come to Moscow I will give you a seat....

From Petersburg I get painful letters, as it were from the damned, [Footnote: From Suvorin.] and it's painful to me as I don't know what to answer, how to behave. Yes, life when it is not a psychological invention is a difficult business....

TO O. L. KNIPPER.

YALTA, September 30, 1899.

At your command I hasten to answer your letter in which you ask me about Astrov's last scene with Elena.

You write that Astrov addresses Elena in that scene like the most ardent lover, "clutches at his feeling like a drowning man at a straw."

But that's not right, not right at all! Astrov likes Elena, she attracts him by her beauty; but in the last act he knows already that nothing will come of it, and he talks to her in that scene in the same tone as of the heat in Africa, and kisses her quite casually, to pass the time. If Astrov takes that scene violently, the whole mood of the fourth act—quiet and despondent—is lost....

TO G. I. ROSSOLIMO.

YALTA, October 11, 1899.

... Autobiography? I have a disease—Auto-biographophobia. To read any sort of details about myself, and still more to write them for print, is a veritable torture to me. On a separate sheet I send a few facts, very bald, but I can do no more....

I, A. P. Chekhov, was born on the 17th of January, 1860, at Taganrog. I was educated first in the Greek School near the church of Tsar Constantine; then in the Taganrog high school. In 1879 I entered the Moscow University in the Faculty of Medicine. I had at the time only a slight idea of the Faculties in general, and chose the Faculty of Medicine I don't remember on what grounds, but did not regret my choice afterwards. I began in my first year to publish stories in the weekly journals and newspapers, and these literary pursuits had, early in the eighties, acquired a permanent professional character. In 1888 I took the Pushkin prize. In 1890 I travelled to the Island of Sahalin, to write afterwards a book upon our penal colony and prisons there. Not counting reviews, feuilletons, paragraphs, and all that I have written from day to day for the newspapers, which it would be difficult now to seek out and collect, I have, during my twenty years of literary work, published more than three hundred signatures of print, of tales, and novels. I have also written plays for the stage.

I have no doubt that the study of medicine has had an important influence on my literary work; it has considerably enlarged the sphere of my observation, has enriched me with knowledge the true value of which for me as a writer can only be understood by one who is himself a doctor. It has also had a guiding influence, and it is probably due to my close association with medicine that I have succeeded in avoiding many mistakes.

Familiarity with the natural sciences and with scientific method has always kept me on my guard, and I have always tried where it was possible to be consistent with the facts of science, and where it was impossible I have preferred not to write at all. I may observe in passing that the conditions of artistic creation do not always admit of complete harmony with the facts of science. It is impossible to represent upon the stage a death from poisoning exactly as it takes place in reality. But harmony with the facts of science must be felt even under those conditions—i.e., it must be clear to the reader or spectator that this is only due to the conditions of art, and that he has to do with a writer who understands.

I do not belong to the class of literary men who take up a sceptical attitude towards science; and to the class of those who rush into everything with only their own imagination to go upon, I should not like to belong....

TO O. L. KNIPPER.

YALTA, October 30, 1899.

... You ask whether I shall be excited, but you see I only heard properly that "Uncle Vanya" was to be given on the twenty-sixth from your letter which I got on the twenty-seventh. The telegrams began coming on the evening of the twenty-seventh when I was in bed. They send them on to me by telephone. I woke up every time and ran with bare feet to the telephone, and got very much chilled; then I had scarcely dozed off when the bell rang again and again. It's the first time that my own fame has kept me awake. The next evening when I went to bed I put my slippers and dressing-gown beside my bed, but there were no more telegrams.

The telegrams were full of nothing but the number of calls and the brilliant success, but there was a subtle, almost elusive something in them from which I could conclude that the state of mind of all of you was not exactly of the very best. The newspapers I have got to-day confirm my conjectures.

Yes, dear actress, ordinary medium success is not enough now for all you artistic players: you want an uproar, big guns, dynamite. You have been spoiled at last, deafened by constant talk about successes, full and not full houses: you are already poisoned with that drug, and in another two or three years you will be good for nothing! So much for you!

How are you getting on? How are you feeling? I am still in the same place, and am still the same; I am working and planting trees.

But visitors have come, I can't go on writing. Visitors have been sitting here for more than an hour. They have asked for tea. They have sent for the samovar. Oh, how dreary!

Don't forget me, and don't let your friendship for me die away, so that we may go away together somewhere again this summer. Good-bye for the present. We shall most likely not meet before April. If you would all come in the spring to Yalta, would act here and rest—that would be wonderfully artistic. A visitor will take this letter and drop it into the post-box....

P.S.—Dear actress, write for the sake of all that's holy, I am so dull and depressed. I might be in prison and I rage and rage....

YALTA,

November 1, 1899.

I understand your mood, dear actress, I understand it very well; but yet in your place I would not be so desperately upset. Both the part of Anna [Footnote: In Hauptmann's "Lonely Lives."] and the play itself are not worth wasting so much feeling and nerves over. It is an old play. It is already out of date, and there are a great many defects in it; if more than half the performers have not fallen into the right tone, then naturally it is the fault of the play. That's one thing, and the second is, you must once and for all give up being worried about successes and failures. Don't let that concern you. It's your duty to go on working steadily day by day, quite quietly, to be prepared for mistakes which are inevitable, for failures—in short, to do your job as actress and let other people count the calls before the curtain. To write or to act, and to be conscious at the time that one is not doing the right thing—that is so usual, and for beginners so profitable!

The third thing is that the director has telegraphed that the second performance went magnificently, that everyone played splendidly, and that he was completely satisfied....

TO GORKY.

YALTA, January 2, 1900.

PRECIOUS ALEXEY MAXIMOVITCH,

I wish you a happy New Year! How are you getting on? How are you feeling? When are you coming to Yalta? Write fully. I have received the photograph, it is very good; many thanks for it.

Thank you, too, for the trouble you have taken in regard to our committee for assisting invalids coming here. Send any money there is or will be to me, or to the executive of the Benevolent Society, no matter which.

My story (i.e., "In the Ravine") has already been sent off to *Zhizn*. Did I tell you that I liked your story "An Orphan" extremely, and sent it to Moscow to first-rate readers? There is a certain Professor Foht in the Medical Faculty in Moscow who reads Slyeptsov capitally. I don't know a better reader. So I have sent your "Orphan" to him. Did I tell you how much I liked a story in your third volume, "My Travelling Companion"? There is the same strength in it as "In the Steppe." If I were you, I would take the best things out of your three volumes and republish them in one volume at a rouble—and that would be something really remarkable for vigour and harmony. As it is, everything seems shaken up together in the three volumes; there are no weak things, but it leaves an impression as though the three volumes were not the work of one author but of seven.

Scribble me a line or two.

TO O. L. KNIPPER.

YALTA, January 2, 1900.

My greetings, dear actress! Are you angry that I haven't written for so long? I used to write often, but you didn't get my letters because our common acquaintance intercepted them in the post.

I wish you all happiness in the New Year. I really do wish you happiness and bow down to your little feet. Be happy, wealthy, healthy, and gay.

We are getting on pretty well, we eat a great deal, chatter a great deal, laugh a great deal, and often talk of you. Masha will tell you when she goes back to Moscow how we spent Christmas.

I have not congratulated you on the success of "Lonely Lives." I still dream that you will all come to Yalta, that I shall see "Lonely Lives" on the stage, and congratulate you really from my heart. I wrote to Meierhold, [Footnote: An actor at the Art Theatre at that time playing Johannes in Hauptmann's "Lonely Lives."] and urged him in my letter not to be too violent in the part of a nervous man. The immense majority of people are nervous, you know: the greater number suffer, and a small proportion feel acute pain; but where—in streets and in houses—do you see people tearing about, leaping up, and clutching at their heads? Suffering ought to be expressed as it is expressed in life—that is, not by the arms and legs, but by the tone and expression; not by gesticulation, but by grace. Subtle emotions of the soul in educated people must be subtly expressed in an external way. You will say—stage conditions. No conditions allow falsity.

My sister tells me that you played "Anna" exquisitely. Ah, if only the Art Theatre would come to Yalta! *Novoye Vremya* highly praised your company. There is a change of tactics in that quarter; evidently they are going to praise you all even in Lent. My story, a very queer one, will be in the February number of *Zhizn*. There are a great number of characters, there is scenery too, there's a crescent moon, there's a bittern that cries far, far away: "Boo-oo! boo-oo!" like a cow shut up in a shed. There's everything in it.

Levitan is with us. Over my fireplace he has painted a moonlight night in the hayfield, cocks of hay, forest in the distance, a moon reigning on high above it all.

Well, the best of health to you, dear, wonderful actress. I have been pining for you.

And when are you going to send me your photograph? What treachery!

TO A. S. SUVORIN.

YALTA, January 8, 1900.

... My health is not so bad. I feel better than I did last year, but yet the doctors won't let me leave Yalta. I am as tired and sick of this charming town as of a disagreeable wife. It's curing me of tuberculosis, but it's making me ten years older. If I go to Nice it won't be before February. I am writing a little; not long ago I sent a long story to *Zhizn*. Money is short, all I have received so far from Marks for the plays is gone by now....

If Prince Baryatinsky is to be judged by his paper, I must own I was unjust to him, for I imagined him very different from what he is. They will shut up his paper, of course, but he will long maintain his reputation as a good journalist. You ask me why the *Syeverny Kurier* is successful? Because our society is exhausted, hatred has turned it as rank and rotten as grass in a bog, and it has a longing for something fresh, free, light—a desperate longing.

I often see the academician Kondakov here. We talk of the Pushkin section of belles-lettres. As Kondakov will take part in the elections of future academicians, I am trying to hypnotize him, and suggest that they should elect Barantsevitch and Mihailovsky. The former is broken down and worn out. He is unquestionably a literary man, is poverty-stricken in his old age.... An income and rest would be the very thing for him. The latter—that is Mihailovsky—would make a good foundation for the new section, and his election would satisfy three-quarters of the brotherhood. But my hypnotism failed, my efforts came to nothing. The supplementary clauses to the statute are like Tolstoy's After-word to the Kreutzer Sonata. The academicians have done all they can to protect themselves from literary men, whose society shocks them as the society of the Russian academicians shocked the Germans. Literary men can only be honorary academicians, and that means nothing—it is just the same as being an honorary citizen of the town of Vyazma or Tcherepovets, there is no salary and no vote attached. A clever way out of it! The professors will be elected real academicians, and those of the writers will be elected honorary academicians who do not live in Petersburg, and so cannot be present at the sittings and abuse the professors.

I hear the muezzin calling in the minaret. The Turks are very religious; it's their fast now, they eat nothing the whole day. They have no religious ladies, that element which makes religion shallow as the sand does the Volga.

You do well to print the martyrology of Russian towns avoided by the extortionate railway contractors. Here is what the famous author Chekhov wrote on the subject in his story "My Life." [Footnote: Appended to the letter was a printed cutting.] Railway contractors are revengeful people; refuse them a trifle, and they will punish you for it all your life—and it's their tradition.

Thanks for your letter, thanks for your indulgence.

TO P. I. KURKIN.

YALTA, January 18, 1900.

DEAR PYOTR IVANOVITCH,

Thank you for your letter. I have long been wanting to write to you, but have never had time, under the load of business and official correspondence. Yesterday was the 17th of January—my name-day, and the day of my election to the Academy. What a lot of telegrams! And what a lot of letters still to come! And I must answer all of them, or posterity will accuse me of not knowing the laws of good manners.

There is news, but I won't tell you it now (no time), but later on. I am not very well. I was ailing all yesterday. I press your hand heartily. Keep well.

TO V. M. SOBOLEVSKY.

YALTA, January 19, 1900.

DEAR VASSILY MIHAILOVITCH,

In November I wrote a story [Footnote: "In the Ravine."] fully intending to send it to *Russkiya Vyedomosti,* but the story lengthened out beyond the sixteen pages, and I had to send it elsewhere. Then Elpatyevsky and I decided to send you a telegram on New Year's Eve, but there was such a rush and a whirl that we let the right moment slip, and now I send you my New Year wishes. Forgive me my many transgressions. You know how deeply I love and respect you, and if the intervals in our correspondence are prolonged it's merely external causes that are to blame.

I am alive and almost well. I am often ill, but not for long at a time; and I haven't once been kept in bed this winter, I keep about though I am ill. I am working harder than I did last year, and I am more bored. It's bad being without Russia in every way.... All the evergreen trees look as though they were made of tin, and one gets no joy out of them. And one sees nothing interesting, as one has no taste for the local life.

Elpatyevsky and Kondakov are here. The former has run up a huge house for himself which towers above all Yalta; the latter is going to Petersburg to take his seat in the Academy—and is glad to go. Elpatyevsky is cheerful and hearty, always in good spirits, goes out in all weathers, in a summer overcoat; Kondakov is irritably sarcastic, and goes about in a fur coat. Both often come and see me and we speak of you.

V. A. wrote that she had bought a piece of land in Tuapse. Oy-oy! but the boredom there is awful, you know. There are Tchetchentsi and scorpions, and worst of all there are no roads, and there won't be any for a long time. Of all warm places in Russia the best are on the south coast of the Crimea, there is no doubt of that, whatever they may say about the natural beauties of the Caucasus. I have been lately to Gurzufa, near Pushkin's rock, and admired the view, although it rained and although I am sick to death of views. In the Crimea it is snugger and nearer to Russia. Let V. A. sell her place in Tuapse or make a present of it to someone, and I will find her a bit of the sea-front with bathing, and a bay, in the Crimea.

When you are in Vosdvizhenka give my respects and greetings to Varvara Alexyevna, Varya, Natasha, and Glyeb. I can fancy how Glyeb and Natasha have grown. Now if only you would all come here for Easter, I could have a look at you all. Don't forget me, please, and don't be angry with me. I send you my warmest good wishes. I press your hand heartily and embrace you.

TO G. I. ROSSOLIMO.

YALTA, January 21, 1900.

DEAR GRIGORY IVANOVITCH,

... I send you in a registered parcel what I have that seems suitable for children—two stories of the life of a dog. And I think I have nothing else of the sort. I don't know how to write for children; I write for them once in ten years, and so-called children's books I don't like and don't believe in. Children ought only to be given what is suitable also for grown-up people. Andersen, "The Frigate Pallada," Gogol, are easily read by children and also by grown-up people. Books should not be written for children, but one ought to know how to choose from what has been written for grown-up people—that is, from real works of art. To be able to select among drugs, and to administer them in suitable doses, is more direct and consistent than trying to invent a special remedy for the patient because he is a child. Forgive the medical comparison. It's in keeping with the moment, perhaps, as for the last four days I have been occupied with medicine, doctoring my mother and myself. Influenza no doubt. Fever and headache.

If I write anything, I will let you know in due time, but anything I write can only be published by one man—Marks! For anything published by anyone else I have to pay a fine of 5,000 roubles (per signature)....

TO O. L. KNIPPER.

YALTA, January 22, 1900.

DEAR ACTRESS,

On January 17th I had telegrams from your mother and your brother, from your uncle Alexandr Ivanovitch (signed Uncle Sasha), and from N. N. Sokolovsky. Be so good as to give them my warm thanks and the expression of my sincere feeling for them.

Why don't you write?—what has happened? Or are you already so fascinated? ... Well, there is no help for it. God be with you!

I am told that in May you will be in Yalta. If that is settled, why shouldn't you make inquiries beforehand about the theatre? The theatre here is let on lease, and you could not get hold of it without negotiating with the tenant, Novikov the actor. If you commission me to do so I would perhaps talk to him about it.

The 17th, my name-day and the day of my election to the Academy, passed dingily and gloomily, as I was unwell. Now I am better, but my mother is ailing. And these little troubles completely took away all taste and inclination for a name-day or election to the Academy, and they, too, have hindered me from writing to you and answering your telegram at the proper time.

Mother is getting better now.

I see the Sredins at times. They come to see us, and I go to them very, very rarely, but still I do go....

So, then, you are not writing to me and not intending to write very soon either.... X. is to blame for all that. I understand you!

I kiss your little hand.

TO F. D. BATYUSHKOV.

YALTA, January 24, 1900.

MUCH RESPECTED F. D.,

Roche asks me to send him the passages from "Peasants" which were cut out by the Censor, but there were no such passages. There is one chapter which has not appeared in the magazine, nor in the book. It was a conversation of the peasants about religion and government. But there is no need to send that chapter to Paris, as indeed there was no need to translate "Peasants" into French at all.

I thank you most sincerely for the photograph; Ryepin's illustration is an honour I had not expected or dreamed of. It will be very pleasant to have the original; tell Ilya Efimovitch [Footnote: Ryepin, who was, at the request of Roche, the French translator, illustrating the French edition of Chekhov's "Peasants."] that I shall expect it with impatience, and that he cannot change his mind now, as I have already bequeathed the original to the town of Taganrog—in which, by the way, I was born.

In your letter you speak of Gorky: how do you like Gorky? I don't like everything he writes, but there are things I like very, very much, and to my mind there is not a shadow of doubt that Gorky is made of the dough of which artists are made. He is the real thing. He's a fine man, clever, thinking, and thoughtful. But there is a lot of unnecessary ballast upon him and in him—for example, his provincialism....

Thanks very much for your letter, for remembering me. I am dull here, I am sick of it, and I have a feeling as though I have been thrown overboard. And the weather's bad too, and I am not well. I still go on coughing. All good wishes.

TO M. O. MENSHIKOV.

YALTA, January 28, 1900.

... I can't make out what Tolstoy's illness is. Tcherinov has sent me no answer, and from what I read in the papers and what you write me now I can draw no conclusion. Ulcers in the stomach and intestines would give different indications: they are not present, or there have been a few bleeding wounds caused by gall-stones which have passed and lacerated the walls. There is no cancer either. It would have shown itself first in the appetite, in the general condition, and above all the face would have betrayed cancer if he had had it. The most likely thing is that L. N. is in good health (apart from the gall-stones), and will live another twenty years. His illness frightened me, and kept me on tenter-hooks. I am afraid of Tolstoy's death. If he were to die there would be a big empty place in my life. To begin with, because I have never loved any man as much as him. I am not a believing man, but of all beliefs I consider his the nearest and most akin to me. Secondly, while Tolstoy is in literature it is easy and pleasant to be a literary man; even recognizing that one has done nothing and never will do anything is not so dreadful, since Tolstoy will do enough for all. His work is the justification of the enthusiasms and expectations built upon literature. Thirdly, Tolstoy takes a firm stand, he has an immense authority, and so long as he is alive, bad tastes in literature, vulgarity of every kind, insolent and lachrymose, all the bristling, exasperated vanities will be in the far background, in the shade. Nothing but his moral authority is capable of maintaining a certain elevation in the moods and tendencies of literature so called. Without him they would be a flock without a shepherd, or a hotch-potch, in which it would be difficult to discriminate anything.

To finish with Tolstoy, I have something to say about "Resurrection," which I have read not piecemeal, in parts, but as a whole, at one go. It is a remarkable artistic production. The least interesting part is all that is said of Nehludov's relations with Katusha; and the most interesting the princes, the generals, the aunts, the peasants, the convicts, the warders. The scene in the house of the General in command of the Peter-Paul Fortress, the spiritualist, I read with a throbbing heart—it is so good! And Madame Kortchagin in the easy chair; and the peasant, the husband of Fedosya! The peasant calls his grandmother "an artful one." That's just what Tolstoy's pen is—an artful one. There's no end to the novel, what there is you can't call an end. To write and write, and then to throw the whole weight of it on a text from the Gospel, that is quite in the theological style. To settle it all by a text from the Gospel is as arbitrary as dividing the convicts into five classes. Why into five and not into ten? He must make us believe in the Gospel, in its being the truth, and then settle it all by texts.

... They write about Tolstoy as old women talk about a crazy saint, all sorts of unctuous nonsense; it's a mistake for him to talk to those people....

They have elected Tolstoy [Footnote: An honorary Academician.]— against the grain. According to notions there, he is a Nihilist. Anyway, that's what he was called by a lady, the wife of an actual privy councillor, and I heartily congratulate him upon it....

TO L. S. MIZINOV.

YALTA, January 29, 1900.

DEAR LIRA,

They have written to me that you have grown very fat and become dignified, and I did not expect that you would remember me and write to me. But you have remembered me—and thank you very much for it, dear. You write nothing about your health: evidently it's not bad, and I am glad. I hope your mother is well and that everything is going on all right. I am nearly well; I am ill from time to time, but not often, and only because I am old—the bacilli have nothing to do with it. And when I see a lovely woman now I smile in an aged way, and drop my lower lip—that's all.

Lika, I am dreadfully bored in Yalta. My life does not run or flow, but crawls along. Don't forget me; write to me now and then, anyway. In your letters just as in your life you are a very interesting woman. I press your hand warmly.

TO GORKY.

YALTA, February 3, 1900.

DEAR ALEXEY MAXIMOVITCH,

Thank you for your letter, for the lines about Tolstoy and about "Uncle Vanya," which I haven't seen on the stage; thanks altogether for not forgetting me. Here in this blessed Yalta one could hardly keep alive without letters. The idleness, the idiotic winter with the temperature always above freezing-point, the complete absence of interesting women, the pig-faces on the sea-front—all this may spoil a man and wear him out in a very short time. I am tired of it; it seems to me as though the winter had been going on for ten years.

You have pleurisy. If so, why do you stay on in Nizhni. Why? What do you want with that Nizhni, by the way? What glue keeps you sticking to that town? If you like Moscow, as you write, why don't you live in Moscow? In Moscow there are theatres and all the rest of it, and, what matters most of all, Moscow is handy for going abroad; while living in Nizhni you'll stick in Nizhni, and never go further than Vasilsursk. You want to see more, to know more, to have a wider range. Your imagination is quick to seize and hold, but it is like a big oven which is not provided with fuel enough. One feels this in general, and in particular in the stories: you present two or three figures in a story, but these figures stand apart, outside the mass; one sees that these figures are living in your imagination, but only these figures—the mass is not grasped. I except from this criticism your Crimean things (for instance, "My Travelling Companion"), in which, besides the figures, there is a feeling of the human mass out of which they have come, and atmosphere and background—everything, in fact. See what a lecture I am giving you—and all that you may not go on staying in Nizhni. You are a young man, strong and tough; if I were you I should make a tour in India and all sorts of places. I would take my degree in two or more faculties—I would, yes, I would! You laugh, but I do feel so badly treated at being forty already, at having asthma and all sorts of horrid things which prevent my living freely. Anyway, be a good fellow and a good comrade, and don't be angry with me for preaching at you like a head priest.

Write to me. I look forward to "Foma Gordeyev," which I haven't yet read properly.

There is no news. Keep well, I press your hand warmly.

TO O. L. KNIPPER.

YALTA, February 10, 1900.

DEAR ACTRESS,

The winter is very cold, I am not well, no one has written to me for nearly a whole month—and I had made up my mind that there was nothing left for me but to go abroad, where it is not so dull; but now it has begun to be warmer, and it's better, and I have decided that I shall go abroad only at the end of the summer, for the exhibition.

And you, why are you depressed? What are you depressed about? You are living, working, hoping, drinking; you laugh when your uncle reads aloud to you—what more do you want? I am a different matter. I am torn up by the roots, I am not living a full life, I don't drink, though I am fond of drinking; I love noise and don't hear it—in fact, I am in the condition of a transplanted tree which is hesitating whether to take root or to begin to wither. If I sometimes allow myself to complain of boredom, I have some grounds for doing so—but you? And Meierhold is complaining of the dulness of his life too. Aie, aie!

By the way, about Meierhold—he ought to spend the whole summer in the Crimea. His health needs it. Only it must be for the whole summer.

Well, now I am all right again. I am doing nothing because I intend to set to work. I dig in the garden. You write that for you, little people, the future is wrapped in mystery. I had a letter from your chief Nemirovitch not long ago. He writes that the company is going to be in Sevastopol, then in Yalta at the beginning of May: in Yalta there will be five performances, then evening rehearsals. Only the precious members of the company will remain for the rehearsals, the others can have a holiday where they please. I trust that you are precious. To the director you are precious, to the author you are priceless. There is a pun for a titbit for you. I won't write another word to you till you send me your portrait.

Thank you for your good wishes in regard to my marriage. I have informed my *fiancee* of your design of coming to Yalta in order to cut her out a little. She said that if "that horrid woman" comes to Yalta, she will hold me tight in her embrace. I observed that to be embraced for so long in hot weather was not hygienic. She was offended and grew thoughtful, as though she were trying to guess in what surroundings I had picked up this *façon de parler*, and after a little while said that the theatre was an evil and that my intention of writing no more plays was extremely laudable—and asked me to kiss her. To this I replied that it was not proper for me to be so free with my kisses now that I am an academician. She burst into tears, and I went away.

In the spring the company will be in Harkov too. I will come and meet you then, only don't talk of that to anyone. Nadyezhda Ivanovna has gone off to Moscow.

TO A. S. SUVORIN.

I have been racking my brains over your fourth act, and have come to no conclusion except, perhaps, that you must not end it up with Nihilists. It's too turbulent and screaming; a quiet, lyrical, touching ending would be more in keeping with your play. When your heroine begins to grow old without arriving at anything or deciding anything for herself, and sees that she is forsaken by all, that she is uninteresting and superfluous, when she understands that the people around her were idle, useless, bad people (her father too), and that she has let her life slip—is not that more dreadful than the Nihilists?

Your letters about "The Russalka" and Korsh are very good. The tone is brilliant, and they are wonderfully written. But about Konovalov and the jury, I think you ought not to have written, however alluring the subject. Let A——t write as much as he likes about it, but not you, for it is not your affair. To treat such questions boldly and with conviction, one must be a man with a single purpose, while you would go off at a tangent halfway through the letter—as you have done—saying suddenly that we all sometimes desire to kill someone, and desire the death of our neighbours. When a daughter-in-law feels sick and tired of an invalid mother-in-law, a spiteful old woman, she, the daughter-in-law, feels easier at the thought that the old woman will soon die: but that's not desiring her death, but weariness, an exhausted spirit, vexation, longing for peace. If that daughter-in-law were ordered to kill the old woman, she would sooner kill herself, whatever desire might have been brooding in her heart.

Why, of course jurymen may make a mistake, but what of that? It does happen by mistake that help is given to the well-fed instead of to the hungry, but whatever you write on that subject, you will reach no result but harm to the hungry. Whether from our point of view the jury are mistaken or not mistaken, we ought to recognize that in each individual case they form a conscious judgment and make an effort to do so conscientiously; and if a captain steers his steamer conscientiously, continually consulting the chart and the compass, and if the steamer is shipwrecked all the same, would it not be more correct to put down the shipwreck not to the captain, but to something else—for instance, to think that the chart is out of date or that the bottom of the sea has changed? Yes, there are three points the jury have to take into consideration: (1) Apart from the criminal law, the penal code and legal procedure, there is a moral law which is always in advance of the established law, and which defines our actions precisely when we try to act on our conscience; thus, for instance, the heritage of a daughter is laid down by law as a seventh part. But you, acting on the dictates of purely moral principle, go beyond the law and in opposition to it, and bequeath her the same share as your sons, for you know that to act otherwise would be acting against your conscience. In the same way it sometimes happens to the jury to be put in a position in which they feel that their conscience is not satisfied by the established law, that in the case they are judging there are fine shades and subtleties which cannot be brought under the provisions of the penal code, and that obviously something else is needed for a just judgment, and that for the lack of that "something" they will be forced to give a judgment in which something is lacking. (2) The jury know that acquittal is not pardon, and that acquittal does not deliver the prisoner from the day of judgment in the other world, from the judgment of his conscience, from the judgment of public opinion; they decide the question only so far as it is a judicial question, and leave A———t to decide whether it is good to kill children or bad. (3) The prisoner comes to the court already exhausted by prison and examination, and he is in an agonizing position at his trial, so that even if he is acquitted he does not leave the court unpunished.

Well, be that as it may, my letter is almost finished, and I seem to have written nothing. We have the spring here in Yalta, no news of interest....

"Resurrection" is a remarkable novel. I liked it very much, but it ought to be read straight off at one sitting. The end is uninteresting and false— false in a technical sense.

TO O. L. KNIPPER.

YALTA, February 14, 1900.

DEAR ACTRESS,

The photographs are very, very good, especially the one in which you are leaning in dejection with your elbows on the back of a chair, which gives you a discreetly mournful, gentle expression under which there lies hid a little demon. The other is good too, but it looks a little like a Jewess, a very musical person who attends a conservatoire, but at the same time is studying dentistry on the sly as a second string, and is engaged to be married to a young man in Mogilev, and whose fiance is a person like M— —. Are you angry? Really, really angry? It's my revenge for your not signing them.

Of the seventy roses I planted in the autumn only three have not taken root. Lilies, irises, tulips, tuberoses, hyacinths, are all pushing out of the ground. The willow is already green. By the little seat in the corner the grass is luxuriant already. The almond-tree is in blossom. I have put little seats all over the garden, not grand ones with iron legs, but wooden ones which I paint green. I have made three bridges over the stream. I am planting palms. In fact, there are all sorts of novelties, so much so that you won't know the house, or the garden, or the street. Only the owner has not changed, he is just the same moping creature and devoted worshipper of the talents that reside at Nikitsky Gate. [Footnote: O. L. Knipper was living at Nikitsky Gate.] I have heard no music nor singing since the autumn, I have not seen one interesting woman. How can I help being melancholy?

I had made up my mind not to write to you, but since you have sent the photographs I have taken off the ban, and here you see I am writing. I will even come to Sevastopol, only I repeat, don't tell that to anyone, especially not to Vishnevsky. I shall be there incognito, I shall put myself down in the hotel-book Count Blackphiz.

I was joking when I said that you were like a Jewess in your photograph. Don't be angry, precious one. Well, herewith I kiss your little hand, and remain unalterably yours.

TO GORKY.

YALTA, February 15, 1900.

DEAR ALEXEY MAXIMOVITCH,

Your article in the Nizhni-Novgorod Listok was balm to my soul. What a talented person you are! I can't write anything but belles-lettres, you possess the pen of a journalist as well. I thought at first I liked the article so much because you praise me in it; afterwards it came out that Sredin and his family and Yartsev were all delighted with it. So peg away at journalism. God bless you!

Why don't they send me "Foma Gordeyev"? I have read it only in bits, and one ought to read it straight through at a sitting as I have just read "Resurrection." Except the relations of Nehludov and Katusha, which are somewhat obscure and made up, everything in the novel made the impression of strength, richness, and breadth, and the insincerity of a man afraid of death and refusing to admit it and clutching at texts and holy Scripture.

Write to them to send me "Foma."

"Twenty-six Men and a Girl" is a good story. There is a strong feeling of the environment. One smells the hot rolls.

They have just brought your letter. So you don't want to go to India? That's a pity. When India is in the past, a long sea voyage, you have something to think about when you can't get to sleep. And a tour abroad takes very little time, it need not prevent your going about in Russia on foot.

I am bored, not in the sense of *weltschmerz*, not in the sense of being weary of existence, but simply bored from want of people, from want of music which I love, and from want of women, of whom there are none in Yalta. I am bored without caviare and pickled cabbage.

I am very sorry that apparently you have given up the idea of coming to Yalta. The Art Theatre from Moscow will be here in May. It will give five performances and then remain for rehearsals. So you come, study the stage at the rehearsals, and then in five to eight days write a play, which I should welcome joyfully with my whole heart.

Yes, I have the right now to insist on the fact that I am forty, that I am a man no longer young. I used to be the youngest literary man, but you have appeared on the scene and I became more dignified at once, and no one calls me the youngest now.

TO V. A. POSSE.

YALTA, February 15, 1900.

MUCH RESPECTED VLADIMIR ALEXANDROVITCH,

"Foma Gordeyev" and in a superb binding too is a precious and touching present; I thank you from the bottom of my heart. A thousand thanks! I have read "Foma" only in bits, now I shall read it properly. Gorky should not be published in parts; either he must write more briefly, or you must put him in whole as the *Vyestnik Evropy* does with Boborykin. "Foma," by the way, is very successful, but only with intelligent well-read people—with the young also. I once overheard in a garden the conversation of a lady (from Petersburg) with her daughter: the mother was abusing the book, the daughter was praising it....

YALTA,

February 29, 1900.

"Foma Gordeyev" is written all in one tone like a dissertation. All the characters speak alike, and their way of thinking is alike too. They all speak not simply but intentionally; they all have some idea in the background; as though there is something they know they don't speak out: but in reality there is nothing they know, and it is simply their *façon de parler*.

There are wonderful passages in "Foma." Gorky will make a very great writer if only he does not weary, does not grow cold and lazy.

TO A. S. SUVORIN,

YALTA, March 10, 1900.

No winter has ever dragged on so long for me as this one, and time merely drags and does not move, and now I realize how stupid it was of me to leave Moscow. I have lost touch with the north without getting into touch with the south, and one can think of nothing in my position but to go abroad. After the spring, winter has begun here again in Yalta—snow, rain, cold, mud—simply disgusting.

The Moscow Art Theatre will be in Yalta in April; it will bring its scenery and decorations. All the tickets for the four days advertised were sold in one day, although the prices have been considerably raised. They will give among other things Hauptmann's "Lonely Lives," a magnificent play in my opinion. I read it with great pleasure, although I am not fond of plays, and the production at the Art Theatre they say is marvellous.

There is no news. There is one great event, though: N.'s "Socrates" is printed in the *Neva* Supplement. I have read it, but with great effort. It is not Socrates but a dull-witted, captious, opinionated man, the whole of whose wisdom and interest is confined to tripping people up over words. There is not a trace or vestige of talent in it, but it is quite possible that the play might be successful because there are words in it such as "amphora," and Karpov says it would stage well.

How many consumptives there are here! What poverty, and how worried one is with them! The hotels and lodging-houses here won't take in those who are seriously ill. You can imagine the awful cases that may be seen here. People are dying from exhaustion, from their surroundings, from complete neglect, and this in blessed Taurida!

One loses all relish for the sun and the sea....

TO O. L. KNIPPER.

YALTA, March 26, 1900.

There is a feeling of black melancholy about your letter, dear actress; you are gloomy, you are fearfully unhappy—but not for long, one may imagine, as soon, very soon, you will be sitting in the train, eating your lunch with a very good appetite. It is very nice that you are coming first with Masha before all the others; we shall at least have time to talk a little, walk a little, see things, drink and eat. But please don't bring with you ...

I haven't a new play, it's a lie of the newspapers. The newspapers never do tell the truth about me. If I did begin a play, of course the first thing I should do would be to inform you of the fact.

There is a great wind here; the spring has not begun properly yet, but we go about without our goloshes and fur caps. The tulips will soon be out. I have a nice garden but it is untidy, moss-grown—a dilettante garden.

Gorky is here. He is warm in his praises of you and your theatre. I will introduce you to him.

Oh dear! Someone has arrived. A visitor has come in. Good-bye for now, actress!

TO HIS SISTER.

YALTA, March 26, 1900.

DEAR MASHA,

... There is no news, there is no water in the pipes either. I am sick to death of visitors. Yesterday, March 25, they came in an incessant stream all day; doctors keep sending people from Moscow and the provinces with letters asking me to find lodgings, to "make arrangements," as though I were a house-agent! Mother is well. Mind you keep well too, and make haste and come home.

TO O. L. KNIPPER.

YALTA, May 20, 1900.

Greetings to you, dear enchanting actress! How are you? How are you feeling? I was very unwell on the way back to Yalta. [Footnote: Chekhov went to Moscow with the Art Theatre Company on their return from Yalta.] I had a bad headache and temperature before I left Moscow. I was wicked enough to conceal it from you, now I am all right.

How is Levitan? I feel dreadfully worried at not knowing. If you have heard, please write to me.

Keep well and be happy. I heard Masha was sending you a letter, and so I hasten to write these few lines. [Footnote: Chekhov's later letters to O. L. Knipper have not been published.]

TO HIS SISTER.

YALTA, September 9, 1900.

DEAR MASHA,

I answer the letter in which you write about Mother. To my thinking it would be better for her to go to Moscow now in the autumn and not after December. She will be tired of Moscow and pining for Yalta in a month, you know, and if you take her to Moscow in the autumn she will be back in Yalta before Christmas. That's how it seems to me, but possibly I am mistaken; in any case you must take into consideration that it is much drearier in Yalta before Christmas than it is after—infinitely drearier.

Most likely I will be in Moscow after the 20th of September, and then we will decide. From Moscow I shall go I don't know where—first to Paris, and then probably to Nice, from Nice to Africa. I shall hang on somehow to the spring, all April or May, when I shall come to Moscow again.

There is no news. There's no rain either, everything is dried up. At home here it is quiet, peaceful, satisfactory, and of course dull.

"Three Sisters" is very difficult to write, more difficult than my other plays. Oh well, it doesn't matter, perhaps something will come of it, next season if not this. It's very hard to write in Yalta, by the way: I am interrupted, and I feel as though I had no object in writing; what I wrote yesterday I don't like to-day....

Well, take care of yourself.

My humblest greetings to Olga Leonardovna, to Vishnevsky, and all the rest of them too.

If Gorky is in Moscow, tell him that I have sent a letter to him in Nizhni-Novgorod.

TO GORKY.

YALTA, October 16, 1900.

DEAR ALEXEY MAXIMOVITCH,

... On the 21st of this month I am going to Moscow, and from there abroad. Can you imagine—I have written a play; but as it will be produced not now, but next season, I have not made a fair copy of it yet. It can lie as it is. It was very difficult to write "Three Sisters." Three heroines, you see, each a separate type and all the daughters of a general. The action is laid in a provincial town, as it might be Perm, the surroundings military, artillery.

The weather in Yalta is exquisite and fresh, my health is improving. I don't even want to go away to Moscow. I am working so well, and it is so pleasant to be free from the irritation I suffered from all the summer. I am not coughing, and am even eating meat. I am living alone, quite alone. My mother is in Moscow.

Thanks for your letters, my dear fellow, thanks very much. I read them over twice. My warmest greetings to your wife and Maxim. And so, till we meet in Moscow. I hope you won't play me false, and we shall see each other.

God keep you.

MOSCOW,

October 22, 1901.

Five days have passed since I read your play ("The Petty Bourgeois"). I have not written to you till now because I could not get hold of the fourth act; I have kept waiting for it, and—I still have not got it. And so I have only read three acts, but that I think is enough to judge of the play. It is, as I expected, very good, written a la Gorky, original, very interesting; and, to begin by talking of the defects, I have noticed only one, a defect incorrigible as red hair in a red-haired man—the conservatism of the form. You make new and original people sing new songs to an accompaniment that looks second-hand, you have four acts, the characters deliver edifying discourses, there is a feeling of alarm before long speeches, and so on, and so on. But all that is not important, and it is all, so to speak, drowned in the good points of the play. Pertchihin—how living! His daughter is enchanting, Tatyana and Pyotr are also, and their mother is a splendid old woman. The central figure of the play, Nil, is vigorously drawn and extremely interesting! In fact, the play takes hold of one from the first act. Only God preserve you from letting anyone act Pertchihin except Artyom, while Alexeyev-Stanislavsky must certainly play Nil. Those two figures will do just what's needed; Pyotr—Meierhold. Only Nil's part, a wonderful part, must be made two or three times as long. You ought to end the play with it, to make it the leading part. Only do not contrast him with Pyotr and Tatyana, let him be by himself and them by themselves, all wonderful, splendid people independently of each other. When Nil tries to seem superior to Pyotr and Tatyana, and says of himself that he is a fine fellow, the element so characteristic of our decent working man, the element of modesty, is lost. He boasts, he argues, but you know one can see what sort of man he is without that. Let him be merry, let him play pranks through the whole four acts, let him eat a great deal after his work—and that will be enough for him to conquer the audience with. Pyotr, I repeat, is good. Most likely you don't even suspect how good he is. Tatyana, too, is a finished figure, only (a) she ought really to be a schoolmistress, ought to be teaching children, ought to come home from school, ought to be taken up with her pupils and exercise-books, and (b) it ought to be mentioned in the first or second act that she has attempted to poison herself; then, after that hint, the poisoning in the third act will not seem so startling and will be more in place. Telerev talks too much: such characters ought to be shown bit by bit between others, for in any case such people are everywhere merely incidental—both in life and on the stage. Make Elena dine with all the rest in the first act, let her sit and make jokes, or else there is very little of her, and she is not clear. Her avowal to Pyotr is too abrupt, on the stage it would come out in too high relief. Make her a passionate woman, if not loving at least apt to fall in love....

July 29, 1902.

I have read your play. [Footnote: "In the Depths."] It is new and unmistakably fine. The second act is very good, it is the best, the strongest, and when I was reading it, especially the end, I almost danced with joy. The tone is gloomy, oppressive; the audience unaccustomed to such subjects will walk out of the theatre, and you may well say good-bye to your reputation as an optimist in any case. My wife will play Vassilisa, the immoral and spiteful woman; Vishnevsky walks about the house and imagines himself the Tatar—he is convinced that it is the part for him. Luka, alas! you must not give to Artyom. He will repeat himself in that part and be exhausted; but he would do the policeman wonderfully, it is his part. The part of the actor, in which you have been very successful (it is a magnificent part), should be given to an experienced actor, Stanislavsky perhaps. Katchalev will play the baron.

You have left out of the fourth act all the most interesting characters (except the actor), and you must mind now that there is no ill effect from it. The act may seem boring and unnecessary, especially if, with the exit of the strongest and most interesting actors, there are left only the mediocrities. The death of the actor is awful; it is as though you gave the spectator a sudden box on the ear apropos of nothing without preparing him in any way. How the baron got into the doss-house and why he is a baron is also not sufficiently clear.

Andreyev's "Thought" is something pretentious, difficult to understand, and apparently no good, but it is worked out with talent. Andreyev has no simplicity, and his talent reminds me of an artificial nightingale. Skitalets now is a sparrow, but he is a real living sparrow....

TO S. P. DYAGILEV.

YALTA, December 30, 1902.

... You write that we talked of a serious religious movement in Russia. We talked of a movement not in Russia but in the intellectual class. I won't say anything about Russia; the intellectuals so far are only playing at religion, and for the most part from having nothing to do. One may say of the cultured part of our public that it has moved away from religion, and is moving further and further away from it, whatever people may say and however many philosophical and religious societies may be formed. Whether it is a good or a bad thing I cannot undertake to decide; I will only say that the religious movement of which you write is one thing, and the whole trend of modern culture is another, and one cannot place the second in any causal connection with the first. Modern culture is only the first beginning of work for a great future, work which will perhaps go on for tens of thousands of years, in order that man may if only in the remote future come to know the truth of the real God—that is not, I conjecture, by seeking in Dostoevsky, but by clear knowledge, as one knows twice two are four. Modern culture is the first beginning of the work, while the religious movement of which we talked is a survival, almost the end of what has ceased, or is ceasing to exist. But it is a long story, one can't put it all into a letter....

TO A. S. SUVORIN.

MOSCOW, June 29, 1903.

... One feels a warm sympathy, of course, for Gorky's letter about the Kishinev pogrom, as one does for everything he writes; the letter is not written though, but put together, there is neither youthfulness in it nor confidence, like Tolstoy's.

July 1, 1903.

You are reading belles-lettres now, so read Veresaev's stories. Begin with a little story in the second volume called "Lizar." I think you will be very much pleased with it. Veresaev is a doctor; I have got to know him lately. He makes a very good impression....

TO S. P. DYAGILEV.

YALTA, July 12, 1903.

... I have been thinking over your letter for a long time, and alluring as your suggestion or offer is, yet in the end I must answer it as neither you nor I would wish.

I cannot be the editor of *The World of Art*, as I cannot live in Petersburg, ... that's the first point. And the second is that just as a picture must be painted by one artist and a speech delivered by one orator, so a magazine must be edited by one man. Of course I am not a critic, and I dare say I shouldn't make a very good job of the reviews; but on the other hand, how could I get on in the same boat with Merezhkovsky, who definitely believes, didactically believes, while I lost my faith years ago and can only look with perplexity at any "intellectual" who does believe? I respect Merezhkovsky, and think highly of him both as a man and as a writer, but we should be pulling in opposite directions....

Don't be cross with me, dear Sergey Pavlovitch: it seems to me that if you go on editing the magazine for another five years you will come to agree with me. A magazine, like a picture or a poem, must bear the stamp of one personality and one will must be felt in it. This has been hitherto the case in the *World of Art*, and it was a good thing. And it must be kept up....

TO K. S. STANISLAVSKY.

YALTA, July 28, 1903.

... My play "The Cherry Orchard" is not yet finished; it makes slow progress, which I put down to laziness, fine weather, and the difficulty of the subject....

I think your part [Translator's Note: Stanislavsky acted Lopahin.] is all right, though I can't undertake to decide, as I can judge very little of a play by reading it....

TO MADAME STANISLAVSKY.

YALTA, September 15, 1903.

... Don't believe anybody—no living soul has read my play yet; I have written for you not the part of a "canting hypocrite," but of a very nice girl, with which you will, I hope, be satisfied. I have almost finished the play, but eight or ten days ago I was taken ill, with coughing and weakness—in fact, last year's business over again. Now—that is to-day—it is warmer and I feel better, but still I cannot write, as my head is aching. Olga will not bring the play; I will send the four acts together as soon as it is possible for me to set to work for a whole day. It has turned out not a drama, but a comedy, in parts a farce, indeed, and I am afraid I shall catch it from Vladimir Ivanitch [Footnote: Nemirovitch Dantchenko.]....

I can't come for the opening of your season, I must stay in Yalta till November. Olga, who has grown fatter and stronger in the summer, will probably come to Moscow on Sunday. I shall remain alone, and of course shall take advantage of that. As a writer it is essential for me to observe women, to study them, and so, I regret to say, I cannot be a faithful husband. As I observe women chiefly for the sake of my plays, in my opinion the Art Theatre ought to increase my wife's salary or give her a pension! ...

TO K. S. STANISLAVSKY.

YALTA, October 30, 1903.

... Many thanks for your letter and telegram. Letters are very precious to me now—in the first place, because I am utterly alone here; and in the second, because I sent the play three weeks ago and only got your letter yesterday, and if it were not for my wife, I should know nothing at all and might imagine any mortal thing. When I was writing Lopahin, I thought of it as a part for you. If for any reason you don't care for it, take the part of Gaev. Lopahin is a merchant, of course, but he is a very decent person in every sense. He must behave with perfect decorum, like an educated man, with no petty ways or tricks of any sort, and it seemed to me this part, the central one of the play, would come out brilliantly in your hands.... In choosing an actor for the part you must remember that Varya, a serious and religious girl, is in love with Lopahin; she wouldn't be in love with a mere money-grubber....

TO V. I. NEMIROVITCH DANTCHENKO.

YALTA, November 2, 1903.

... About the play.

1. Anya can be played by anyone you like, even by a quite unknown actress, so long as she is young and looks like a girl, and speaks in a youthful singing voice. It is not an important part.

(2) Varya is a more serious part.... She is a character in a black dress, something of a nun, foolish, tearful, etc.

... Gorky is younger than you or I, he has his life before him.... As for the Nizhni theatre, that's a mere episode; Gorky will try it, "sniff it and reject it." And while we are on this subject, the whole idea of a "people's" theatre and "people's" literature is foolishness and lollipops for the people. We mustn't bring Gogol down to the people but raise the people up to Gogol....

TO A. L. VISHNEVSKY.

YALTA, November 7, 1903.

... As I am soon coming to Moscow, please keep a ticket for me for "The Pillars of Society"; I want to see the marvellous Norwegian acting, and I will even pay for my seat. You know Ibsen is my favourite writer....

TO K. S. STANISLAVSKY.

YALTA, November 10, 1903.

DEAR KONSTANTIN SERGEYITCH,

Of course the scenery for III. and IV. can be the same, the hall and the staircase. Please do just as you like about the scenery, I leave it entirely to you; I am amazed and generally sit with my mouth wide open at your theatre. There can be no question about it, whatever you do will be excellent, a hundred times better than anything I could invent....

TO F. D. BATYUSHKOV.

MOSCOW, January 19, 1904.

... At the first performance of "The Cherry Orchard" on the 17th of January, they gave me an ovation, so lavish, warm, and really so unexpected, that I can't get over it even now....

TO MADAME AVILOV.

MOSCOW, February 14, 1904.

... All good wishes. Above all, be cheerful; don't look at life so much as a problem—it is, most likely, far simpler. And whether it—life, of which we know nothing—is worth all the agonizing reflections which wear out our Russian wits, is a question.

TO FATHER SERGEY SHTCHUKIN.

MOSCOW, May 27, 1904.

DEAR FATHER SERGEY,

Yesterday I talked to a very well-known lawyer about the case in which you are interested, and I will tell you his opinion. Let Mr. N. immediately put together *all* the necessary documents, let his fiancee do the same, and go off to another province, such as Kherson, and there get married. When they are married let them come home and live quietly, saying nothing about it. It is not a crime (there is no consanguinity), but only a breach of a long established tradition. If in another two or three years someone informs against them, or finds out and interferes, and the case is brought into court, anyway the children would be legitimate. And when there is a lawsuit (a trivial one anyway), then they can send in a petition to the Sovereign. The Sovereign does not sanction what is forbidden by law (so it is no use to petition for permission for the marriage), but the Sovereign enjoys the fullest privilege of pardon and does as a rule pardon what is inevitable.

I don't know whether I am putting it properly. You must forgive me, I am in bed, ill, and have been since the second of May, I have not been able to get up once all this time. I cannot execute your other commissions....

TO HIS SISTER.

BERLIN, Sunday, June 6, 1904.

... I write to you from Berlin, where I have been now for twenty-four hours. It turned very cold in Moscow after you went away; we had snow, and it was most likely through that that I caught cold. I began to have rheumatic pains in my arms and legs, I did not sleep for nights, got very thin, had injections of morphia, took thousands of medicines of all sorts, and remember none of them with gratitude except heroin, which was once prescribed me by Altschuller....

On Thursday I set off for foreign parts, very thin, with very lean skinny legs. We had a good and pleasant journey. Here in Berlin we have taken a comfortable room in the best hotel. I am enjoying being here, and it is a long time since I have eaten so well, with such appetite. The bread here is wonderful, I eat too much of it. The coffee is excellent and the dinners beyond description. Anyone who has not been abroad does not know what good bread means. There is no decent tea here (we have our own), there are no hors d'oeuvres, but all the rest is magnificent, though cheaper than with us. I am already the better for it, and to-day I even took a long drive in the Thiergarten, though it was cool. And so tell Mother and everyone who is interested that I am getting better, or indeed have already got better; my legs no longer ache, I have no diarrhoea, I am beginning to get fat, and am all day long on my legs, not lying down....

BERLIN,

June 8.

. . . The worst thing here which catches the eye at once is the dress of the ladies. Fearfully bad taste, nowhere do women dress so abominably, with such utter lack of taste. I have not seen one beautiful woman, nor one who was not trimmed with some kind of absurd braid. Now I understand why taste is so slowly developed in Germans in Moscow. On the other hand, here in Berlin life is very comfortable. The food is good, things are not dear, the horses are well fed—the dogs, who are here harnessed to little carts, are well fed too. There is order and cleanliness in the streets....

BADENWEILER,

June 12.

I have been for three days settled here, this is my address—Germany, Badenweiler, Villa Fredericke. This Villa Fredericke, like all the houses and villas here, stands apart in a luxuriant garden in the sun, which shines and warms us till seven o'clock in the evening (after which I go indoors). We are boarding in the house; for fourteen or sixteen marks a day we have a double room flooded with sunshine, with washing-stands, bedsteads, etc., with a writing-table, and, best of all, with excellent water, like Seltzer water. The general impression: a big garden, beyond the garden, mountains covered with forest, few people, little movement in the street. The garden and the flowers are splendidly cared for. But to-day, apropos of nothing, it has begun raining; I sit in our room, and already begin to feel that in another two or three days I shall be thinking of how to escape.

I am still eating butter in enormous quantities and with no effect. I can't take milk. The doctor here, Schworer, married to a Moscow woman, turns out to be skilful and nice.

We shall perhaps return to Yalta by sea from Trieste or some other port. Health is coming back to me not by ounces but by stones. Anyway, I have learned here how to feed. Coffee is forbidden to me absolutely, it is supposed to be relaxing; I am beginning by degrees to eat eggs. Oh, how badly the German women dress!

I live on the ground floor. If only you knew what the sun is here! It does not scorch, but caresses. I have a comfortable low chair in which I can sit or lie down. I will certainly buy the watch, I haven't forgotten it. How is Mother? Is she in good spirits? Write to me. Give her my love. Olga is going to a dentist here....

June 16.

I am living amongst the Germans and have already got used to my room and to the regime, but can never get used to the German peace and quiet. Not a sound in the house or outside it; only at seven o'clock in the morning and at midday there is an expensive but very poor band playing in the garden. One feels there is not a single drop of talent in anything nor a single drop of taste; but, on the other hand, there is order and honesty to spare. Our Russian life is far more talented, and as for the Italian or the French, it is beyond comparison.

My health has improved. I don't notice now as I go about that I am ill; my asthma is better, nothing is aching. The only trace left of my illness is extreme thinness; my legs are thin as they have never been. The German doctors have turned all my life upside down. At seven o'clock in the morning I drink tea in bed—for some reason it must be in bed; at half-past seven a German by way of a masseur comes and rubs me all over with water, and this seems not at all bad. Then I have to lie still a little, get up at eight o'clock, drink acorn cocoa and eat an immense quantity of butter. At ten o'clock, oatmeal porridge, extremely nice to taste and to smell, not like our Russian. Fresh air and sunshine. Reading the newspaper. At one o'clock, dinner, at which I must not taste everything but only the things Olga chooses for me, according to the German doctor's prescription. At four o'clock the cocoa again. At seven o'clock supper. At bedtime a cup of strawberry tea—that is as a sleeping draught. In all this there is a lot of quackery, but a lot of what is really good and useful—for instance, the porridge. I shall bring some oatmeal from here with me....

June 21.

Things are going all right with me, only I have begun to get sick of Badenweiler. There is so much German peace and order here. It was different in Italy. To-day at dinner they gave us boiled mutton—what a dish! The whole dinner is magnificent, but the maitres d'hotel look so important that it makes one uneasy.

June 28.

... It has begun to be terribly hot here. The heat caught me unawares, as I have only winter suits here. I am gasping and dreaming of getting away. But where to go? I should like to go to Italy, to Como, but everyone is running away from the heat there. It is hot everywhere in the south of Europe. I should like to go from Trieste to Odessa by steamer, but I don't know how far it is possible now, in June and July.... If it should be rather hot it doesn't matter; I should have a flannel suit. I confess I dread the railway journey. It is stifling in the train now, particularly with my asthma, which is made worse by the slightest thing. Besides, there are no sleeping carriages from Vienna right up to Odessa; it would be uncomfortable. And we should get home by railway sooner than we need, and I have not had enough holiday yet. It is so hot one can't bear one's clothes, I don't know what to do. Olga has gone to Freiburg to order a flannel suit for me, there are neither tailors nor shoemakers in Badenweiler. She has taken the suit Dushar made me as a pattern.

I like the food here very much, but it does not seem to suit me; my stomach is constantly being upset. I can't eat the butter here. Evidently my digestion is hopelessly ruined. It is scarcely possible to cure it by anything but fasting—that is, eating nothing—and that's the end of it. And the only remedy for the asthma is not moving.

There is not a single decently dressed German woman. The lack of taste makes one depressed.

Well, keep well and happy. My love to Mother, Vanya, George, and all the rest. Write!

I kiss you and press your hand.

Yours,

A.

THE END

Lightning Source UK Ltd.
Milton Keynes UK
UKHW010943281222
414514UK00004B/233

9 789356 718326